Concrete New York

Allison C. Meier
Jason R. Woods

Blue Crow Media

Introduction

Concrete makes New York monumental. It holds the weight of the glass and steel soaring over Manhattan and provides the structures for its buildings to reach ever higher into the clouds. It encircles the subway and infrastructure tunnels down below; it is in the sidewalks and roads that keep the constant flow of people moving through the boroughs above. It is ubiquitous yet frequently invisible in these utilitarian spaces. To make this modest material the focus of a building is to expose something elemental about the city. Concrete is everywhere—it's often cited as the most used substance in the world after water—but the buildings in this book celebrate rather than hide it, drawing your attention to its tactile textures, imposing materiality, and possibilities for forms that no other material can achieve.

As a writer on architecture who has lived in New York for 16 years, exploring the city through this very specific lens has changed the way I see it. It's introduced me to lesser-known works by Modernist masters, including Marcel Breuer's elegant 1950s designs at Lehman College in the Bronx [28], and revealed how radical 20th-century styles were expressed at a neighborhood scale, such as the 1969 Church of the Crucifixion [19] that transported the raw concrete forms of Le Corbusier to Harlem. My research into the relationship between concrete and the city brought together its most successful and detrimental architecture, from revolutionary masterpieces like Frank Lloyd Wright's 1959 Guggenheim Museum [44] in Manhattan to isolating fortresses of public housing like the 1970s Morrisania Air Rights [36] in the

Bronx. And it highlighted just how much concrete has consumed the city and reduced its green space into small islands. Despite appreciating the grand architectural gestures, I'm cheered by nature's resilience against this heavy concrete footprint every time I see a tree root rippling through a sidewalk or a bit of flora finding a place to grow on a wall.

Concrete's dominance across the five boroughs started about 150 years ago. Although the mixing of cement, sand, gravel, and water to make a building material has centuries of history, with the Colosseum and Pantheon demonstrating the endurance of ancient Roman concrete, it is a relatively recent addition to New York construction. Before the 19th century, this was a city of stone and wood. Susceptible to fires, it kept at a low profile compared to the skyscrapers that would follow. An early shift can be found in the Gowanus neighborhood of Brooklyn, where the city's oldest surviving concrete building stands. It was completed in 1873 to demonstrate the new possibilities of Beton Coignet, a concrete developed by French industrialist François Coignet and marketed as a cost-saving replacement for stone. Passing by the building at Third Street and Third Avenue, you might mistake its two-story Italianate façade for limestone, as, unlike the later Modernist concrete works, it was being molded to mimic carved stone. You can also find Beton Coignet in nearby Prospect Park, where it shapes the patterned flourishes of the 1872 Cleft Ridge Span, considered by historians to be the first cast concrete arch erected in the United States.

Yet it would take until the 20th century for concrete to truly transfigure the city into a metropolis. Concrete reinforced with steel supported the towering statements of the Art Deco age; stone block and brick streets were paved over as automobiles eclipsed horse-drawn transportation in the first decades of the 1900s. Still, the major early architectural works of exposed concrete were designed for function. Along the Brooklyn waterfront are the warehouses of the World War I-era Brooklyn Army Terminal—among the largest concrete structures in the world at its completion—and the vast 1922 Red Hook Grain Terminal [39]. Only after World War II did the Modernist sensibility for an honesty of materials and the need for more affordability in construction make unadorned concrete a popular aesthetic choice.

Many of the proponents of this new mode of design in the United States had fled the rise of fascism in Europe. Walter Gropius, who founded the trailblazing Bauhaus design school in Germany, became part of the Harvard Graduate School of Design; Italian architectural sculptor Costantino Nivola found a home in New York's Greenwich Village. In Europe, concrete became an essential material for rebuilding from the rubble of war. (Some of the debris even made it to New York as ship ballast, with stones and bricks from the bombed city of Bristol, England, used to shape new land at Manhattan's Bristol Basin.) One of the polarizing styles of this era became known as Brutalism, its name derived from *béton brut* ("raw concrete"), a term coined by Swiss-born French architect Le Corbusier while he was building his 1952 Unité d'Habitation housing blocks in Marseille, France. As architectural critic Reyner Banham observed in his 1966 book *The New Brutalism*, Le Corbusier in this influential project "decided to recognise that concrete starts life as a messy soup of suspended dusts, grits and slumpy aggregate, mixed and poured under conditions subject to the vagaries of weather and human fallibility..."

In the United States, the same practicality of simple forms following function, without sacrificing good design, fueled a postwar building boom. Hard lines, an absence of ornamentation, and an unmasking of the inner workings of buildings through exterior staircases and protrusions for infrastructure were all fixtures of architecture in the 1950s, '60s, and '70s. The concrete used was rugged and rough. The architects embraced its robust character rather than hide it beneath layers of plaster, paint, or brick, as it had been in the past. There was little nostalgia in these designs for architectural styles that had come before, for why look back to the history that had brought such ruinous violence?

But these economical forms did not take shape in concrete in New York as much as they did in the sharp angles of plate glass and steel that became known as the International Style. A glance at the skyline will reveal the Bauhaus visionary whose ideas most redefined the midcentury city: the school's last director, Ludwig Mies van der Rohe. The curtain wall of his 1958 Seagram Building acts as a dark mirror to Park Avenue and has been mimicked endlessly in office buildings around the city and far beyond, although usually with less exacting taste. Just south is Gropius's stern 1963 Pan Am Building [34], providing a heftier silhouette in precast concrete as it hulks over Grand Central Terminal. While New York doesn't have as many Brutalist giants as some American cities like Boston and Albany, it has major landmarks by its champions, such as Le Corbusier, Paul Rudolph, and Breuer, another Bauhaus alumnus, who stated in a 1973 interview, "I believe the architect can fully express himself as an artist by means of concrete."

The impact of concrete on the 20th-century growth of the city cannot be discussed without acknowledging how the material was weaponized by Robert Moses, the urban planner who amassed incredible power as New York City's parks commissioner. A proponent of the car over pedestrianization and public transportation, he plowed freeways indiscriminately through neighborhoods and ringed the city with those "cloverleafs and broad ribbons of concrete that to him represented beauty and that were his trademark," as Robert Caro wrote in his 1974 biography, *The Power Broker*. Slum clearance further leveled blocks of housing and businesses, which were replaced with gargantuan developments. Despite the socialist spirit of these urban renewal projects in attempting to improve housing with denser blocks that left space for green lawns and pedestrian plazas, many fell short of their utopian ambitions. Over the years, their concrete streaked and degraded, reflecting the neglect of these properties as the optimism for addressing the city's issues through design waned.

Contemporary architects working with concrete have to grapple with this complex legacy of what the material represents in the city. Many are also reckoning with its environmental costs by incorporating more sustainable production systems and utilizing stronger concrete that will hold up to the urban elements. Manufacturing concrete is a notoriously polluting process, with significant carbon emissions from the production of cement, and involves massive amounts of water. All those years of covering the city with concrete have additionally contributed to the heat-island effect, as the material absorbs the warmth of the day, so it swelters long after sunset.

The pioneering concrete buildings of the 20th century are now showing their age, their once gleaming gray façades mottled and sometimes cracked as the interior rebar rusts and expands. As their stark geometries have fallen out of favor, and the demands for maintenance frequently outweigh the desire to preserve and upgrade them, many concrete buildings have been torn down. The 1964 Holy Trinity Chapel at New York University, designed by Eggers & Higgins with striking Brutalist lines, was razed in 2009. I. M. Pei's 1969 design for JFK Airport's Terminal 6—known as the Sundrome for its enclosure of steel and green glass floating on cylindrical concrete columns—was demolished in 2011. The 1965 Guggenheim Bandshell, also by Eggers & Higgins at Lincoln Center, with its graceful curve of concrete, may be gone before this book is published, replaced with an updated outdoor concert space and amphitheater.

What is the value of caring for these sometimes clunky, often idiosyncratic, concrete behemoths? Few other building materials have allowed architects to treat their designs like art and shape them into gravity-defying swoops, arches, and blocky stacks. Buildings once deemed eyesores are now being reevaluated for their innovation in constructing something that had never before been possible. The most exciting 21st-century concrete architecture likewise showcases both the material's imperfections and dramatic capabilities, from the grainy shotcrete caves and canyons of Studio Gang's 2023 Gilder Center [11] to the color variations on the craggy exterior of Dattner Architects's 2015 Spring Street Salt Shed [45].

Meanwhile, architecture associated with harmful legacies of urban renewal can be rejuvenated to better support its communities. The environmental toll of the construction of these buildings can be contained instead of releasing it through their demolition and beginning a new cycle of construction, especially crucial when the contemporary building industry continues to have a colossal carbon footprint. The successful rejuvenation of Albert C. Ledner's 1964 National Maritime Union [29] into a medical center and Eero Saarinen's 1962 TWA Flight Center [52] into a hotel demonstrates how modern architecture can be adapted after its original purpose becomes obsolete. Other concrete buildings are less visible and were envisioned by less prominent architects. Understanding their history and the intentions behind their designs can help them survive the relentless redevelopment of the city. In this book, there are not just architectural icons but also branch libraries, playgrounds, neighborhood churches, and parking garages. Rather than footnotes in the city's story, they deserve to be recognized for their own bold, inventive designs that were part of the postwar attempt to build a better future, and they can still stand the test of time if given the right care.

What is most powerful to me in looking closely at concrete architecture is discovering how it carries the imprint of the time, place, and people who created it. The word "concrete" can be traced back to the Latin *concrescere*, a verb meaning "to grow together." Made from different components into a solid whole, concrete evokes connection both in its name and textures. The molds from the plywood boards that shaped the spiral of the Guggenheim Museum are still detectable beneath the off-white paint of its façade; the interior walls of Breuer's Whitney Museum [07]—now a headquarters for Sotheby's—were bush hammered to give them an organic feel and expose fragments of black obsidian mixed with the cement. Even the silky concrete used in newer architecture often features the circular tie holes from the molding process. Brownstone, granite, glass, and steel don't convey the same evidence of who made a building, those countless laborers behind the name of a singular architect or firm. Then there are the unintended ways concrete freezes a moment, whether a stray falling leaf that left an impression or the blemish from someone who couldn't resist pressing a hand or writing a name in it as it hardened. I encourage you to pause and seek out those signs of life in the concrete architecture near you. Each molding mark or scar from time is a reminder of the people who have transformed a place through the formidable potential of this humble material.

List of buildings

29 Lenox Health Greenwich Village (National Maritime Union)
30 Little Island
31 Macy's Queens
32 Manhattan Church of Christ
33 Maritime Hotel (National Maritime Union)
34 MetLife Building (Pan Am Building)
35 Middletown Plaza
36 Morrisania Air Rights
37 Motorgate
38 New York State Pavilion
39 Red Hook Grain Terminal
40 Rockefeller University: Benjamin and Irma G. Weiss Research Building
41 St. Mary's Catholic Church of the Byzantine Rite
42 Silver Towers (University Village)
43 Society of St. Paul (Alba House)
44 Solomon R. Guggenheim Museum
45 Spring Street Salt Shed
46 Spuyten Duyvil Library
47 Stephen Wise Towers Playground Horses
48 Studio Museum in Harlem
49 Terrace on the Park (Port Authority Heliport)
50 Tracey Towers
51 Tribeca Synagogue (Civic Center Synagogue)
52 TWA Flight Center
53 United Nations General Assembly Building
54 West 67th Street Adventure Playground

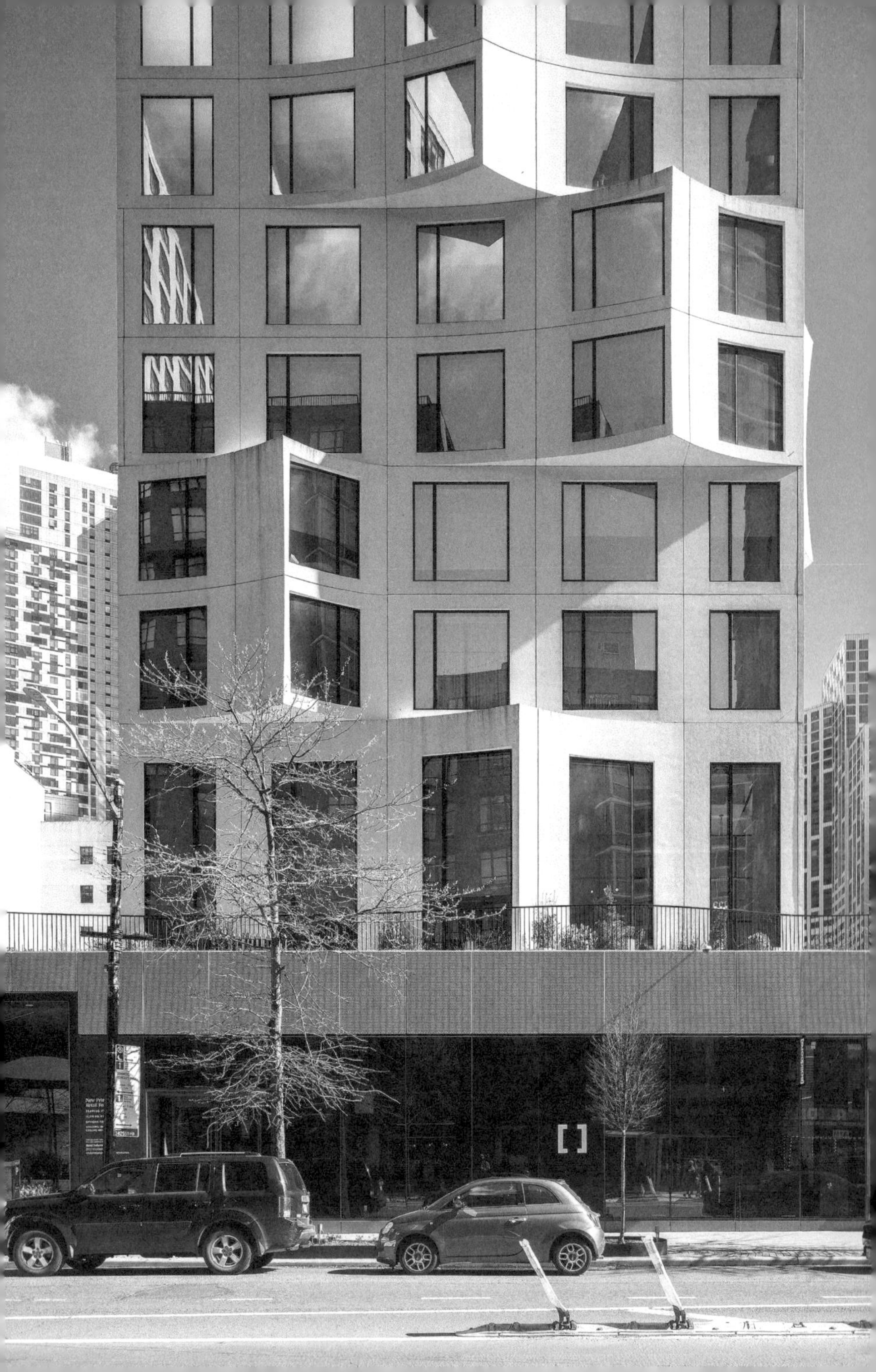

01

11 Hoyt

Studio Gang, 2015–21
11 Hoyt Street, Brooklyn, 11201

The once sparse skyline of Downtown Brooklyn has been radically developed with numerous luxury condominium. Whereas many of these are unimaginative metal and glass monoliths, 11 Hoyt has a façade that ripples with patterns of precast concrete. More than 1,200 concrete panels, some flat, some scalloped, were sandblasted to a bright white. Installed on the 620-foot-tall high-rise, their diagonal arrangements of contours make them appear windswept.

The Chicago-based Studio Gang, led by Jeanne Gang, collaborated with Hill West Architects to design the project on the former site of a parking garage. Despite standing out from its fellow new neighbors with its rhythmic concrete, 11 Hoyt is far less experimental in its use of industrial materials than the firm's 2023 Gilder Center [11] at Manhattan's American Museum of Natural History. Still, in its more muted design approach are thoughtful flourishes like a private garden on its podium base that is intended not just as an amenity for residents but also a stop for migrating birds and butterflies. And in contrast to the creamy concrete on its exterior, an interior yoga studio is dominated by exposed concrete trusses.

The meandering concrete panels additionally extend the living spaces arranged across the 57 stories, offering built-in seats to look out the large aluminum-framed windows, a contemporary update on Brooklyn's iconic brownstone bay window.

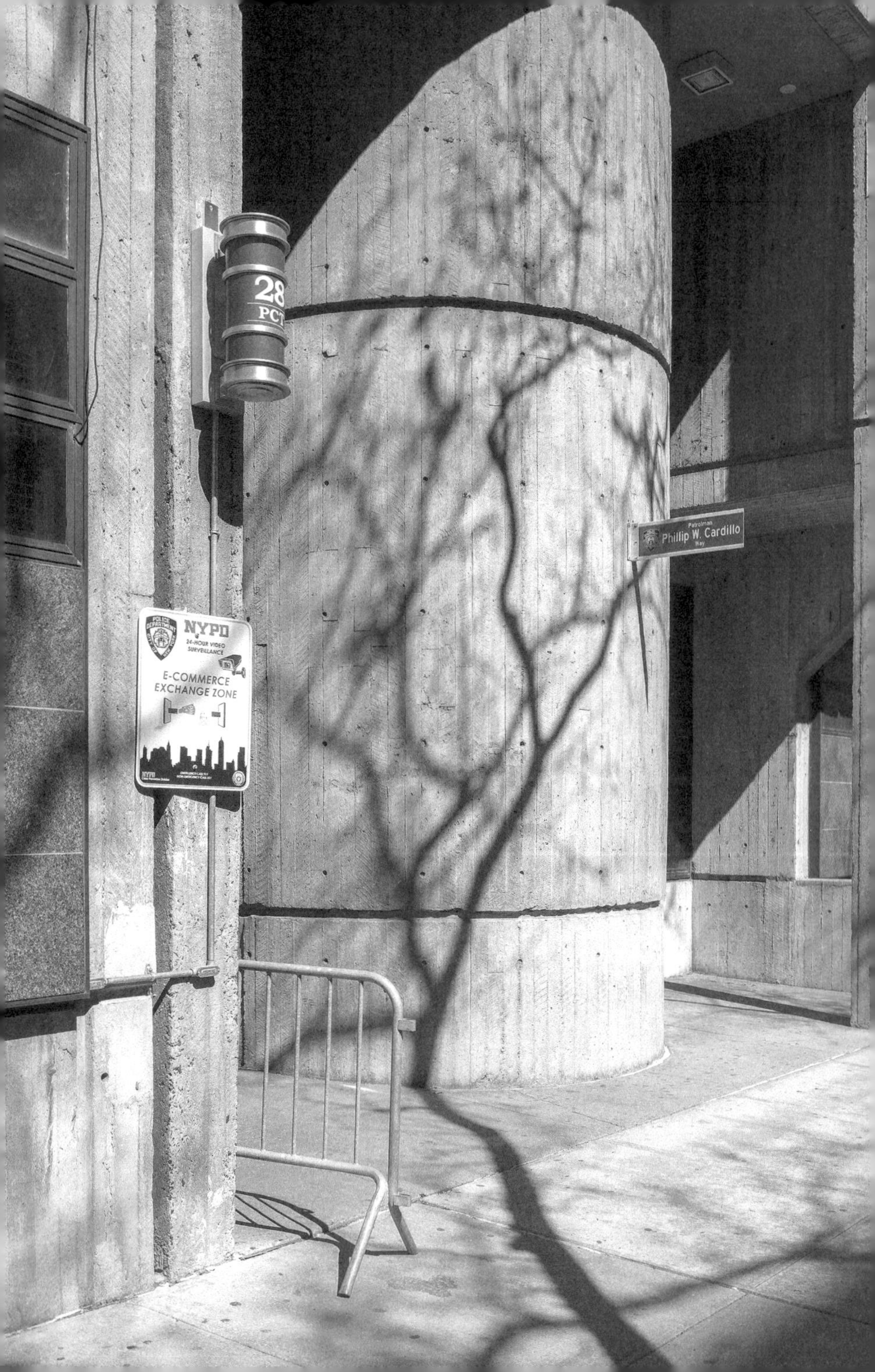
28
PCT
NYPD
24-HOUR VIDEO
SURVEILLANCE
E-COMMERCE
EXCHANGE ZONE
Patrolman
Phillip W. Cardillo
Way

(02) 28th Precinct NYPD

Lehrecke & Tonetti, 1974
2271–89 Frederick Douglass Boulevard, Manhattan, 10027

When the new 28th Precinct for the New York City Police Department was dedicated in October 1975, Police Commissioner Michael J. Codd said that "the opening of a new station house can no longer be regarded as something that has pertinence only to the police." The 28th's previous home was an 1890s brick building that still stands at 177–179 East 104th Street, a lovely civic structure, but not suited to the current needs of the department. ("I'm enjoying not walking up four flights of stairs to get to my locker," one officer told the *New York Times*.) The hard lines and exposed concrete of the new two-story station gave the precinct a freshly modern and fortified presence. It neatly fits into its triangular lot in Harlem, with a concrete wall extending around its parking lot. Its imposing shape is given character through textural details from its board-formed cast-in-place concrete surfaces, as well as curved volumes that break up the blocky façade. Sections of the second story project over slight recesses on the first floor, creating added depth and visual interest.

Although it was a novel approach in presenting a show of force that did not overwhelm its community, the aged concrete now looks hostile. An interesting comparison is the newer 40th Precinct station in the South Bronx, completed by Bjarke Ingels Group (BIG) in 2024. Volumes that appear like stacked boxes are covered in smooth, sandblasted precast concrete panels. The intent is to be more open to the surrounding neighborhood, even while still using this hard material to express law and order.

NEVER FORGET

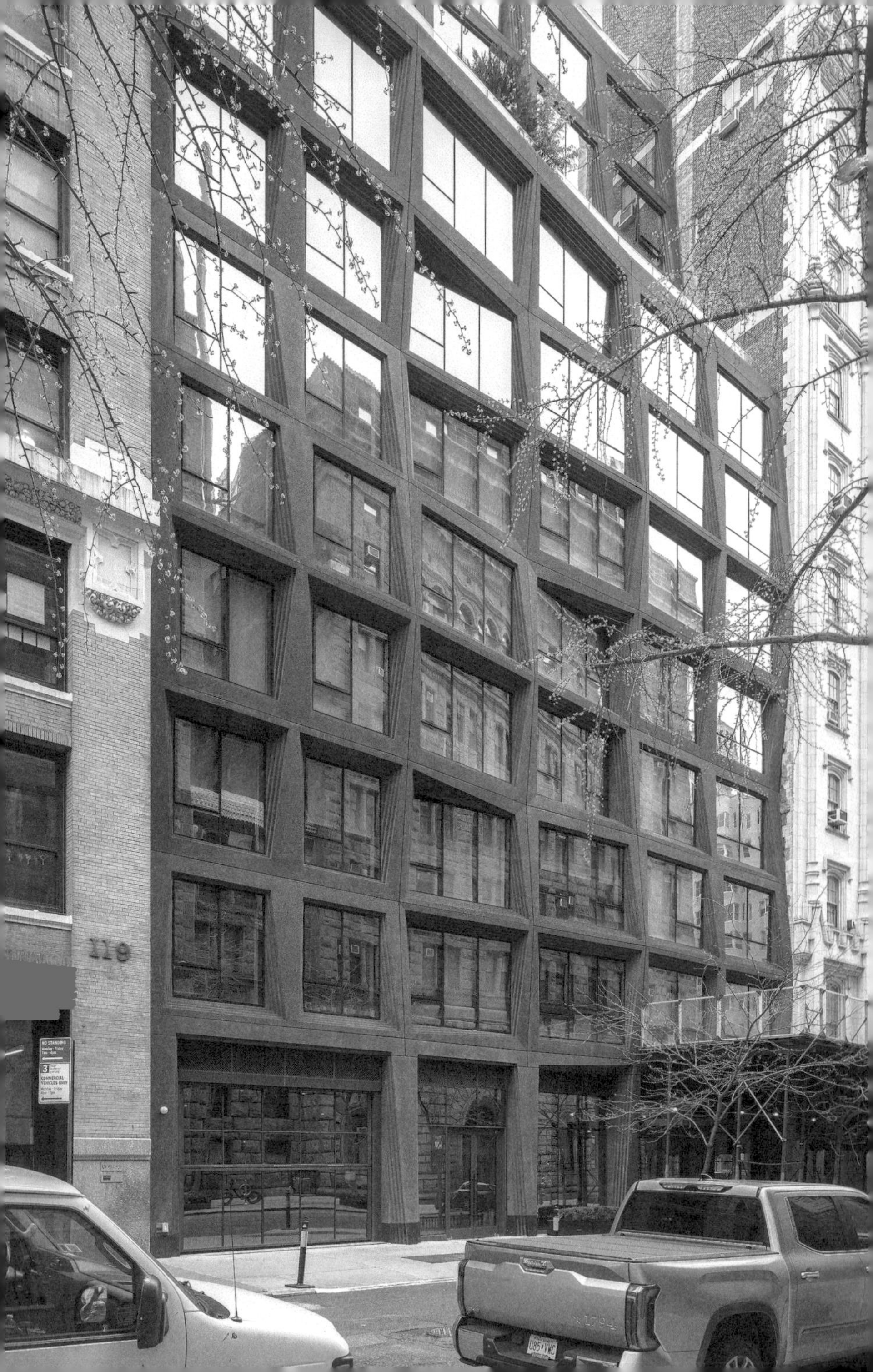
119
NO STANDING
COMMERCIAL VEHICLES ONLY

03 121 East 22nd

OMA, 2016–19
121 East 22nd Street, Manhattan, 10010

At the corner of East 23rd Street and Lexington Avenue, the black precast concrete panels framing the windows of this residential complex burst into prismatic angles. It's the most theatrical moment of the first ground-up building completed by OMA in New York, surprising given the significant impact the city had on its co-founder Rem Koolhaas. His influential *Delirious New York: A Retroactive Manifesto for Manhattan* (1978), inspired by his intensive research of the city, was published just after OMA was established in 1975. He wrote of Manhattan's rigid grid system, dating back to 1811, "The city becomes a mosaic of episodes, each with its own particular life span, that contest each other through the medium of the Grid."

So how does this structure that touches on three different faces of its block—Lexington Avenue, East 23rd Street, and East 22nd Street—offer its own episode? Designed by OMA partner Shohei Shigematsu, it has two towers on an L-shaped site, linked by a courtyard. This is inaccessible to those who don't live in its luxury apartments; what is at street level nods to what came before in its pattern of shapes. Rectangular windows mimic those of its prewar neighbors. A closer look at the concrete reveals small differences, with the outer area darker and sandblasted, while the inner texture is acid-etched with a smoother lightness. This gives the façade a muted gradient appearance, a subtle modern contribution to the ever-evolving grid.

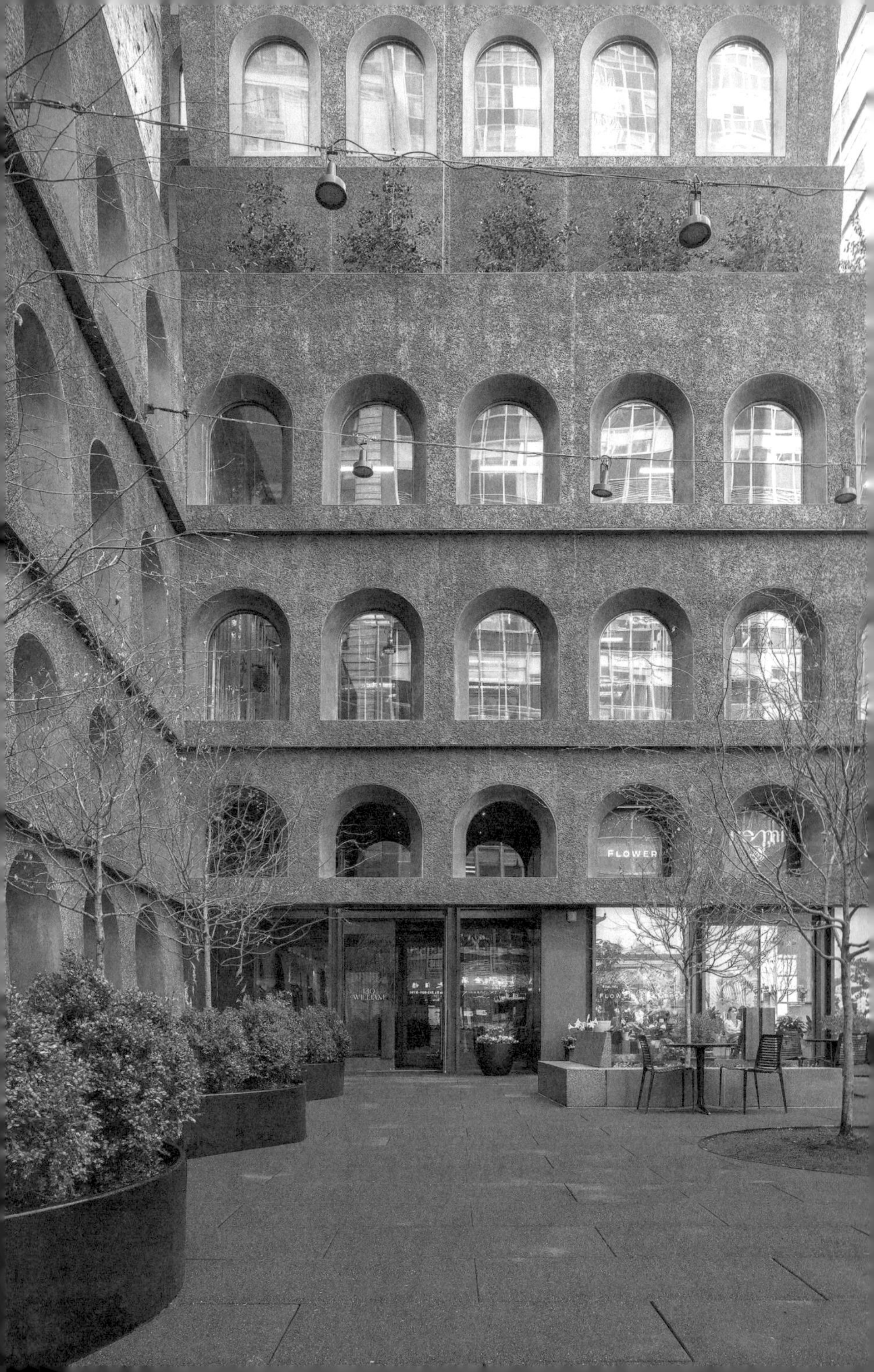
FLOWER

(04) 130 William

Adjaye Associates, 2017-23
130 William Street, Manhattan, 10038

A façade of hand-cast concrete arches resembles volcanic rock, looking like something more primordial than a new addition to New York City's luxury condo market. Rising 800 feet, its somber tones and serrated edges set it apart from the glassy skyscrapers of the Financial District. It's one of several recently completed local projects designed by Ghanaian-British architect David Adjaye, including the 2025 Studio Museum in Harlem [48] and the 2014 Sugar Hill Housing Development, also in Harlem, all involving graphite-colored concrete and textural forms.

Here, the 66 stories of the tower have uniform grids of arches until the top, where they flip upside down into loggias, giving a suggestion of an inverted ziggurat. Adjaye stated that he was inspired by Lower Manhattan's history of masonry architecture, and the structural arches of mercantile warehouses from when the waterfront bustled with maritime industry. The recessed windows that echo these historic vaults are framed with bronze to complement the mottled concrete.

Adjaye Associates worked on 130 William in partnership with Hill West Architects and the developer Lightstone. The arch panels were cast in Canada, with pigment, granite chips, and black stones creating their smoky color. While the interior of this pillar of concrete is restricted to the residents of its luxury apartments, there is an open courtyard at its ground level. In this plaza, the public can sit on benches between two walls of concrete arches, as if taking refuge in a modern ruin.

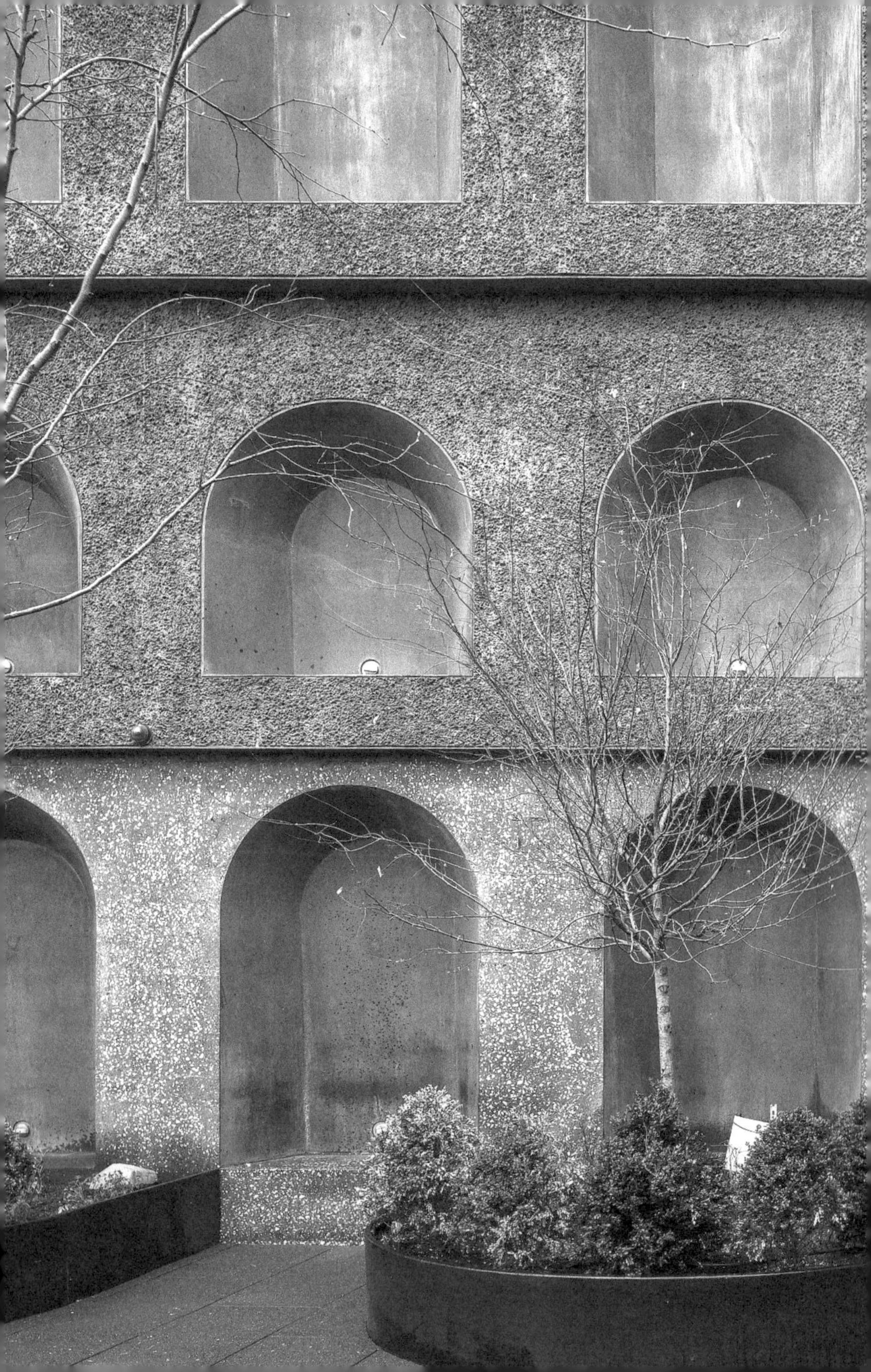

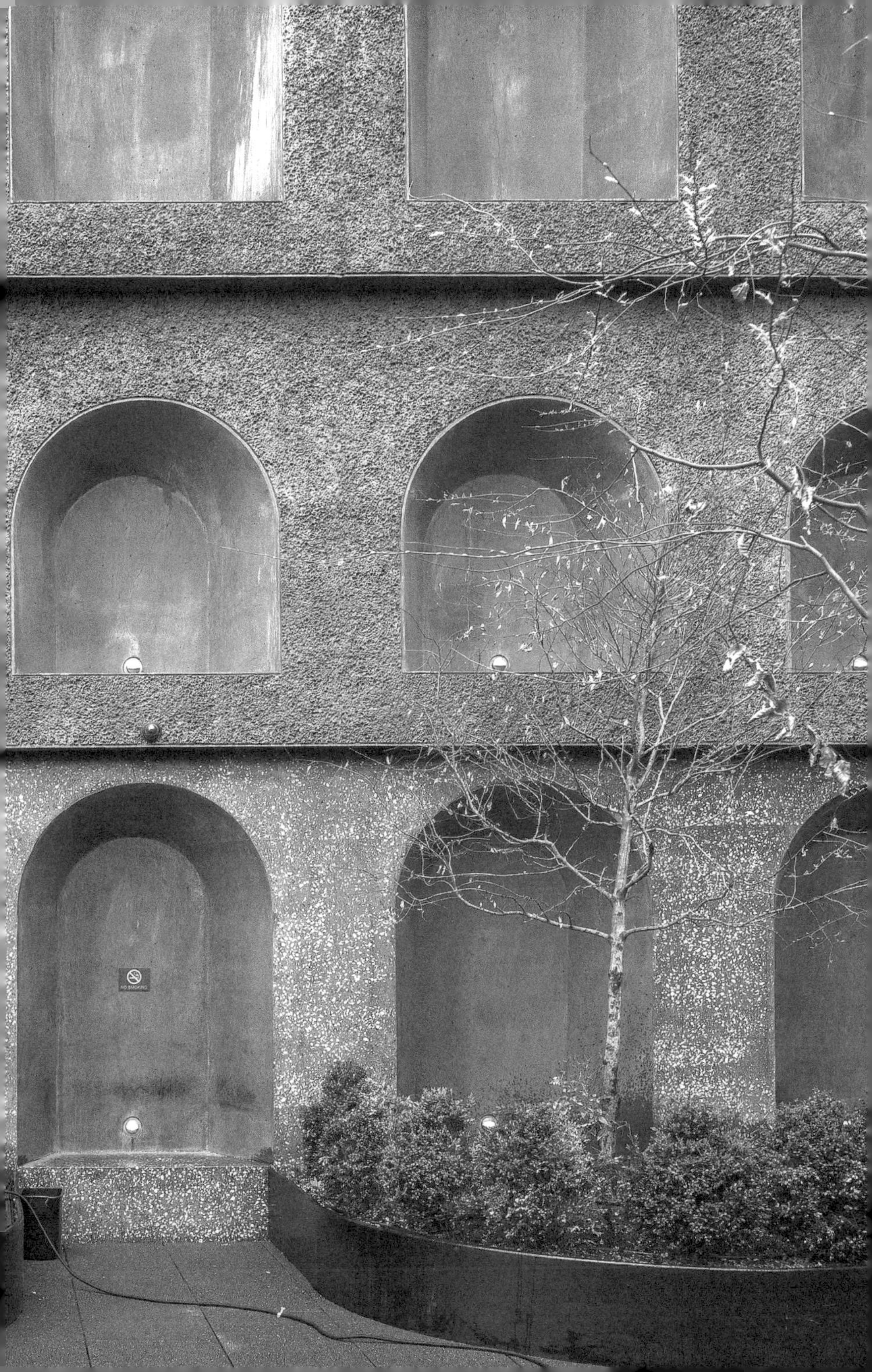

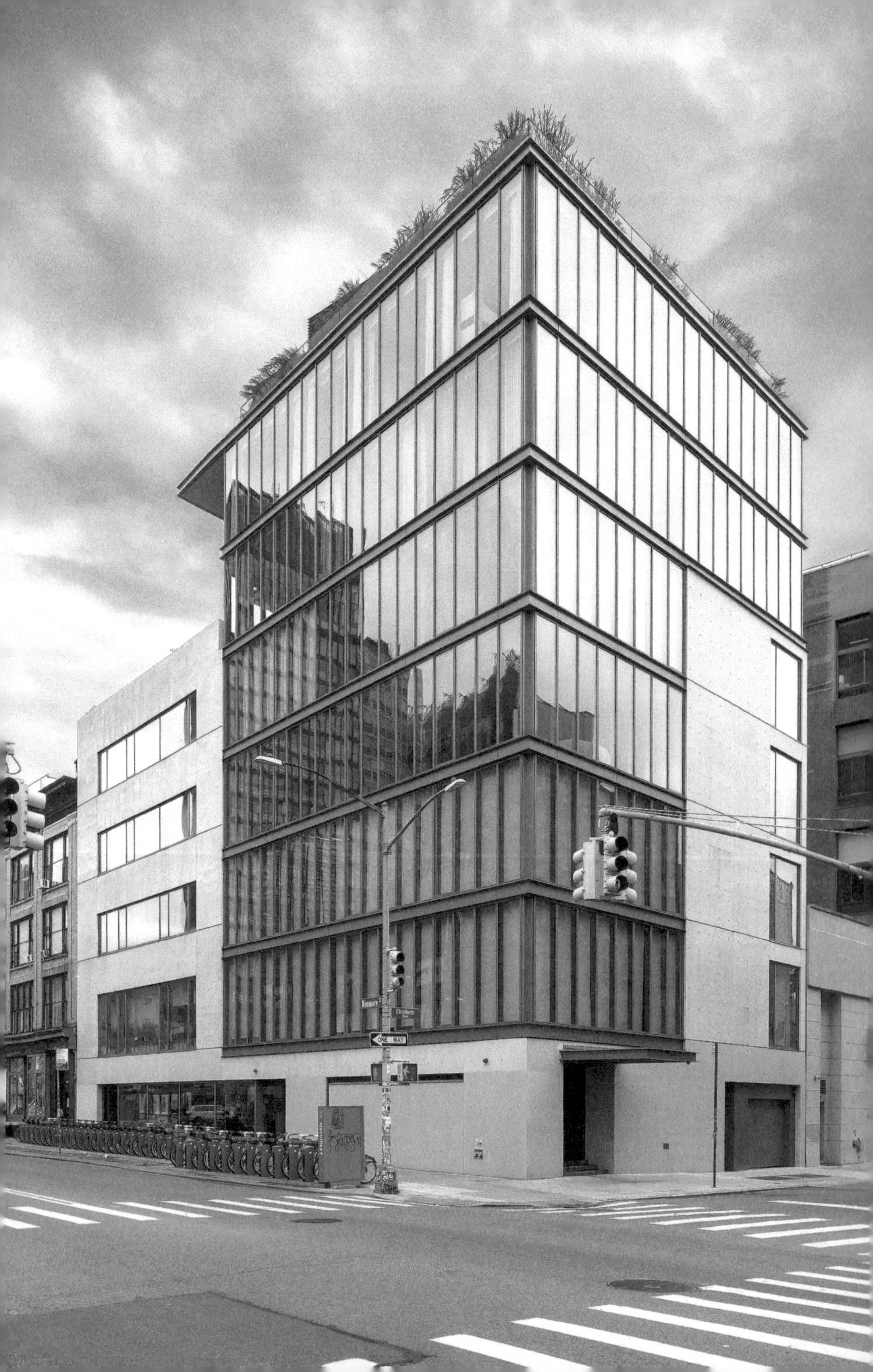
ONE WAY

05 152 Elizabeth Street

Tadao Ando Architect & Associates, 2014-17
152 Elizabeth Street, Manhattan, 10012

Japanese architect Tadao Ando is known for his artful mixing of concrete, glass, and metal in his designs. For his first ground-up New York City building, he instilled his minimalist touch into a seven-story ultra-high-end apartment building. It's an understated and relatively small-scale work for the first major Manhattan project by the Pritzker Prize-winner, but it incorporates all the carefully balanced ingredients that have brought him international acclaim, including that silky smooth polished concrete. It lines much of the corner façade at Elizabeth Street and Kenmare Street, with his signature, evenly spaced formwork ties left unfilled on the poured-in-place material. The rest is floor-to-ceiling glass windows and metal, with the more extravagant details, like a fog and light installation in the lobby and a large green wall high on its southern side, kept largely hidden from passersby.

Previously, Ando had only worked on interiors in the city, such as the concrete column-lined Morimoto restaurant (now closed) in Chelsea. 152 Elizabeth Street was realized on the former site of a parking garage with American architect Michael Gabellini and developers Sumaida + Khurana. It includes a concrete-walled retail space, as of this writing occupied by Issey Miyake's Pleats Please. Even if you are not among the few who spent millions to live in this concrete and glass jewel box, you can still enjoy the feel of its walls at street level. These demonstrate how Ando transmutes tough concrete into something tantalizingly tactile.

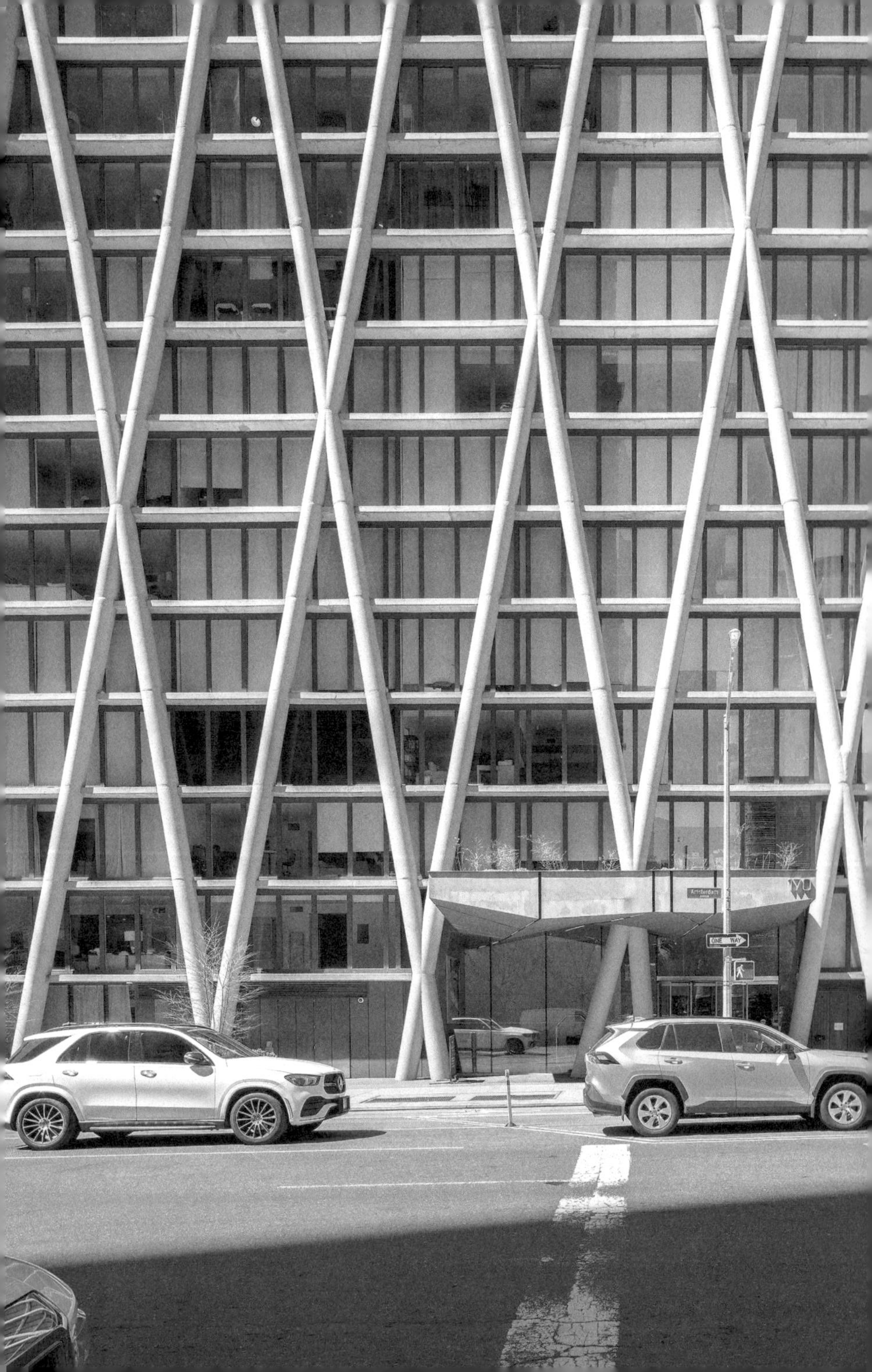
Amsterdam
ONE WAY

06

170 Amsterdam

Handel Architects, 2012-15
170 Amsterdam Avenue, Manhattan, 10023

An exoskeleton of reinforced concrete makes this building more eye-catching than most other residential developments on the Upper West Side. The intersecting angles of the exposed material form large Xs on a diagonal axis in what's known as a diagrid. (Norman Foster also employed the diagrid structural system on the 2006 Hearst Tower on Eighth Avenue.) This maximized the apartment floors of the long, slender 20-story tower. Instead of having the support columns take up space inside the building, they zigzag over the floor-to-ceiling walls of windows. Only a few interior columns were needed, and these were used as dynamic details. Exposed concrete columns erupt from the floor and walls of the lobby and other common areas. On the roof, the concrete exoskeleton extends upward and folds over to create a lattice over a terrace.

Handel Architects worked with DeSimone Consultants as the structural engineers. They purposefully used concrete with a smooth finish and color suggestive of limestone to echo the historic architecture in the neighborhood. The firm has completed numerous building projects around the city, with those involving exposed concrete each having a unique approach to the material. For instance, Inspīr Carnegie Hill on the Upper East Side pairs board-formed concrete with wood detailing, while 255 Hudson Street in Hudson Square has precast concrete walls that appear woven together.

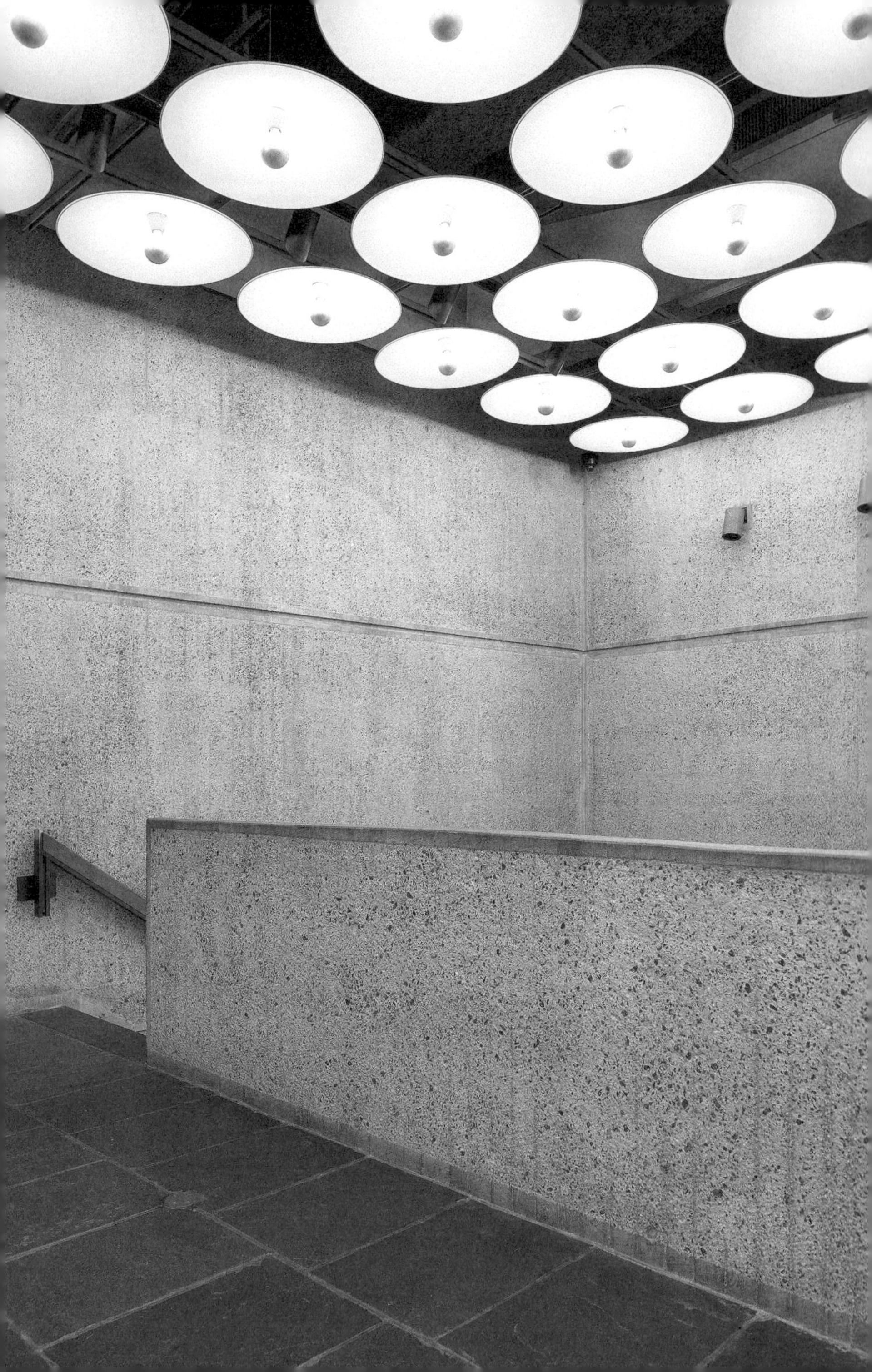

07 945 Madison Avenue (Breuer Building)

Marcel Breuer & Associates, 1963-66
945 Madison Avenue, Manhattan, 10021

"What should a museum look like, a museum in Manhattan?" Marcel Breuer asked the Whitney's Board of Trustees on November 12, 1963. He presented a design for "the building itself as a sculpture." It would stand out from the genteel Upper East Side with an invitation to enter into a sanctuary for art. This encounter would begin at street level, with a concrete bridge crossing a sunken sculpture garden. Inside, textural concrete would contribute to an aura of contemplation, making the galleries an urban retreat.

His gambit was a success, and his commission for a new kind of museum—Manhattan's first dedicated to American art—was underway. The Hungarian-born, Bauhaus-trained master was then at the height of his powers in employing concrete in spectacular forms, such as the 1961 St. John's Abbey Church in Minnesota. For the Whitney, he worked with his partner Hamilton P. Smith. He was inspired by ancient ziggurats, creating an inverted tier of concrete and gray granite punched with trapezoidal windows. A variety of treatments were used on the exposed concrete within, some smooth, some coarsely bush-hammered to reveal the dark chips of obsidian embedded in the material.

Many hated it when it debuted, calling it the "Madison Avenue Monster." It is now widely lauded for its daring design. Its exterior and lobby are landmarked, although the galleries are still vulnerable to change. After the Whitney moved downtown in 2014, the building served as an extension of the Frick and the Metropolitan Museum of Art before opening as a new headquarters for Sotheby's in 2025.

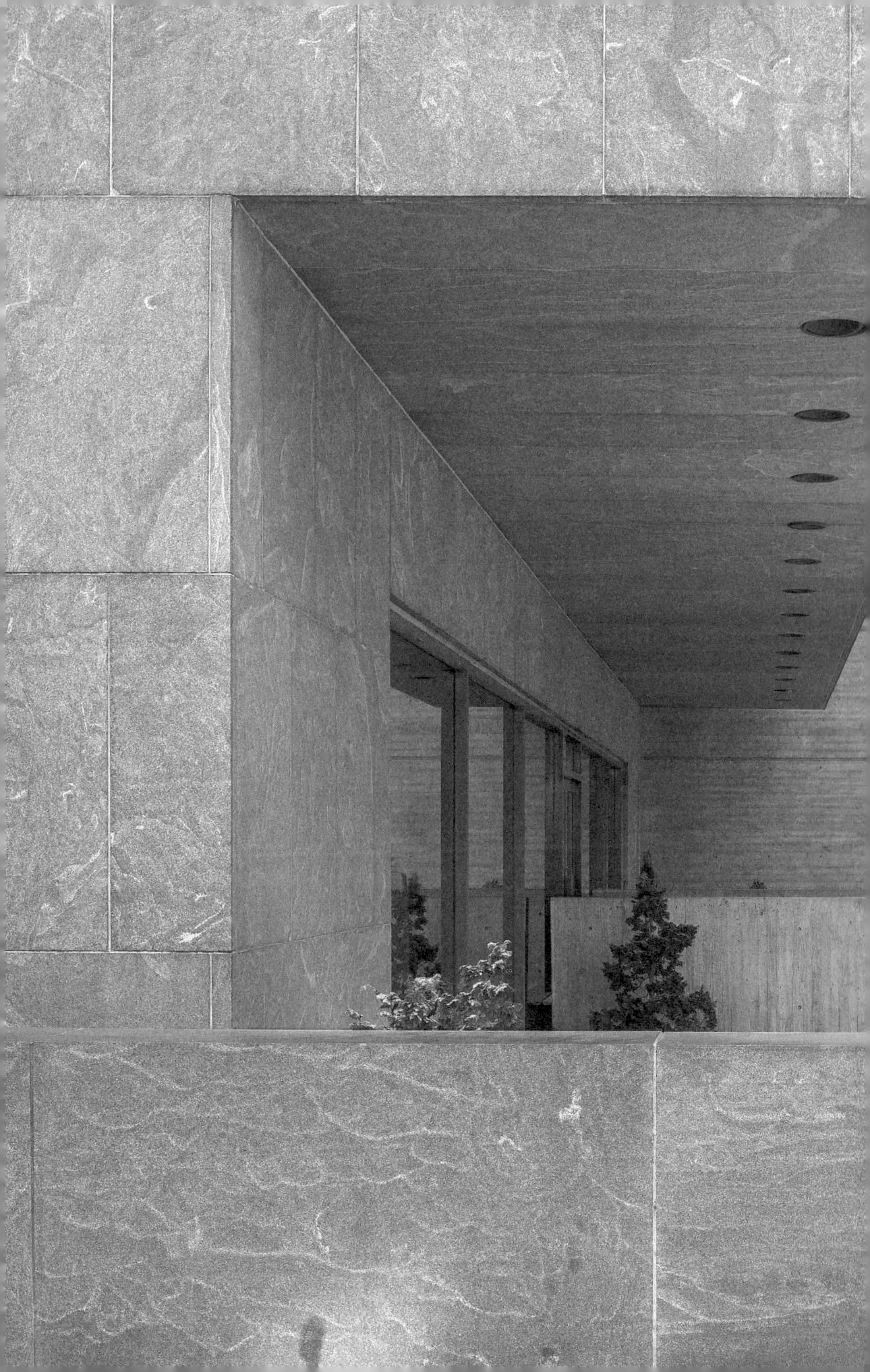

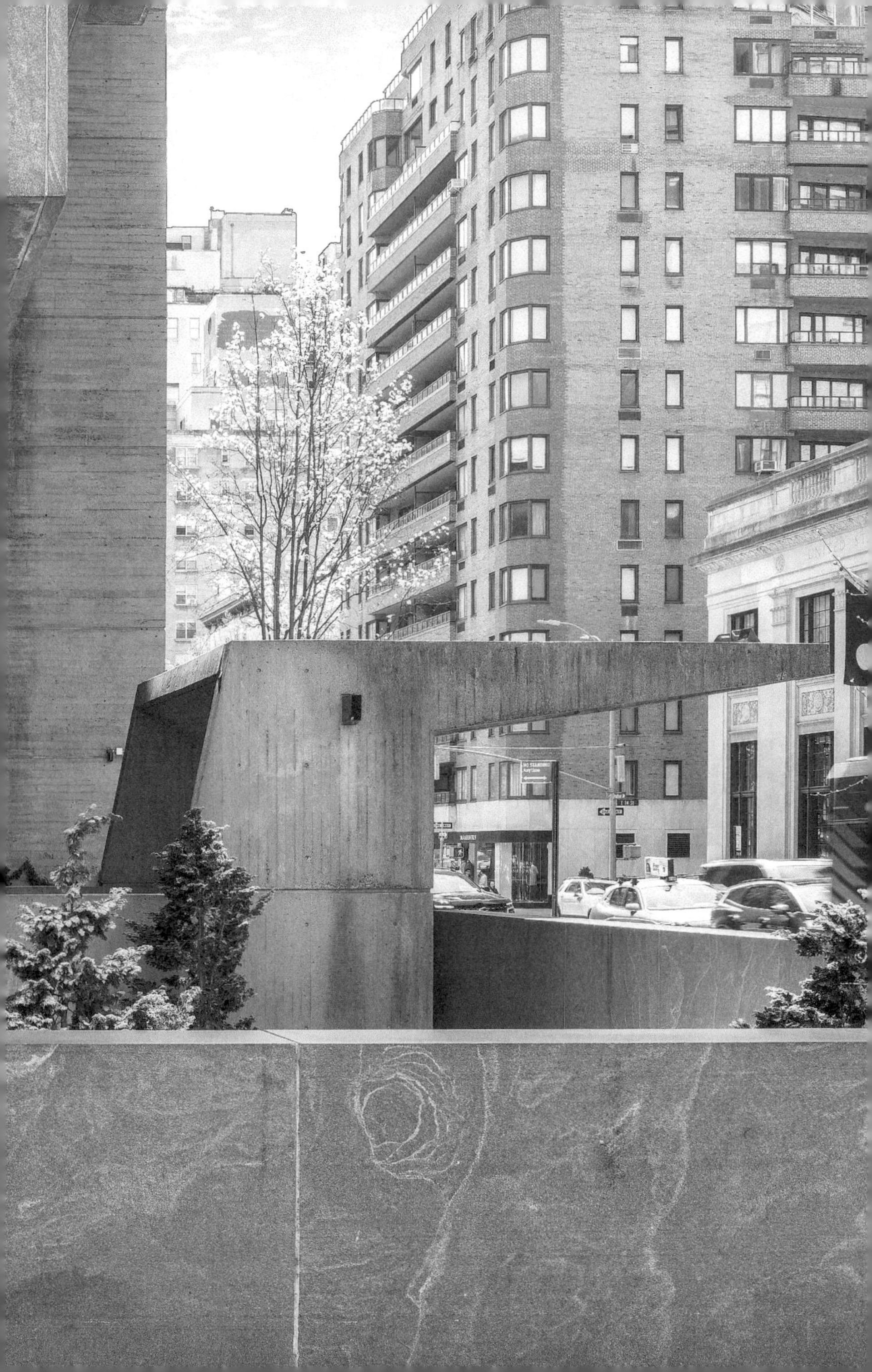

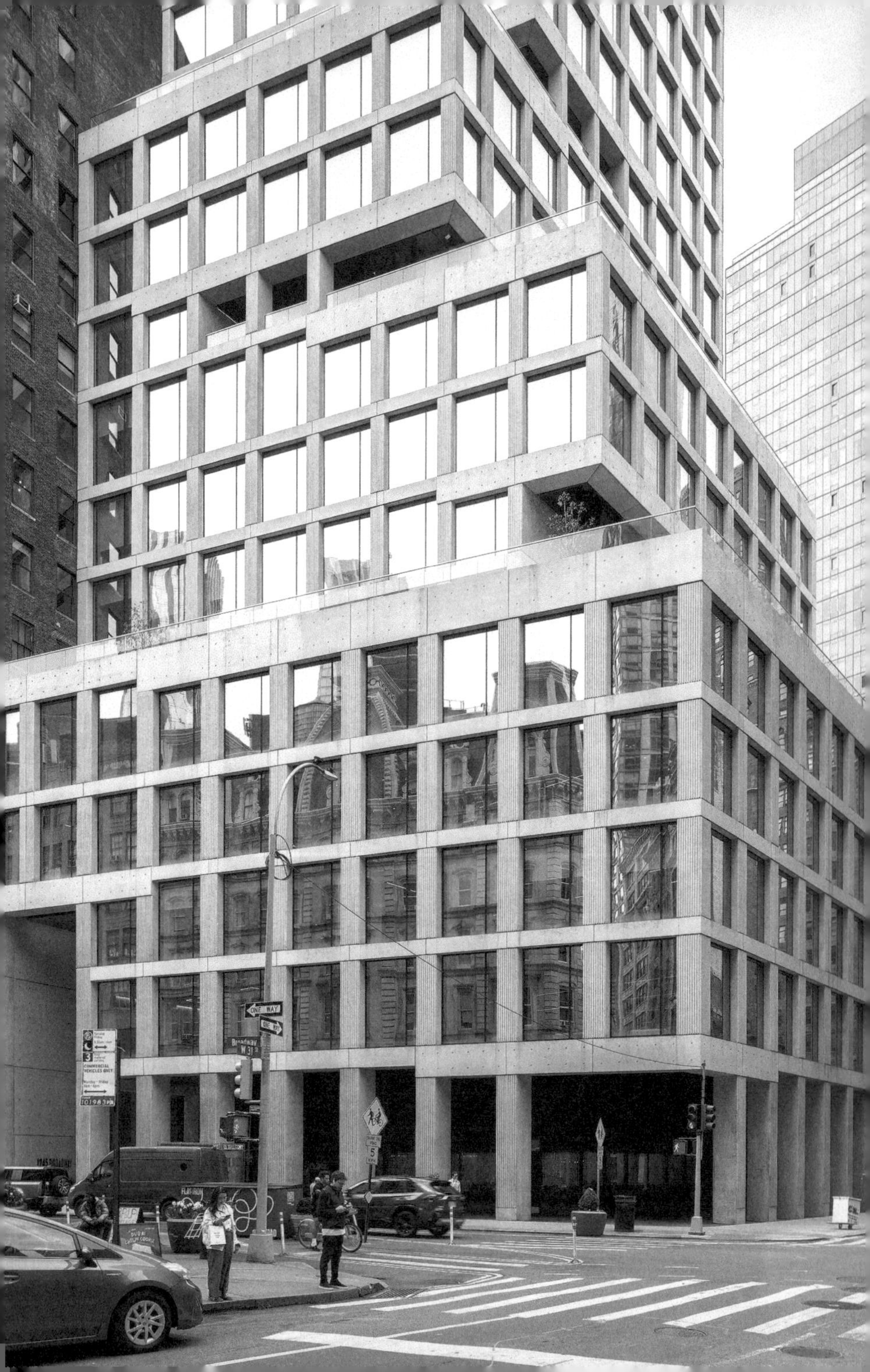
ONE WAY
ONE WAY
Broadway

08 1245 Broadway

Skidmore, Owings & Merrill (SOM), 2019–22
1245 Broadway, Manhattan, 10001

A deep arcade of fluted exposed concrete columns welcomes pedestrians to enjoy the shade beneath this office building. Various textures of the material are used on the façade and interior, preserving traces of how the poured-in-place concrete was cast. The ribbed grooves of the columns were made with a concrete formliner, while the tie-bolt holes were left unfilled on the smooth panels of concrete. These evenly spaced dots in the material's surface, formed from the pouring process, offer a motif that continues into the lobby. There, the concrete contrasts and frames the organic veins of marble, and it also forms a long bench.

SOM, working with the developers GDSNY and Klövern AB, focused on concrete for this building at the corner of West 31st Street and Broadway as something that would give the structure character. Most other new commercial developments in Manhattan's NoMad neighborhood are dominated by glass and steel. They were also considering sustainability to make the building LEED Gold certified, as the reinforced concrete doesn't require additional cladding or finishing.

The building's 23 stories appear like a skewed version of the wedding-cake-style tiers of older Manhattan high-rises that were made to conform to the city's zoning and setback regulations. Four off-kilter forms of differing sizes, gridded with bare concrete around recessed windows and incorporating open-air corners, are cantilevered over outdoor terraces.

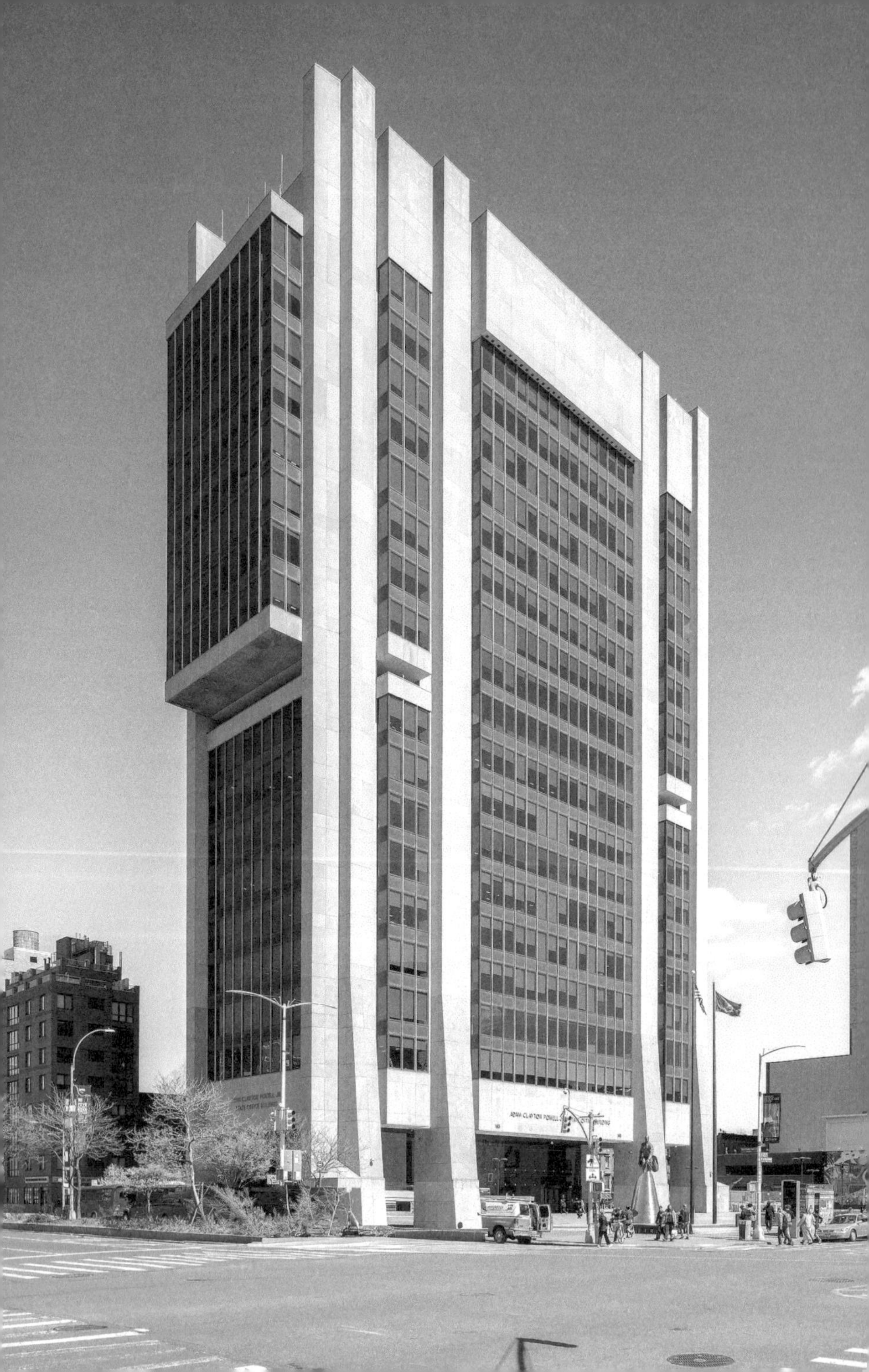
ADAM CLAYTON POWELL

09 Adam Clayton Powell, Jr. State Office Building

Ifill Johnson Hanchard, 1968-74
163 West 125th Street, Manhattan, 10027

The pioneering African American architectural firm Ifill Johnson Hanchard designed Harlem's tallest building. A façade of limestone and granite cladding over concrete is offset by a sweeping metal and dark glass curtain wall. Immense structural columns support its steel-framed 19 stories. Some viewers have interpreted the design as an abstracted African mask. Rectangular volumes extend on either side of the narrow building's top floors next to eye-like slits.

Construction spanned years of controversy, including a three-month sit-in in 1969 at the planned site. Local activists viewed it as an imposition of the state government that would not serve the community. In response, there was an effort to involve Black leadership in every aspect of its design, including the Black-owned Finley & Madison as the consulting engineers. Ifill Johnson Hanchard, led by Percy C. Ifill and Conrad Johnson, was brought in after Philip Johnson and John Burgee stepped away. The firm had previously worked on smaller-scale civic and commercial projects, including apartment buildings, churches, and schools.

It was erected at the same time that Albany's Empire State Plaza, with its many Brutalist giants, was being built. When the Harlem State Office Building opened in May 1974, opinions were mixed. (Critic Paul Goldberger remarked that at least the state was consistent in creating the "same mediocre architecture it dishes out everywhere else.") In September 1983, it was renamed for Adam Clayton Powell, Jr., the first Black Congressman elected from New York.

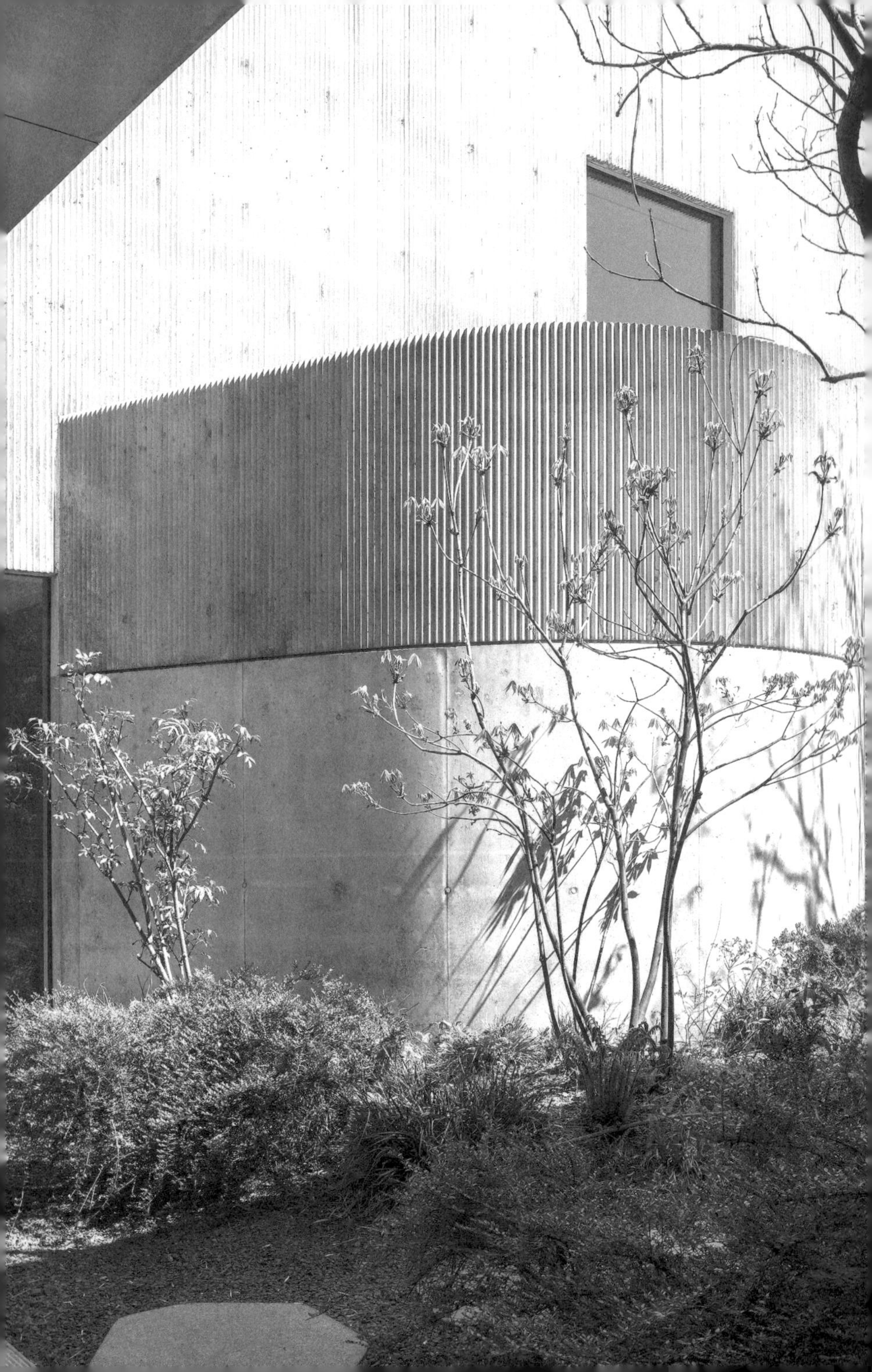

10 Amant

SO-IL, 2016-21
315 Maujer Street, Brooklyn, 11206

The architecture here is all about the surfaces. Four small buildings spread over three blocks are the campus of Amant, an international arts organization that also has an outpost in Siena, Italy. Design started in 2016, with groundbreaking in 2018, allowing for careful consideration of how it would be embedded among the warehouses and industrial spaces of East Williamsburg.

With concrete, brick, and steel, the Brooklyn-based firm SO-IL designed a sanctum using materials that characterize the gritty neighborhood. Volumes of smooth exposed concrete are set against concrete with corrugated lines. Asymmetry reigns as walls curve and intersect in blocks of texture, including white bricks rotated to create a jagged pattern. On one façade, a single amorphous window bores through a thick concrete wall. Precast concrete stepping stones and textured concrete pathways invite visitors to explore courtyards and corridors between spaces holding galleries, studios, offices, a bookstore, and a café. Inside, ripples of felt line a reading nook, a nod to the exterior banded concrete.

In many of its recent projects, SO-IL has been using concrete in ways that resist its sometimes bleak associations. Elsewhere in Brooklyn, 450 Warren Street, completed in 2022, features suspended concrete walkways winding to its apartments, while another residential project at 144 Vanderbilt, completed in 2025, is covered with interlocking precast concrete panels tinted a dusty rose.

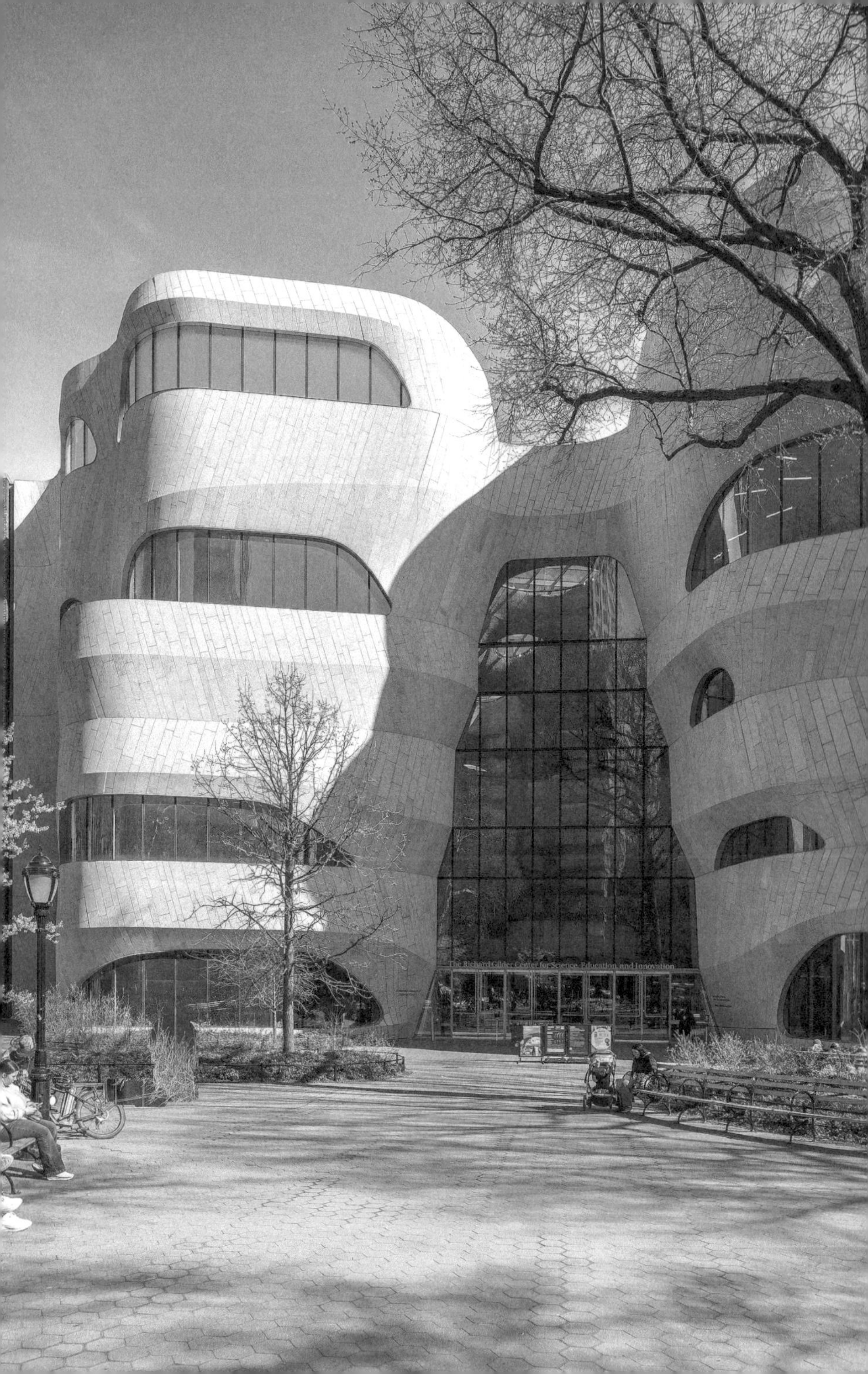
The Richard Gilder Center for Science, Education, and Innovation

11 American Museum of Natural History: Gilder Center

Studio Gang, 2019-23
415 Columbus Avenue, Manhattan, 10024

Since the American Museum of Natural History opened its home alongside Central Park in 1877, it has sprawled into a hodgepodge of more than 25 interconnected buildings enveloping four city blocks. Each has its own character, from the Romanesque Revival addition on West 77th Street to the contemporary Rose Center for Earth and Space with its sphere suspended in a glass cube. To blend seamlessly into such a mélange would be impossible, so for the latest wing, Studio Gang presented something singular in this architectural constellation: a design inspired by nature's raw power.

A cavernous atrium, soaring six stories, forms the Gilder Center's interior core. Skylights and bridges cut through the space in organic forms, with the amorphous interior informed by the way wind and water shape geologic formations. Its surfaces are covered with shotcrete, in which concrete is sprayed directly onto mesh and rebar armatures. It's a technique more frequently used in infrastructure, such as underground subway tunnels. Earlier renderings of the project depicted its interior concrete walls as smooth and white. The completed surfaces are instead a grainy gray, their rough texture suggesting something eroded from rock. These contrast with details in wood and glass, including windows that give glimpses into labs and visible storage. In the fourth-floor library, the concrete bursts into a mushroom-like form that sprouts over a reading room. On every level are portals outward, opening former dead ends and creating new points of connection for the labyrinthine museum.

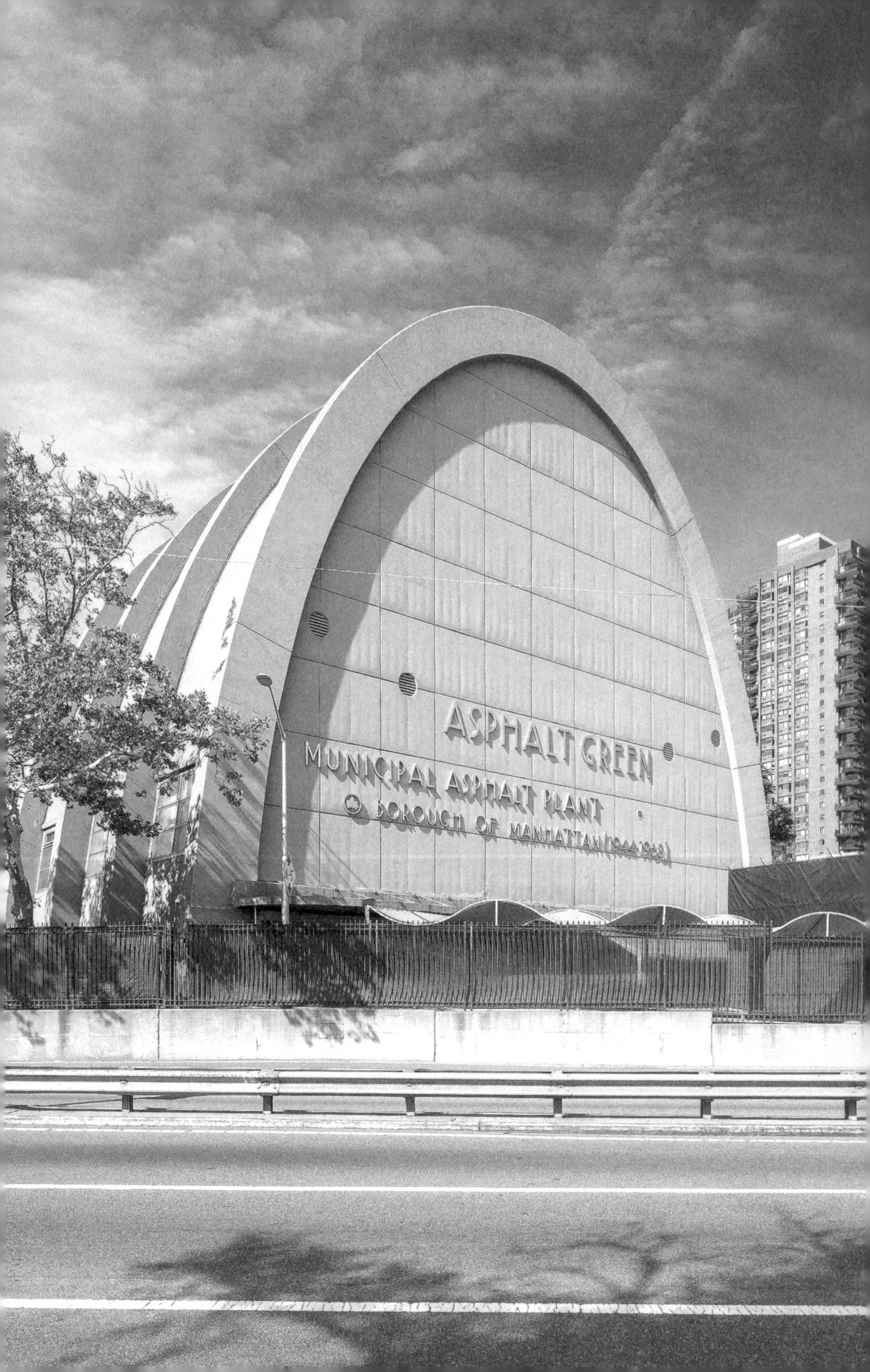
ASPHALT GREEN
MUNICIPAL ASPHALT PLANT
BOROUGH OF MANHATTAN 1944-1968

12 Asphalt Green (Municipal Asphalt Plant)

Kahn & Jacobs, 1941–44
555 East 90th Street, Manhattan, 10128

Robert Moses, New York City's cantankerous parks commissioner, mocked the Municipal Asphalt Plant as a "Cathedral of Asphalt" before it was completed in 1944. The Museum of Modern Art responded by celebrating it in an exhibition that year, with curator Elizabeth Mock stating of its efficient use of space, "The bold semi-ellipse of the mixing plant is no affectation." Now that the controversy around this elegant example of industrial Modernism has faded, it has become a landmark of the East River waterfront.

It replaced a 1914 plant for mixing street asphalt with one that was cleaner, quieter, and more attractive. Its architects, Ely Jacques Kahn and Robert Allan Jacobs, had recently become partners in 1940. Kahn brought his experience making mountainous modern towers and Jacobs his knowledge of concrete's possibilities from working for Le Corbusier in Paris. He had also studied Eugène Freyssinet's concrete dirigible hangars at Orly Airport.

The most remarkable element of the complex is what survives: the elongated curve of the first reinforced concrete parabolic-arched structure in the country. Its four nearly 90-foot-tall ribbed arches bend over walls and a roof of exposed cast-in-place concrete. After the plant's operations ended in 1968, much of it was demolished. A grassroots fight protected this pioneering building as the showpiece of the Asphalt Green recreation center. It opened in 1984, with a running track and basketball courts within its concrete shell.

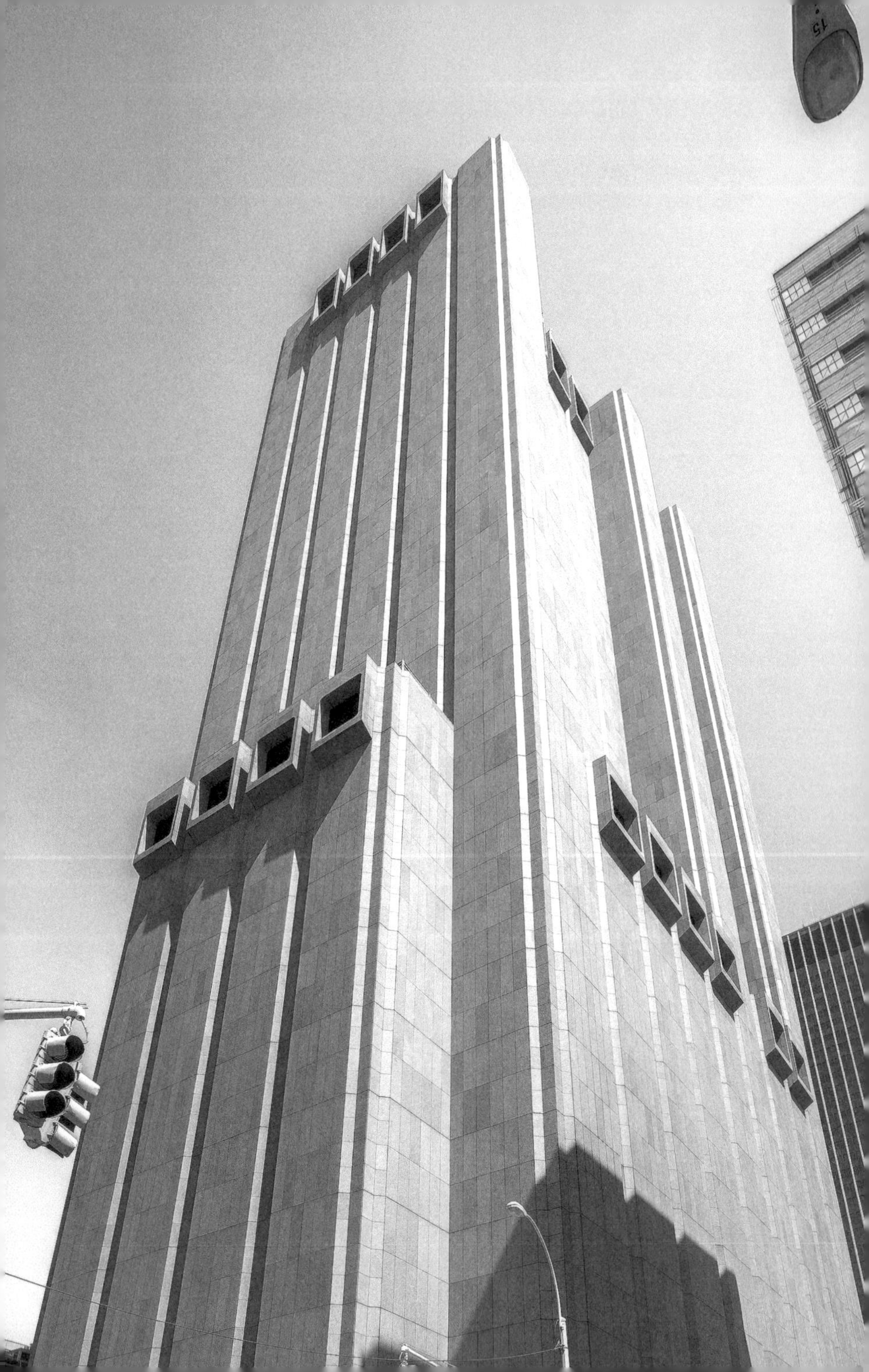

13 AT&T Long Lines Building

John Carl Warnecke & Associates, 1969–74
33 Thomas Street, Manhattan, 10007

No windows interrupt the approximately 550 feet of this Tribeca skyscraper. The sole apertures in the walls of precast concrete clad in reddish-brown granite are boxy ventilation openings. These protrude from the middle and top of huge columns like an array of giant periscopes.

This is a building created for the needs of machines instead of people. It was designed to house switching equipment for the AT&T Long Lines Department. Telecommunications structures dot Manhattan, chronicling the changing infrastructural needs as technology advanced. Nearby is AT&T's 1932 Art Deco building at 32 Avenue of the Americas, a mountain of brick that housed what was then the largest long-distance switchboard in the country. The facility at 33 Thomas became one of the largest centers in the world for long-distance telephone calls and required fewer human workers with increasing automation.

The Washington, DC-based architect John Carl Warnecke also worked on a number of government buildings, including offices for the Senate. The muscular AT&T tower has been referred to as one of the most secure buildings in the United States. The Cold War-era colossus is even prepared to endure a nuclear blast and offer shelter and supplies for its staff in the fallout. Its bizarre and clandestine appearance has led to conspiracy theories around its current use, with investigative reporting revealing its role as a National Security Agency (NSA) surveillance post.

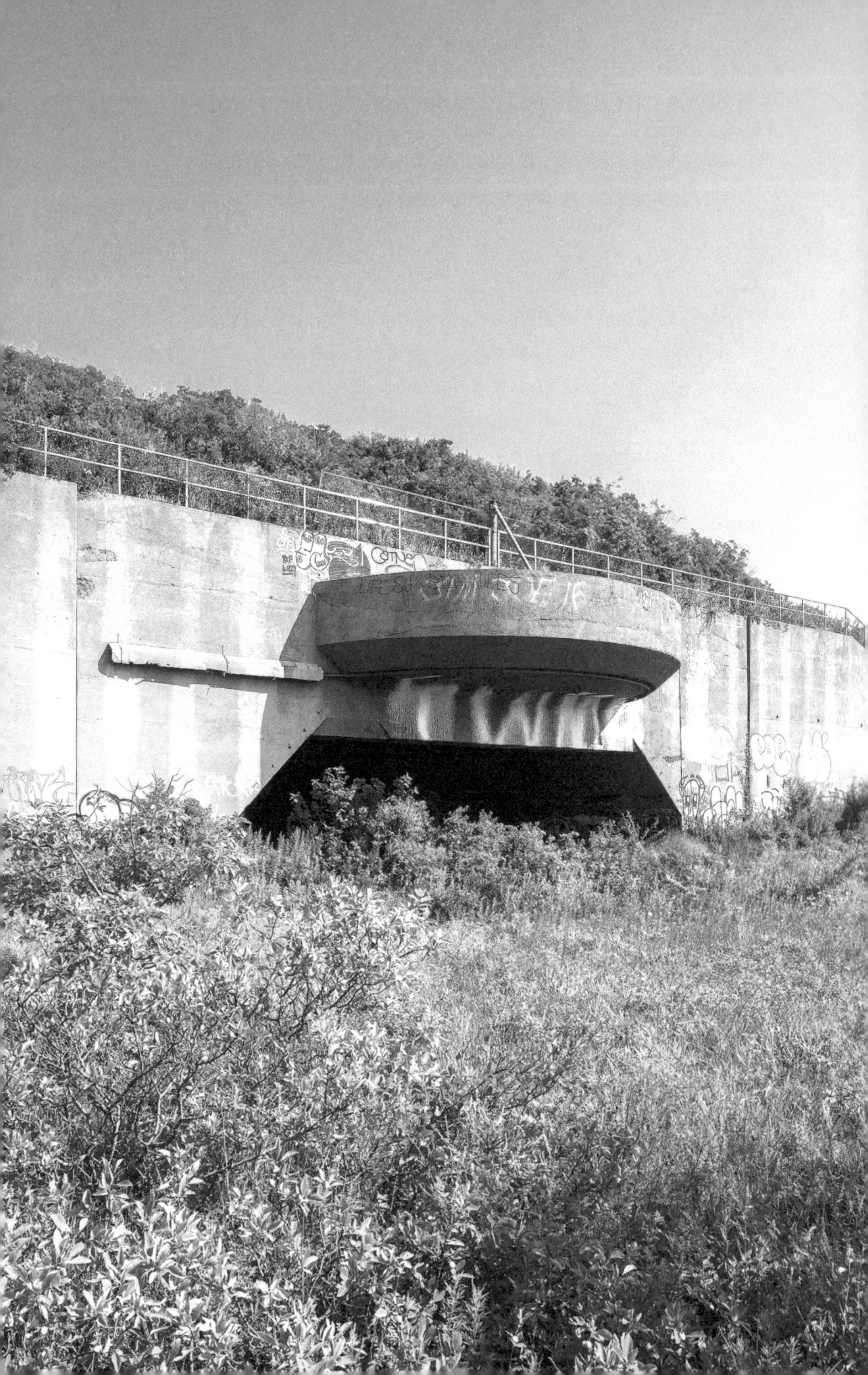

(14) Battery Harris at Fort Tilden

United States Army, 1941-43
Gateway National Recreation Area, Queens, 11697

The two mammoth concrete casemates collectively known as Battery Harris are almost invisible until you come upon them, hunched in the dunes and marine forest just beyond the beach. They were once part of the city's coastal defense system, holding anti-aircraft guns and cannons capable of shooting 25 miles out to sea. This artillery was initially in the open air when first installed in the 1920s; it was enhanced with concrete shelters in the World War II era to protect the 16-inch M1919 guns from aerial bombing. The two bunkers were built into the sand dunes with low, wide openings leading to interior rooms for gunpowder, artillery shells, and other supplies. The arc of concrete hanging over their entrances not only protected the guns from aerial attacks but also limited their rotation so they could not be turned on Manhattan if an enemy took over the site.

The US Army fort on the Rockaway Peninsula dates from 1917, although military use of its sandy coast goes back to the War of 1812. Fort Tilden was active through the Cold War, updated over the decades for shifting threats, from German U-boats to Soviet nuclear strikes. Decommissioned in the 1970s, it is now overseen by the National Park Service. Concrete bunkers and ammunition magazines, overgrown with vegetation and tagged with graffiti, still scatter the area.

While some sites are off limits due to safety concerns, like the old Nike missile silos, Battery Harris is open to explore. On Battery Harris East, stairs lead up to a viewing platform where the Manhattan skyline rises in the distance.

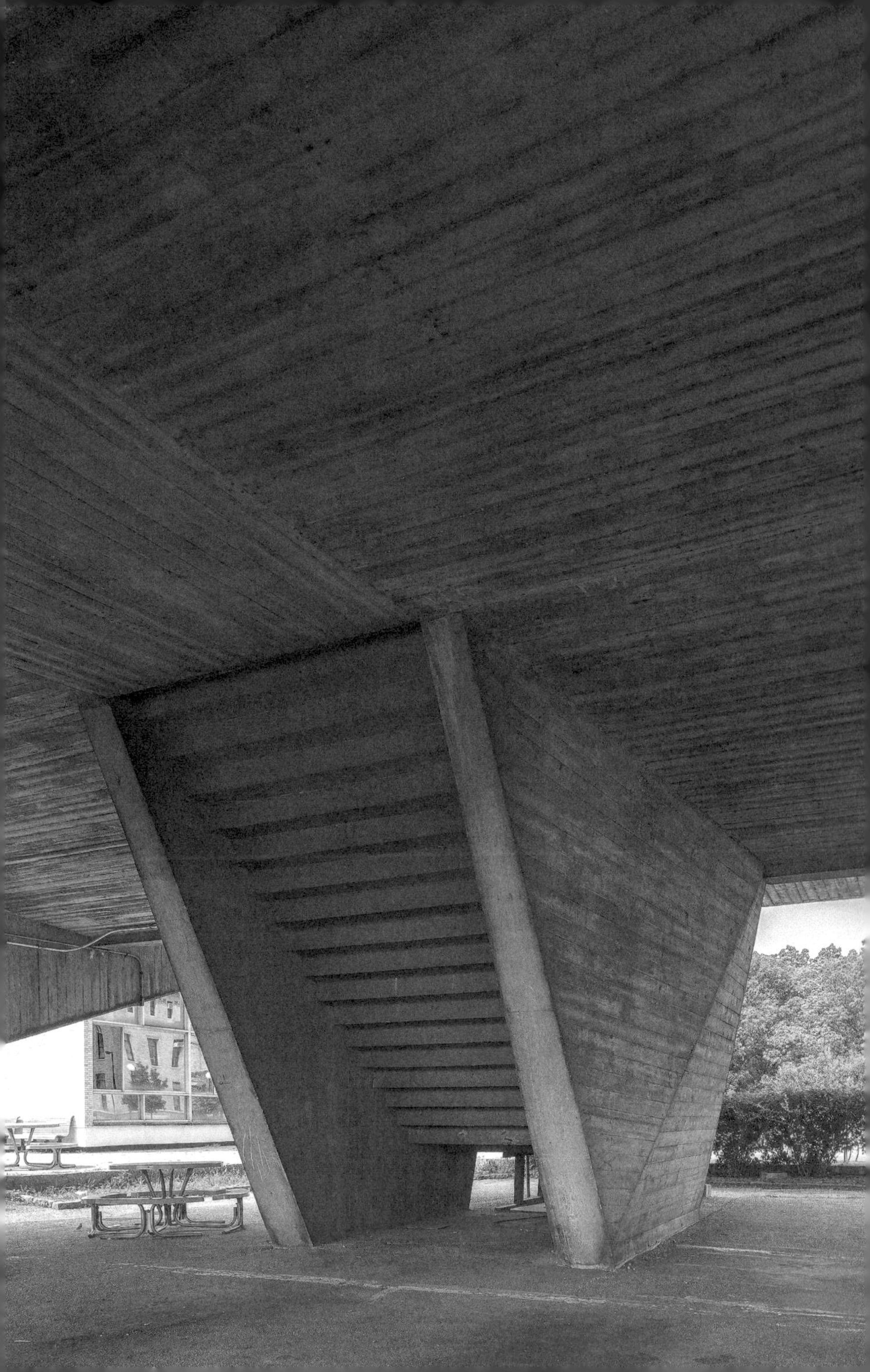

15 Bronx Community College: Breuer Buildings

Marcel Breuer & Associates, 1956–67
2155 University Avenue, The Bronx, 10453

In 1956, New York University commissioned Marcel Breuer for a master plan to expand its uptown campus. What the architect proposed was a bold counterpoint to the Beaux-Arts buildings by Stanford White that made up the historic core. Where those have a classically inspired sense of order in granite and marble, Breuer's additions are more informal and employ the fluidity of concrete for a series of geometric forms. Five of Breuer's buildings were ultimately completed here: Colston Hall (1960, previously Silver Hall), Community Hall (1960), Carl Polowczyk Hall (1960, previously Gould Technology), Begrisch Hall (1961), and Meister Hall (1967, previously Tech II).

In 1973, the campus became Bronx Community College. The buildings chronicle how Breuer's use of reinforced, exposed concrete and steel evolved. The earlier works are expressively sculptural, especially the most outstanding—Begrisch Hall—that slopes downward from each end. Its bulk of trapezoidal concrete, which holds two lecture halls, looks lightly balanced on a triangular support. An enclosed concrete bridge connects it to Carl Polowczyk Hall. A sweeping slab of concrete canopies the entrance of the V-shaped Colston Hall. The last completed, Meister Hall, is a more succinct statement as it stands on Y-shaped legs and has a wall of concrete panels in a grid pattern. Everywhere is Breuer's poetic attention to every aspect of a building, which gave his Brutalist structures detail on a human scale.

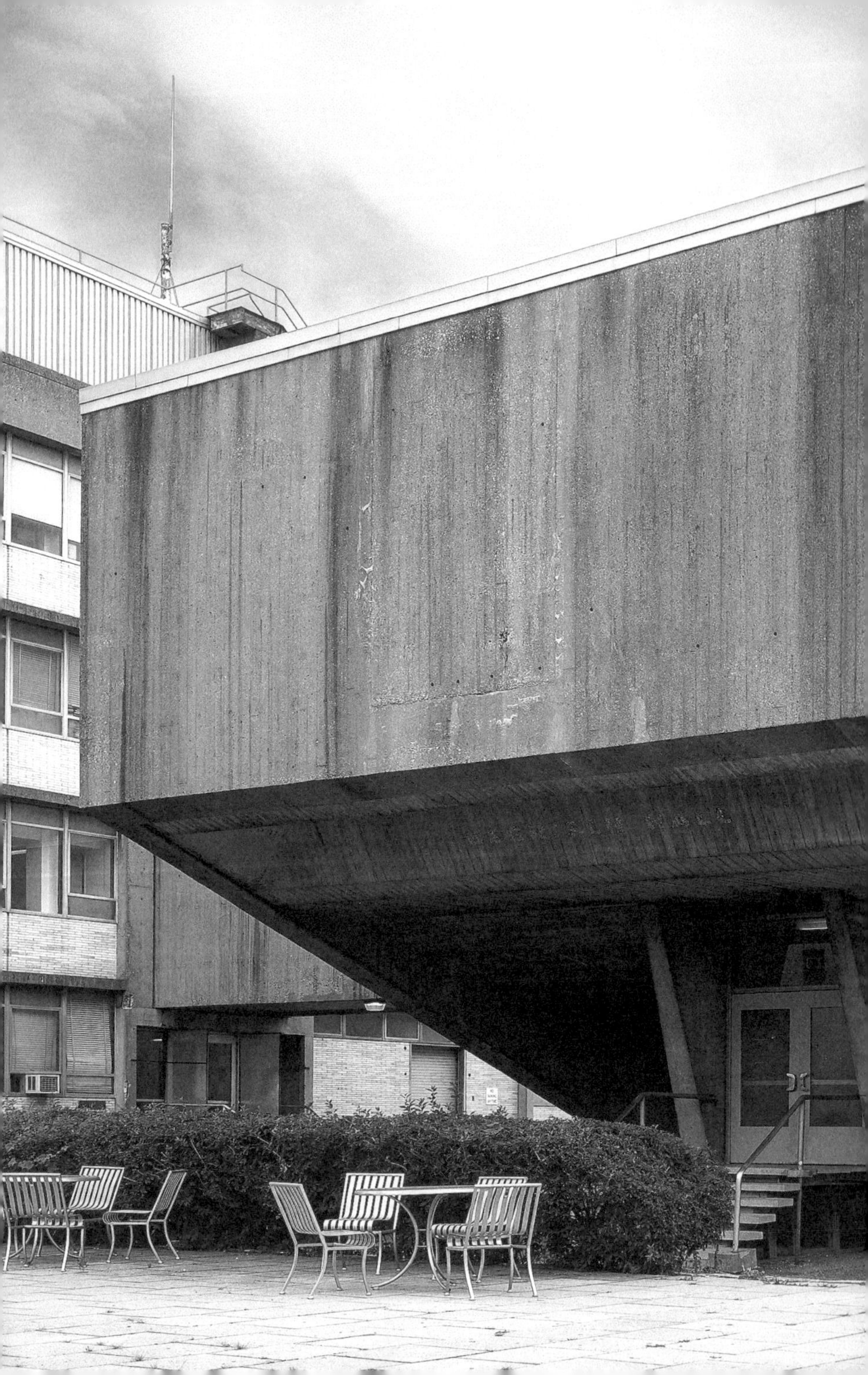

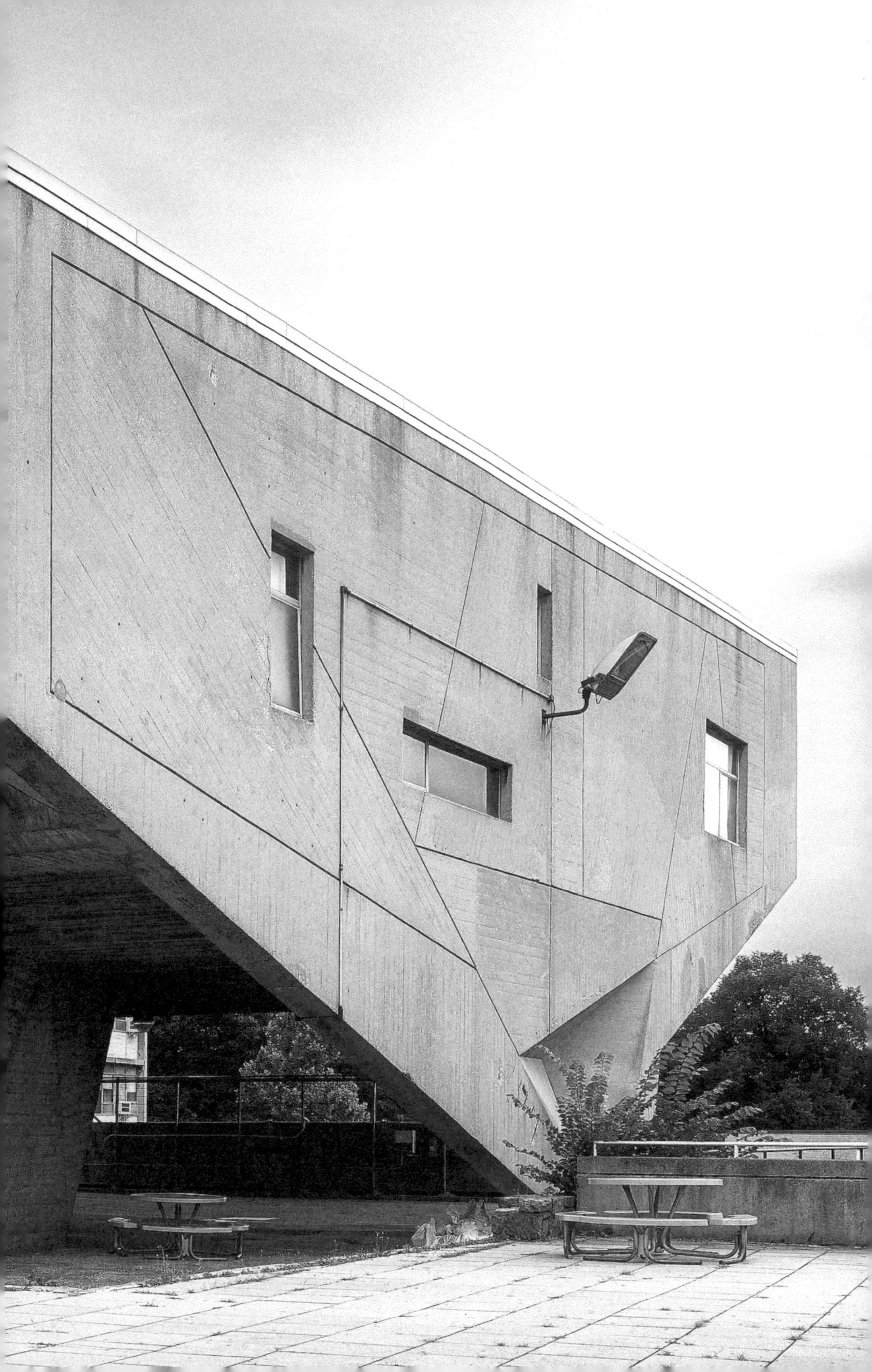

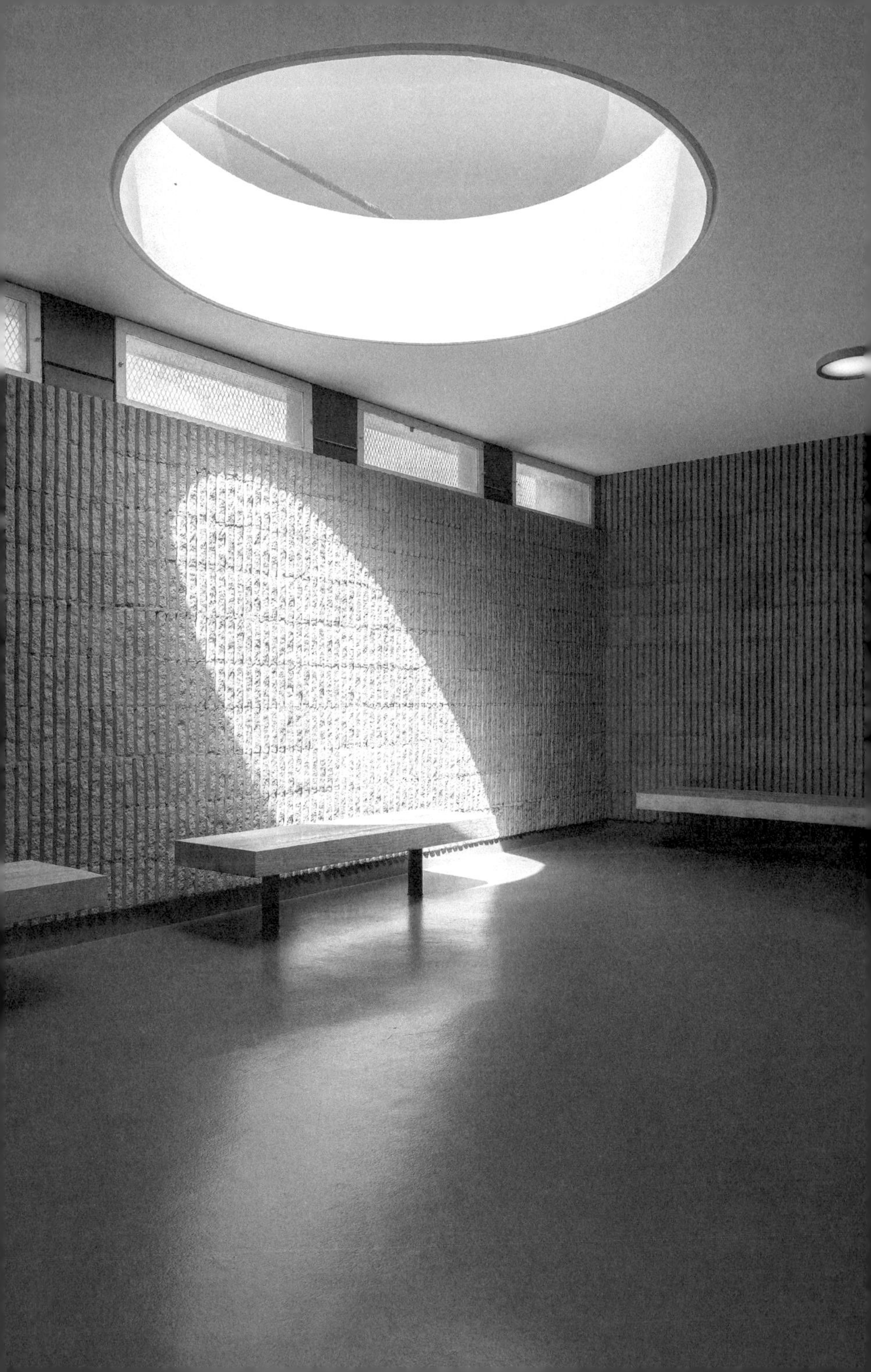

16

Bronx Zoo: The World of Birds

Morris Ketchum, Jr. & Associates, 1971-72
2300 Southern Boulevard, The Bronx, 10460

Morris Ketchum, Jr. described the rough-hammered concrete circling the avian habitats in this building as a "protective skin." Some aspects, like the painted backdrops, may appear dated now, but the World of Birds was revolutionary zoo design when it debuted. Dividers, even glass, were removed between visitors and the birds. The needs of the animals, not the architecture, were central, a divergence with the Bronx Zoo's earlier ornate Beaux-Arts buildings.

The structure's cylindrical volumes vary in height, which helps keep shadows from being cast on the angled skylights. Reinforced concrete ramps lead visitors up through two floors, each offering different perspectives on the habitats. The project followed Ketchum's work on the zoo's 1969 World of Darkness. That windowless facility, made with large slabs of precast concrete surfaced with black granite, reverses day and night for its nocturnal animals. This complex of aviaries is even more ambitious and came in at twice its expected budget, generously funded by *Reader's Digest* co-founder Lila Acheson Wallace. The architects worked closely with the zoo team, resulting in a 30,000-square-foot space supporting hundreds of species. Its 24 areas range from rainforests with simulated thunderstorms to arid deserts. Although visitors encounter a global diversity of birds—like critically endangered maleos from Indonesia and bee-eaters from Africa that catch crickets in midair—a waterfall element was made close to home: water cascades over a 40-foot cliff cast from the New Jersey Palisades.

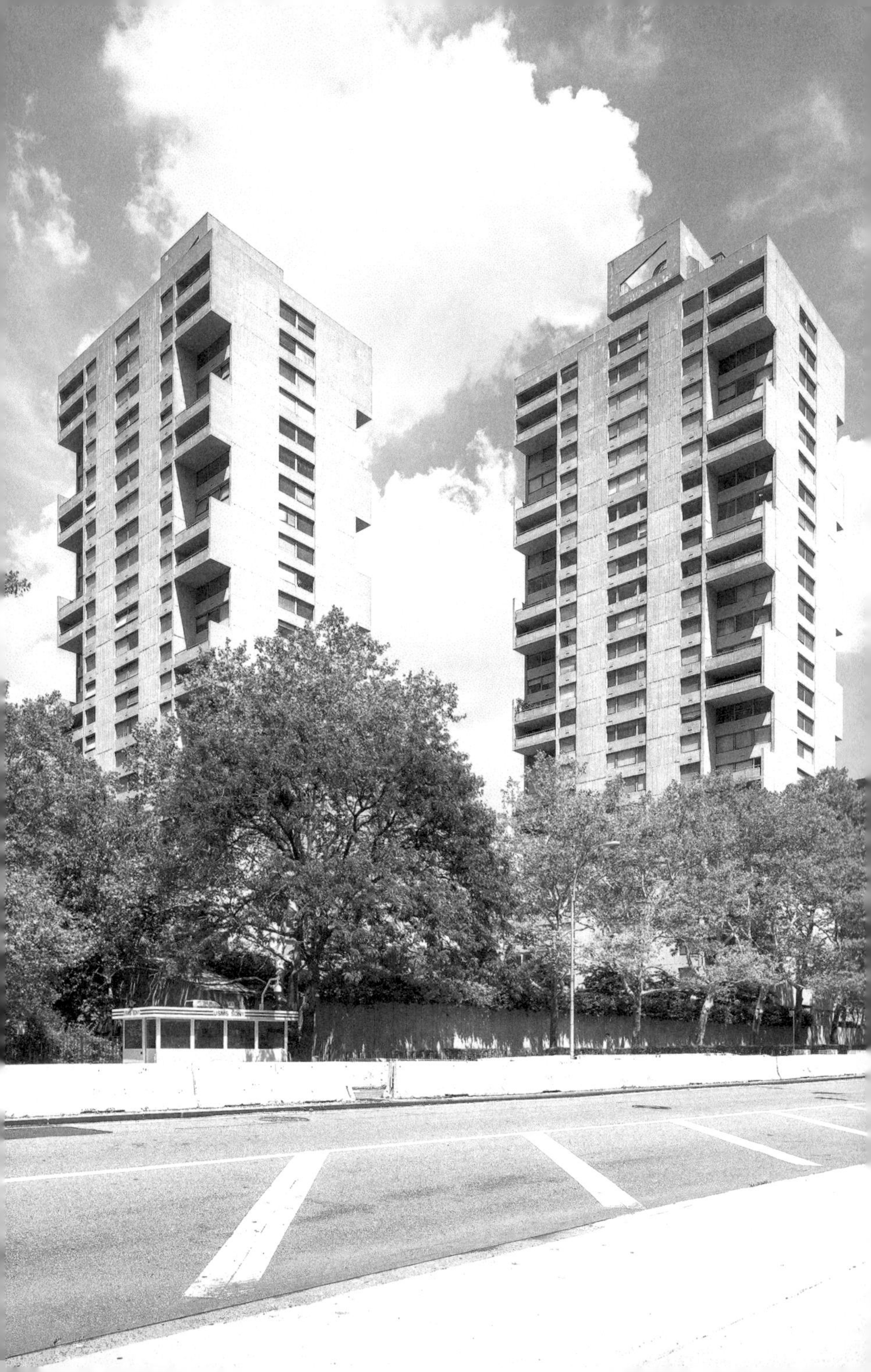

17

Chatham Towers

Kelly & Gruzen, 1959–65
170 and 180 Park Row, Manhattan, 10038

These two 25-story towers were some of the first Manhattan housing to feature exposed concrete. An earlier design proposed steel. The switch in material allowed for maximizing space by putting the load-bearing support on the exterior rather than the interior columns. But the aesthetics of the choice are also flaunted, such as the wood grain imprints from the board forms of the poured-in-place material. Even the rooftop mechanical equipment is concealed by concrete. A rhythm of two floors with terraces, then two without, gives the towers a distinctive syncopated appearance, like stacks of oversized blocks.

Although apartments here can now go for over a million dollars, when Chatham Towers was completed, it was a middle-income co-op. One of its key amenities was a roof garden designed by M. Paul Friedberg atop the parking garage, decorated with exposed concrete tree planters and reflecting pools.

To showcase city views, a defining feature of the apartments, the architects were among the first to employ large Swedish-designed extruded aluminum windows that pivot open (often compared to train or bus windows). Measuring five by seven feet, they have double panes of glass set in a rounded-corner metal frame, with a Venetian blind set between the panes—an innovation long before integral blinds became commonplace. George Shimamoto led the project for Kelly & Gruzen; the team included Cuban architect Mario Romanach, who had worked on 1950s Modernist housing in Havana.

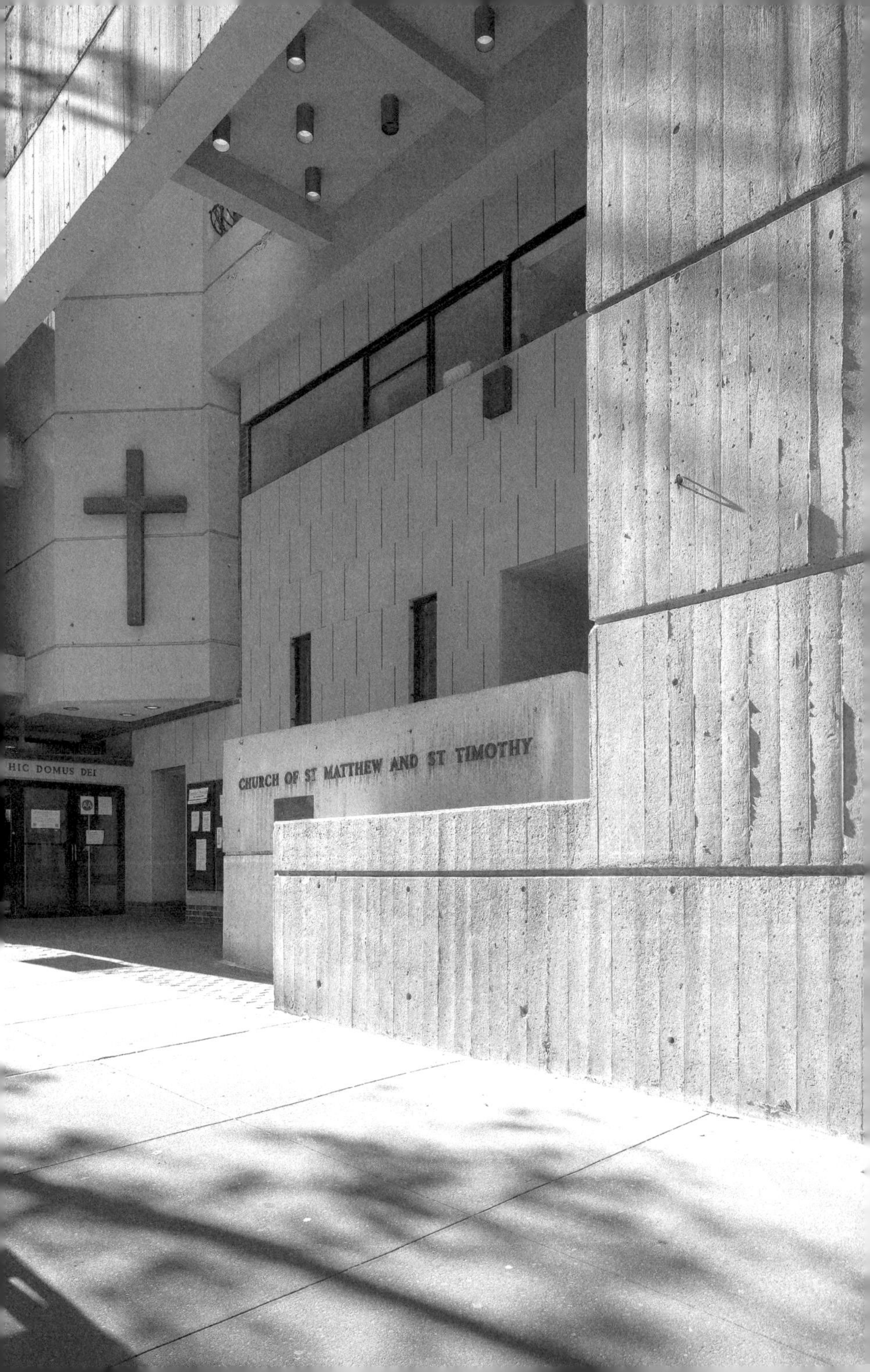
HIC DOMUS DEI
CHURCH OF ST MATTHEW AND ST TIMOTHY

18 Church of St. Matthew and St. Timothy

Victor Christ-Janer & Associates, 1967–70
26 West 84th Street, Manhattan, 10024

Hic Domus Dei—"Here is the house of God"—reads the inscription over the entrance to this citadel of a church. Cast-in-place concrete dominates its edifice in the middle of an Upper West Side block of apartment buildings. Yet as hinted by its geometric opening packed with windows, doorways, and protrusions—including a turret of concrete adorned with a cross—it uses the protective nature of the material to shelter a haven within. While the exterior is all gray, inside the exposed concrete harmonizes with the warm wood of the pews and organ and the white of the walls. Members of this Episcopal congregation access the sanctuary through a long corridor, setting a contemplative tone. The space for worship is intimate; a second-level balcony hangs low to bring everyone close to the central altar, over which is suspended a large mosaic cross.

The church's dual name comes from a 1922 merger of two parishes. Its previous home was an 1890s Gothic structure by ecclesiastical architect William Halsey Wood that was razed after a 1965 fire. The architect of this new building was Victor Christ-Janer, known for his use of concrete and glass at a human rather than a monumental scale. Most of his other local religious work has not survived, such as a stark 1966 façade of orange brick on the Tenth Church of Christ, Scientist on McDougal Street (removed in 2008) and the austere concrete community center for the Church of the Master on Morningside Avenue, replaced with a gleaming white edifice in 2013.

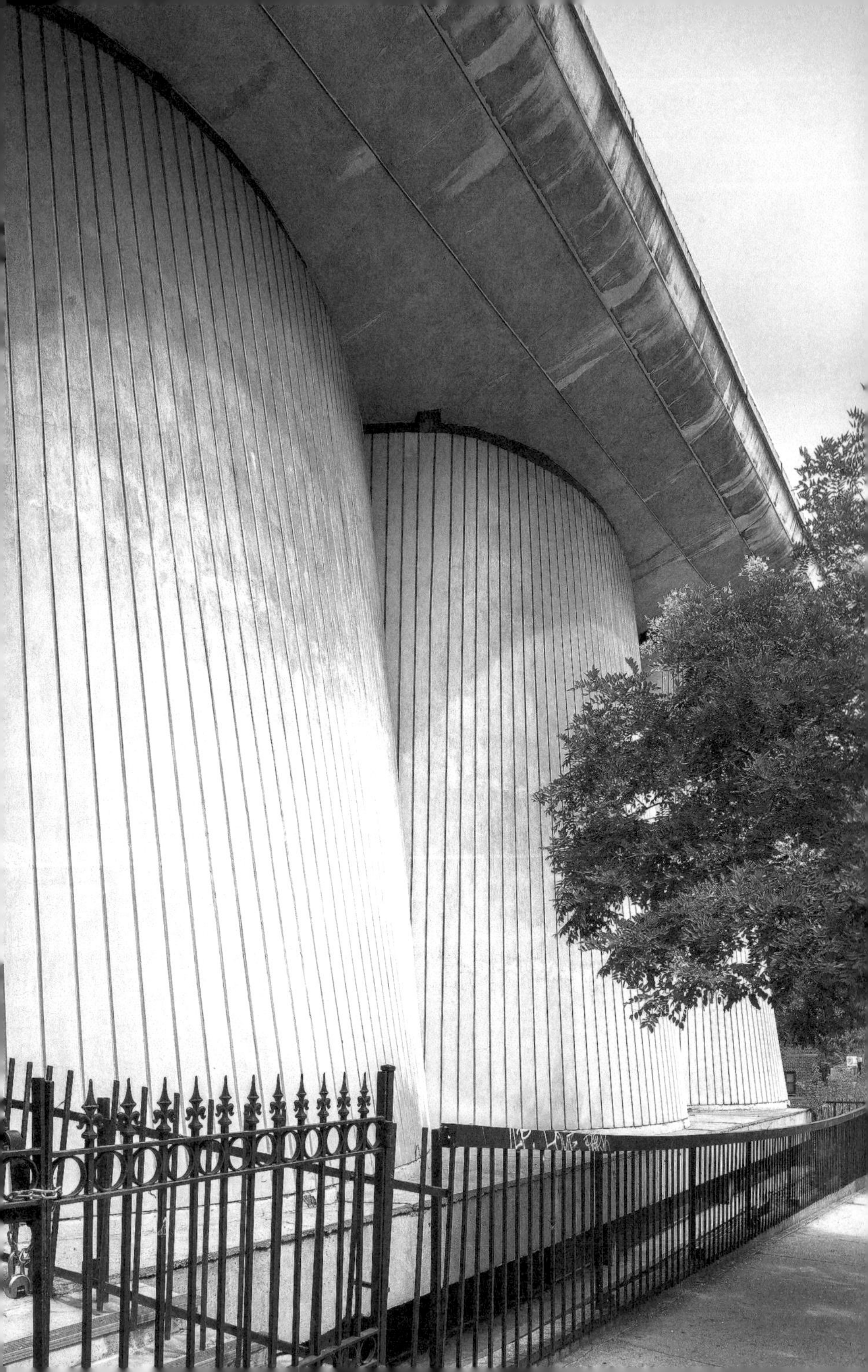

19 Church of the Crucifixion

Costas Machlouzarides, 1965–69
459 West 149th Street, Manhattan, 10031

The year that Le Corbusier died, one of his most famous works was echoed in Manhattan. The Cyprus-born architect Costas Machlouzarides's design for this Episcopal church is strongly reminiscent of the 1950s Notre-Dame du Haut in Ronchamp, France. A buoyant exposed concrete roof, topped by a steel cross, appears to float on cylinders of reinforced concrete that all slant in a slightly different way. This gives the base a sense of movement, with three conical forms on one side of its corner lot and one large swoop on another. Inside, these create a barrel-vault effect. Where these windowless walls meet the roof, light streams in through a strip of windows, radiating a halo over the sanctuary.

In a quiet but dense residential area of Harlem, the church manages to be a gentle giant, even though its chunky curves look like nothing else around it. Machlouzarides once said he wanted to generate through his architecture "a certain elation for people who use the space." Although visually disparate, his New York works share a whimsical exuberance, from the multicolored 1966 Greater Refuge Temple [25] to the 1975 Calhoun School at the corner of West End Avenue and West 81st Street, with its two gaping façades of travertine and glass that resemble colossal television sets. The Church of the Crucifixion congregation's previous home was the Hamilton Grange Reformed Dutch Church, a Gothic-style building destroyed by a fire in March 1963. The Modernist rebuild opened in 1969, and you can still see traces of the old church's granite foundation below the concrete.

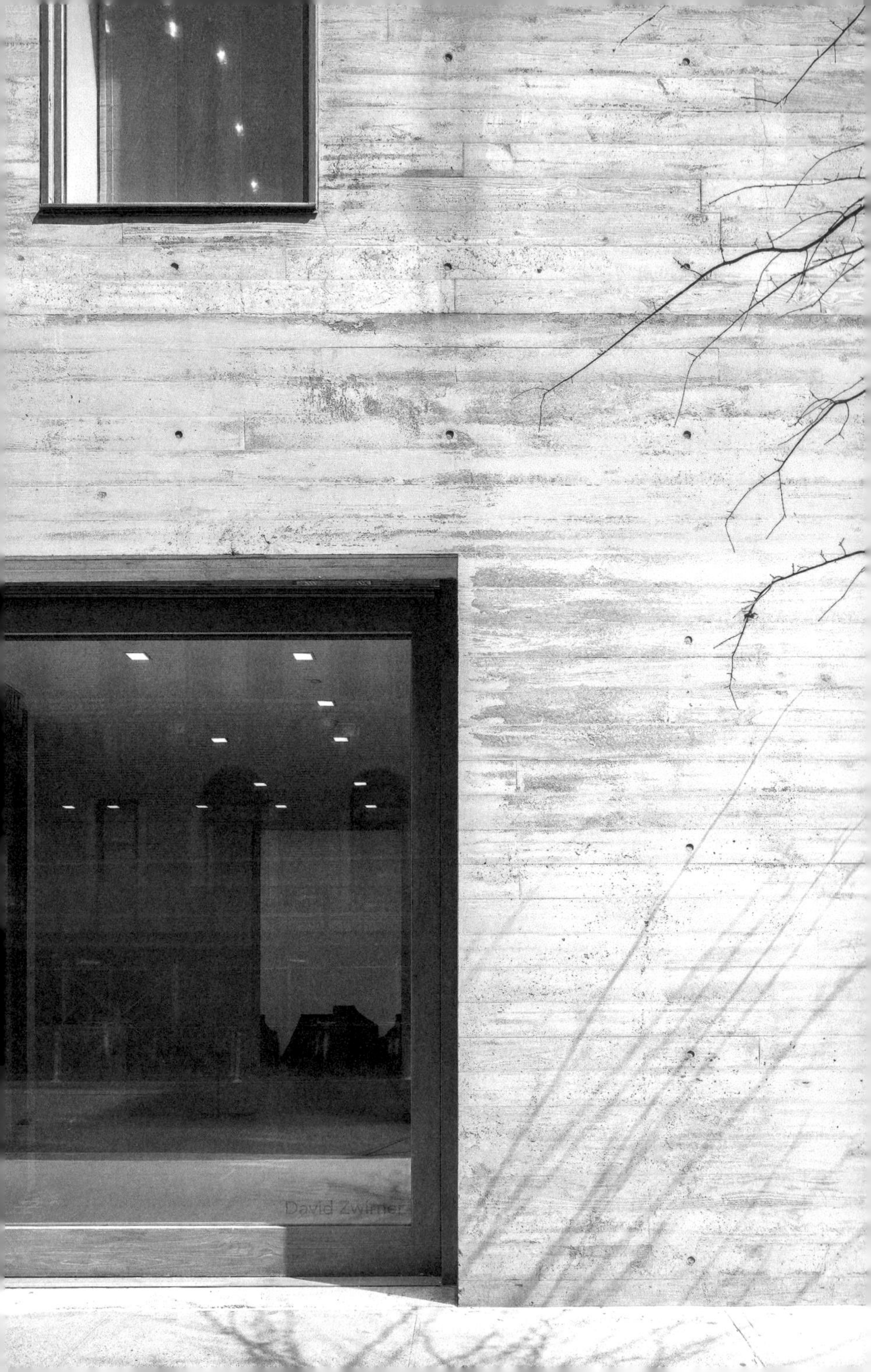
David Zwirner

(20) David Zwirner

Selldorf Architects, 2013
537 West 20th Street, Manhattan, 10011

The striated concrete façade of this gallery makes it stand out from its brick warehouse neighbors. Imprints from the pine boards used in a poured-in-place process keep its five stories of exposed concrete, accentuated with teak-framed windows, from becoming monotonous. Inside, a large columnless 5,000-square-foot gallery space has a poured concrete floor; smaller galleries and offices are on the upper levels. The most dramatic feature is its central staircase. Concrete steps appear to levitate as they cantilever off walls of board-formed concrete, the stairwell warmly illuminated by a skylight. It's a building signature that Selldorf Architects later echoed in a Los Angeles gallery for David Zwirner, completed in 2024.

Selldorf has a longstanding relationship with Zwirner, having designed several of its outposts. While many of these projects adapted existing structures, this was a ground-up project. The restrained material palette, where the rough is side-by-side with the refined, complements a roster of modern and contemporary artists. (The first exhibition at the West 20th Street gallery was of Minimalist work by Dan Flavin and Donald Judd.)

Selldorf also worked on the nearby Hauser & Wirth gallery on West 22nd Street, completed in 2020. Concrete is also a dominant element but used in a distinct way, with a dark gray façade that involves zinc panels and concrete blocks made with recycled glass.

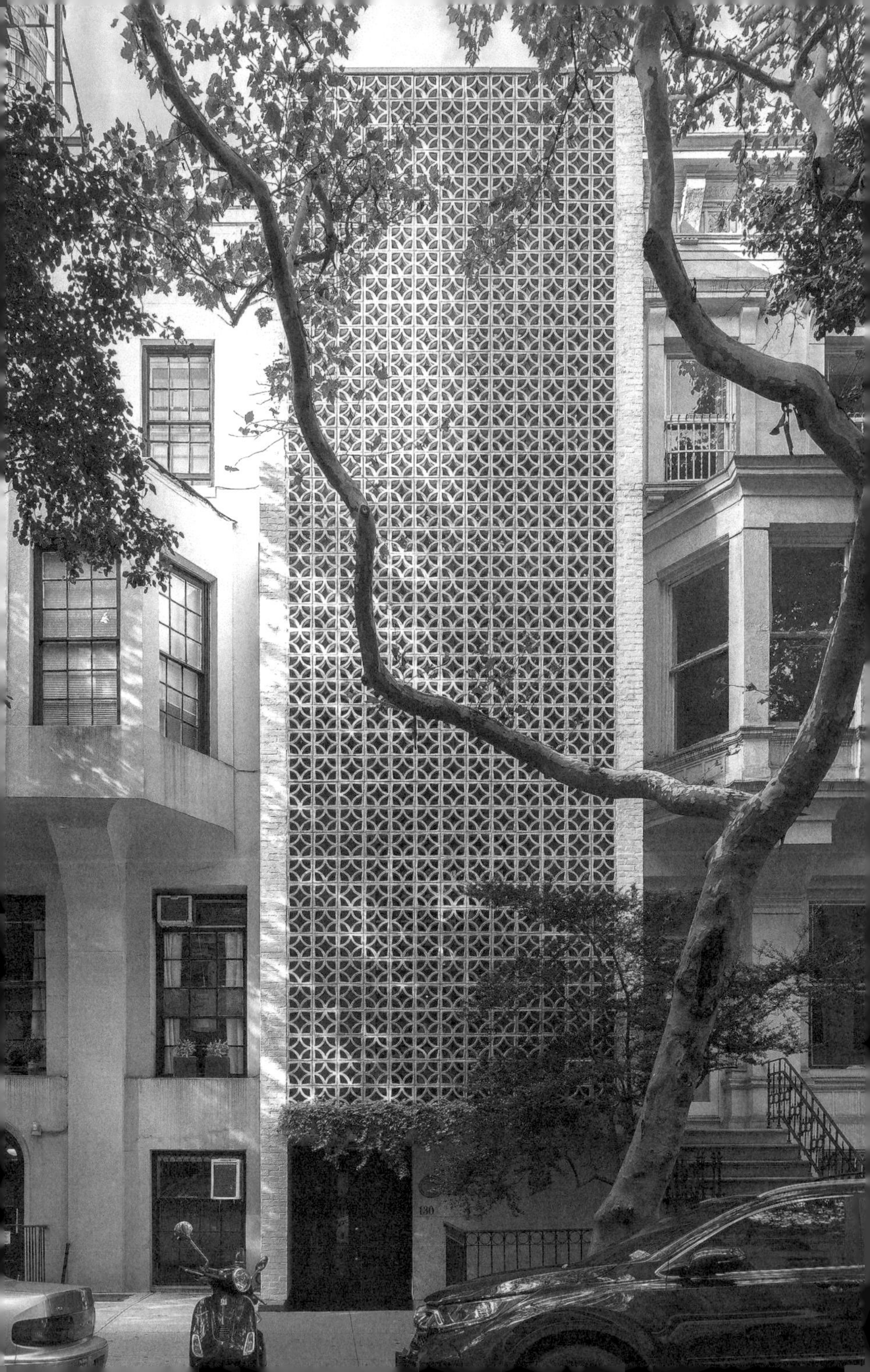
130

21 Edward Durell Stone Townhouse

Edward Durell Stone, 1956
130 East 64th Street, Manhattan, 10065

Edward Durell Stone was not averse to design that stood out from what had come before, as seen in the sleek Modernism of his work with Philip Goodwin on the 1939 Museum of Modern Art and the decadent sky-high lines of marble on the 1968 General Motors Building that towers over Fifth Avenue. His home on the Upper East Side was no different. In 1956, he completely overhauled an 1878 building in the middle of a block of rowhouses, stripping its façade and adding a large skylight and picture windows. The metamorphosis was masked with a concrete grille that offered a privacy screen for those big windows and diffused the light within. Compared to its townhouse neighbors, it was an architectural oddity.

The concrete grille's geometric pattern of interconnecting circles and squares was inspired by Stone's work on the US Embassy in New Delhi, India, which opened in 1959. It introduced a screen block of perforated concrete that he would replicate on many of his subsequent projects. This shift to the ornamental broke with his earlier embrace of the glass and steel of the International Style. As he said in a 1958 *Vogue* article, he had become "discontented with the uncompromising purity and aridness" of these ascetic designs. Stone died in 1978, and this ostentatious chimera of a Victorian home was landmarked as part of the Upper East Side Historic District in 1981.

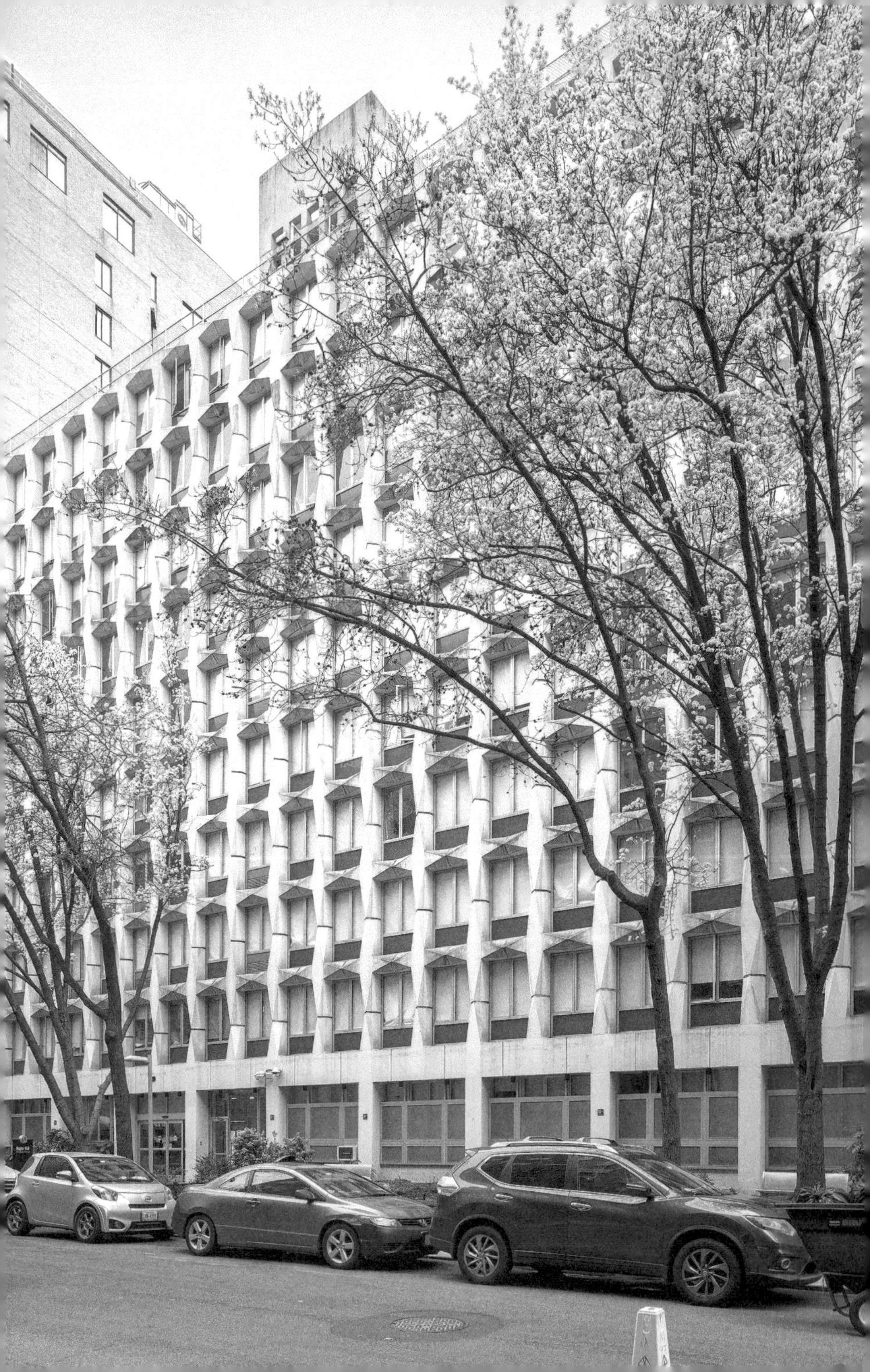

22 Fashion Institute of Technology: Nagler Residence Hall

DeYoung & Moscowitz, 1962
220 West 27th Street, Manhattan, 10001

A grid of precast concrete cruciforms covers this ten-story dormitory. Windows are deep-set within these faceted crosses on the mid-block building. It was one of several structures that Philip de Young and Benjamin Moscowitz worked on for the Fashion Institute of Technology (FIT) campus in Chelsea. Despite being overseen by the same architects, each of these buildings has its own adventurous take on Modernism. In the compendium *New York 1960: Architecture and Urbanism Between the Second World War and the Bicentennial* (1995) by Robert A. M. Stern, David Fishman, and Thomas Mellins, the authors observed that the addition of Nagler Residence Hall was "setting the campus on a course leading to cacophony."

There is a brazen diversity to the buildings here. There's also something fitting to their eclectic façades, as if they were huge sheets of different textile patterns from the nearby Garment District. FIT was founded in 1944 to promote training in the clothing industry, but it didn't have its first dedicated building until 1959. Right across the street from Nagler Hall is one of the earliest buildings designed for the campus by De Young, Moscowitz & Rosenberg (when the firm included Karl Rosenberg). It is covered with large aluminum panels with an origami bend that have weathered from their original blue to a copper color. Next door is a later dorm that the firm worked on—CoEd Hall—which has textural concrete blocks that protrude from its top like turrets.

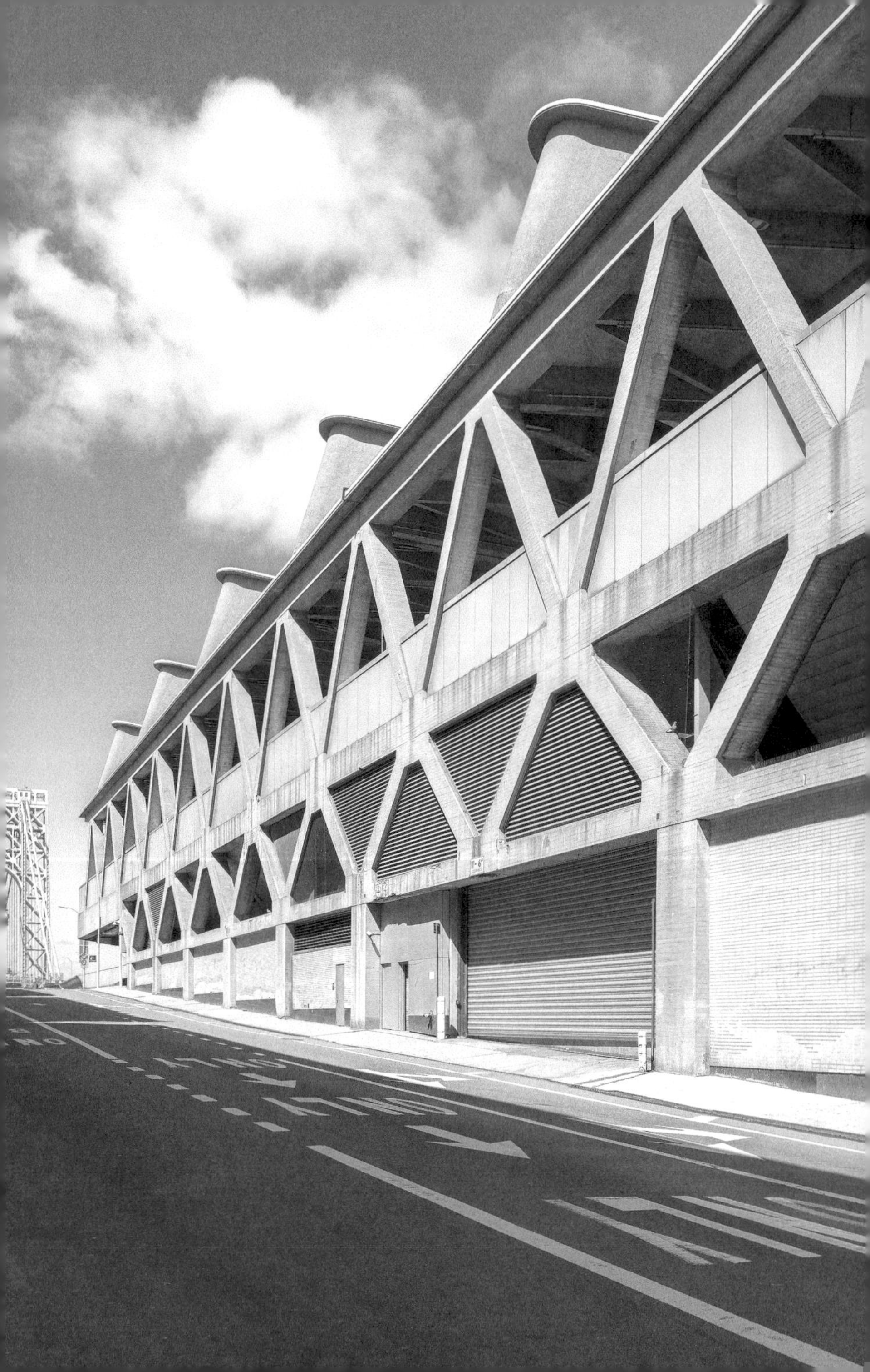

23 George Washington Bridge Bus Station

Pier Luigi Nervi, 1960-63
4211 Broadway, Manhattan, 10033

For what would be his first building in the United States, Italian architect and engineer Pier Luigi Nervi was hired in 1960 by the Port Authority of New York and New Jersey to design a terminal that would consolidate commuter buses that loaded on the streets. The resulting three-level structure spans the Trans-Manhattan Expressway on huge concrete trusses. Despite its magnitude, it exemplifies why Nervi was a maestro at making reinforced concrete appear weightless. Unlike his better-known stadium projects in Italy, with their graceful curves—such as the swerving staircases of the 1931 Stadio Artemio Franchi in Florence and the flying buttresses of the Palazzetto dello Sport built for the 1960 Summer Olympics in Rome—the George Washington Bridge Bus Station is all about angles. Yet, like all of Nervi's work, it reaches toward the sky.

Opened on January 17, 1963, the structure's most arresting feature is the roof. Triangular forms of precast concrete rise like butterfly wings from crisscrossing columns that extend to the ground. Their chalky gray color contrasts with sky-blue panels accenting the exterior. The patterns of the concrete emulate the latticework of the exposed steel towers on the adjacent George Washington Bridge that connects the buses from Upper Manhattan to New Jersey. Following years of decay, a refurbishment of the station completed in 2017 improved access and added commercial space while respecting Nervi's vision of creating soaring structures from simple materials.

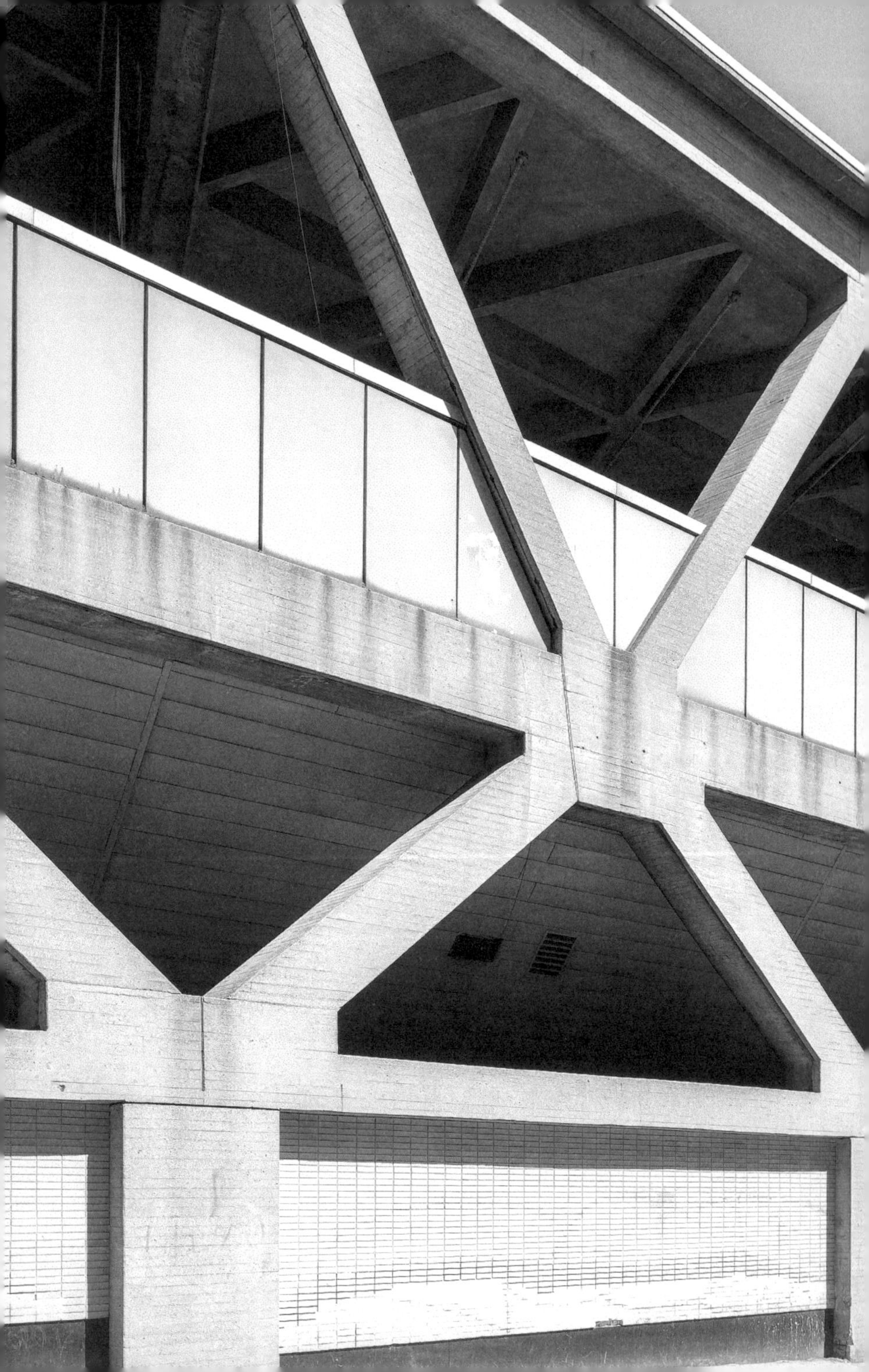

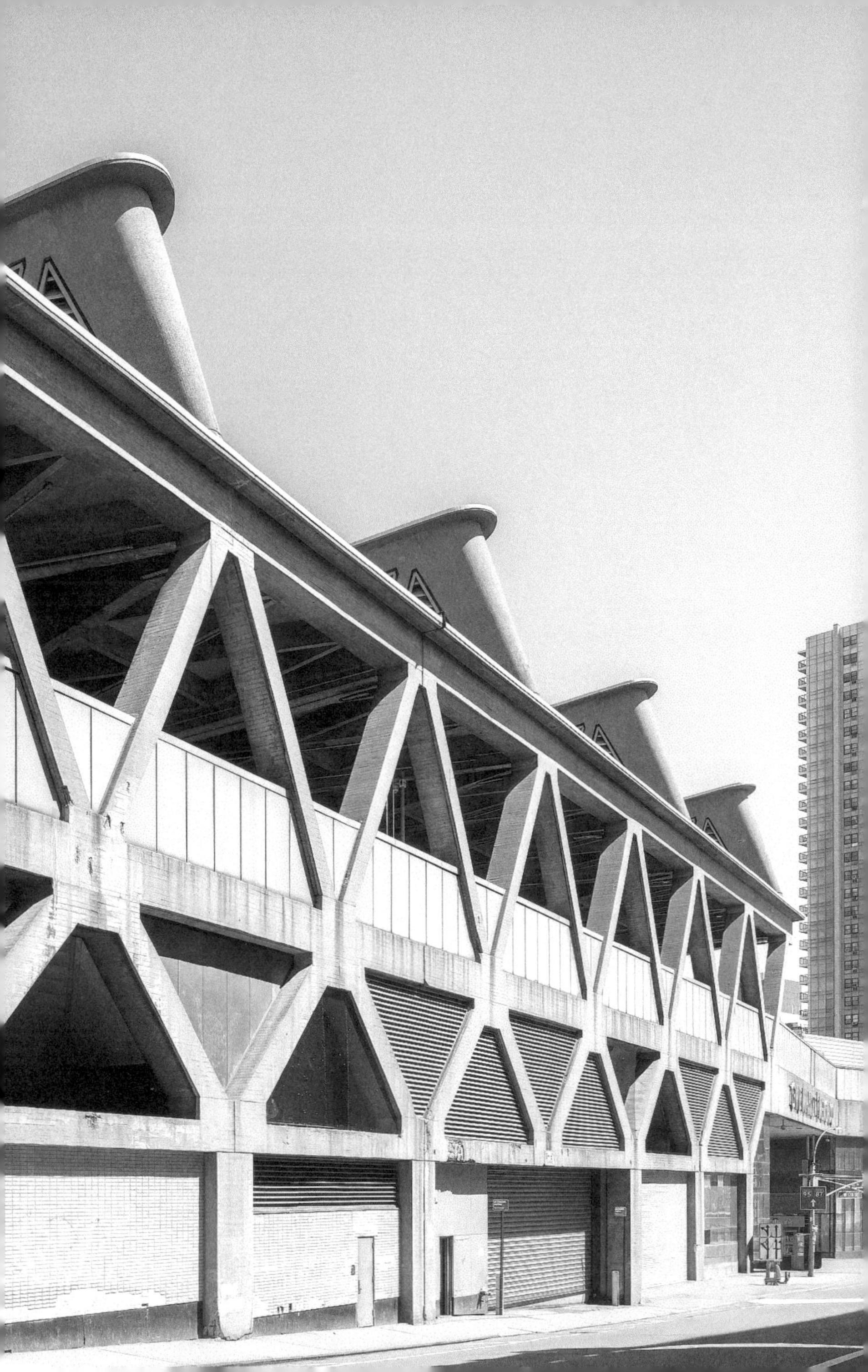

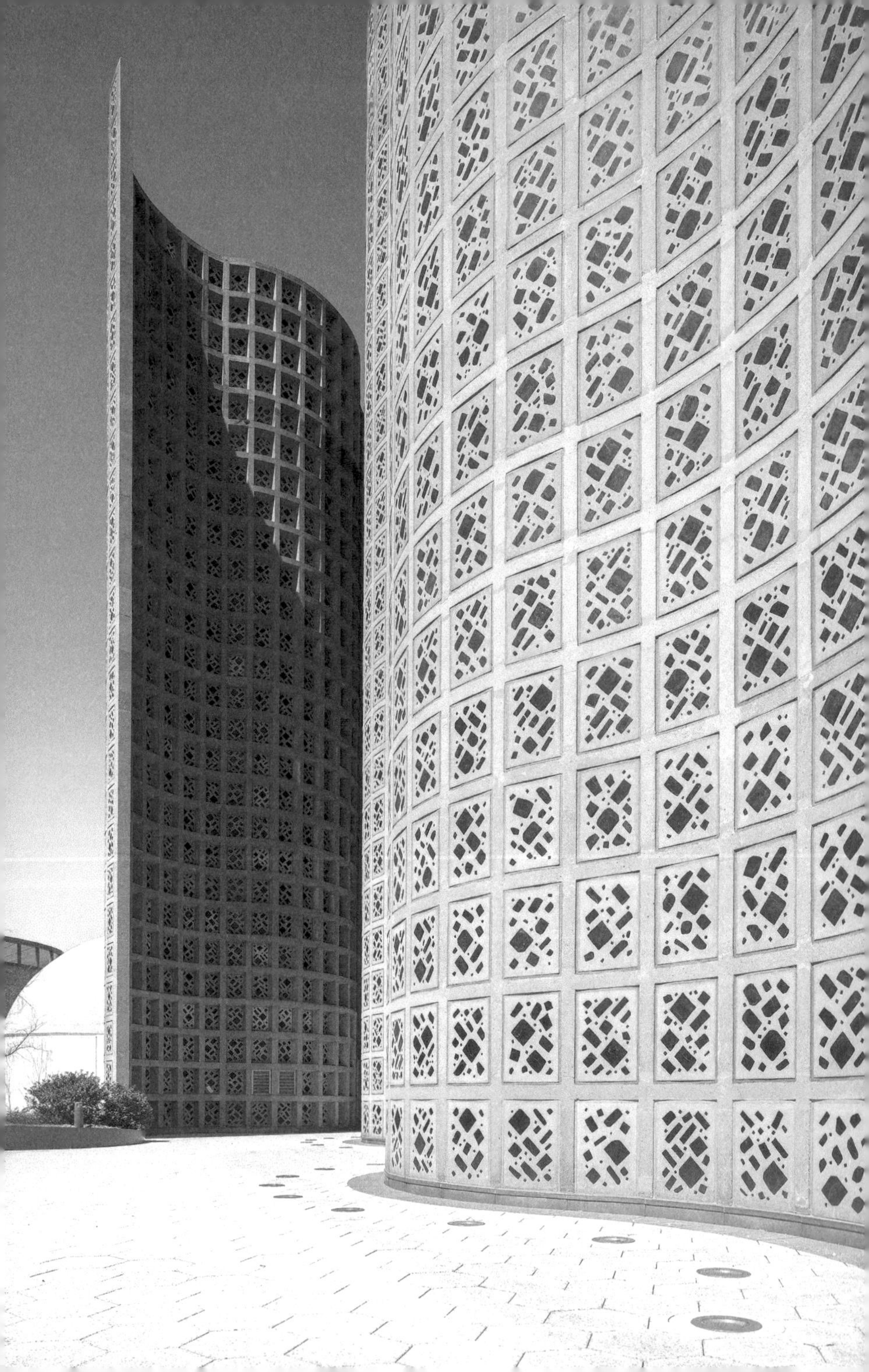

24 Great Hall of the New York Hall of Science

Harrison & Abramovitz, 1963-64
47-01 111th Street, Queens, 11368

The Space Race was in full swing during the 1964 World's Fair, with the Americans and the Soviets both having successfully launched people into orbit. For this Hall of Science on the fairgrounds in Queens, architect Wallace K. Harrison wanted to give visitors the impression of entering deep space. Using the *dalle de verre* technique he had previously employed at the 1958 First Presbyterian Church in Stamford, Connecticut, he designed a pavilion that is illuminated by the dappled light of around 5,400 concrete two-by-three-foot panels embedded with segments of cobalt blue glass. Sporadically, there is a peppering of yellow and red. These panels make up the 80-foot-high walls that curl around the darkened free-form interior, the lack of right angles creating a sense of the limitlessness of the universe.

During the World's Fair, a multimedia show featured a simulated docking between models of a space shuttle and a space station suspended overhead. The structure is now the Great Hall of the New York Hall of Science and is one of the few vestiges of the fair built to be permanent rather than temporary (along with the nearby New York State Pavilion [38] and Terrace on the Park [49]). At night, its honeycombed concrete is illuminated in a blue glow. A multimillion-dollar restoration completed in 2015 meticulously cleaned each of the glass and concrete panels and color-matched replacements so this retro-future "cathedral of science" still glimmers with the mysteries of the cosmos.

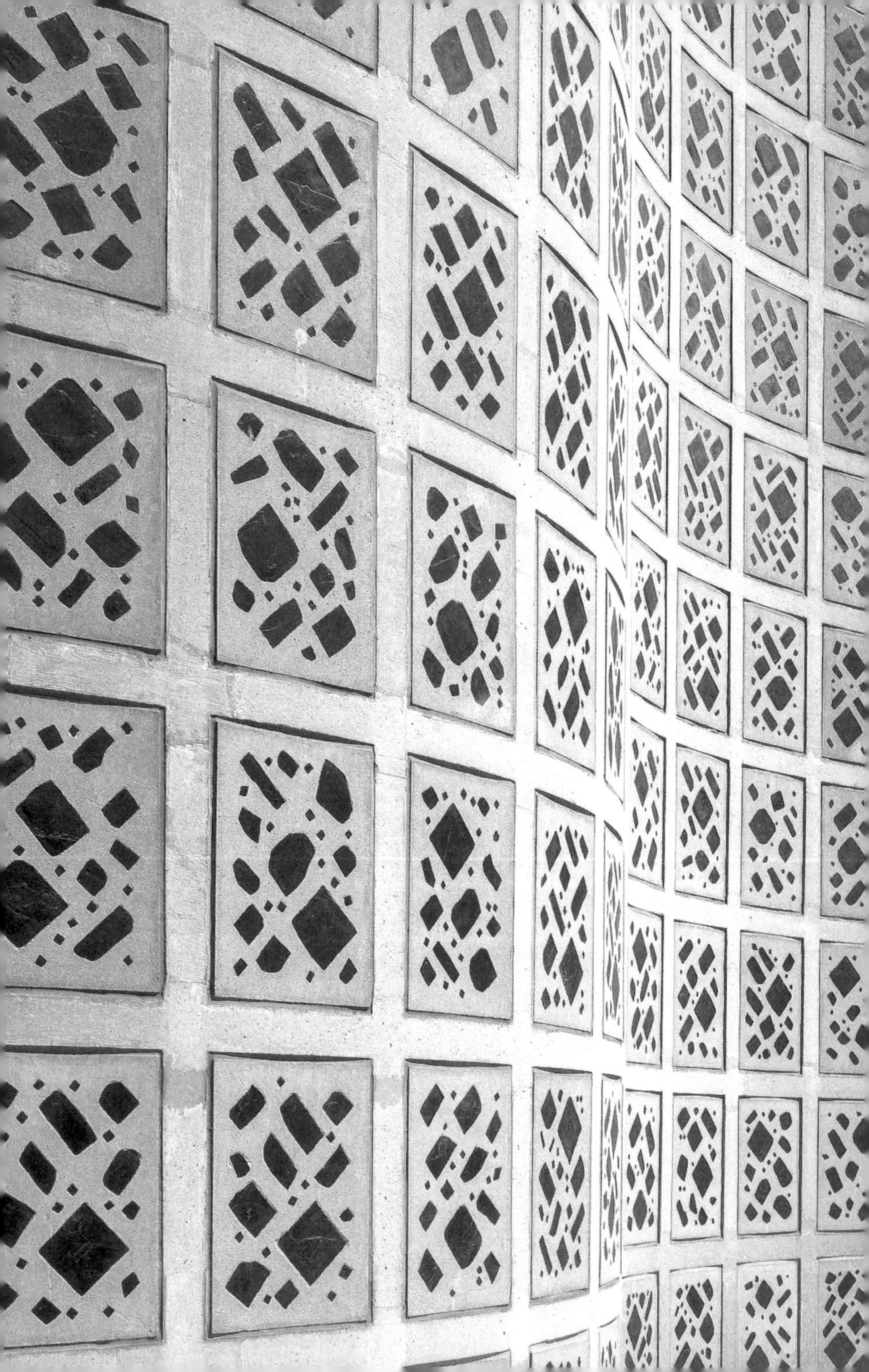

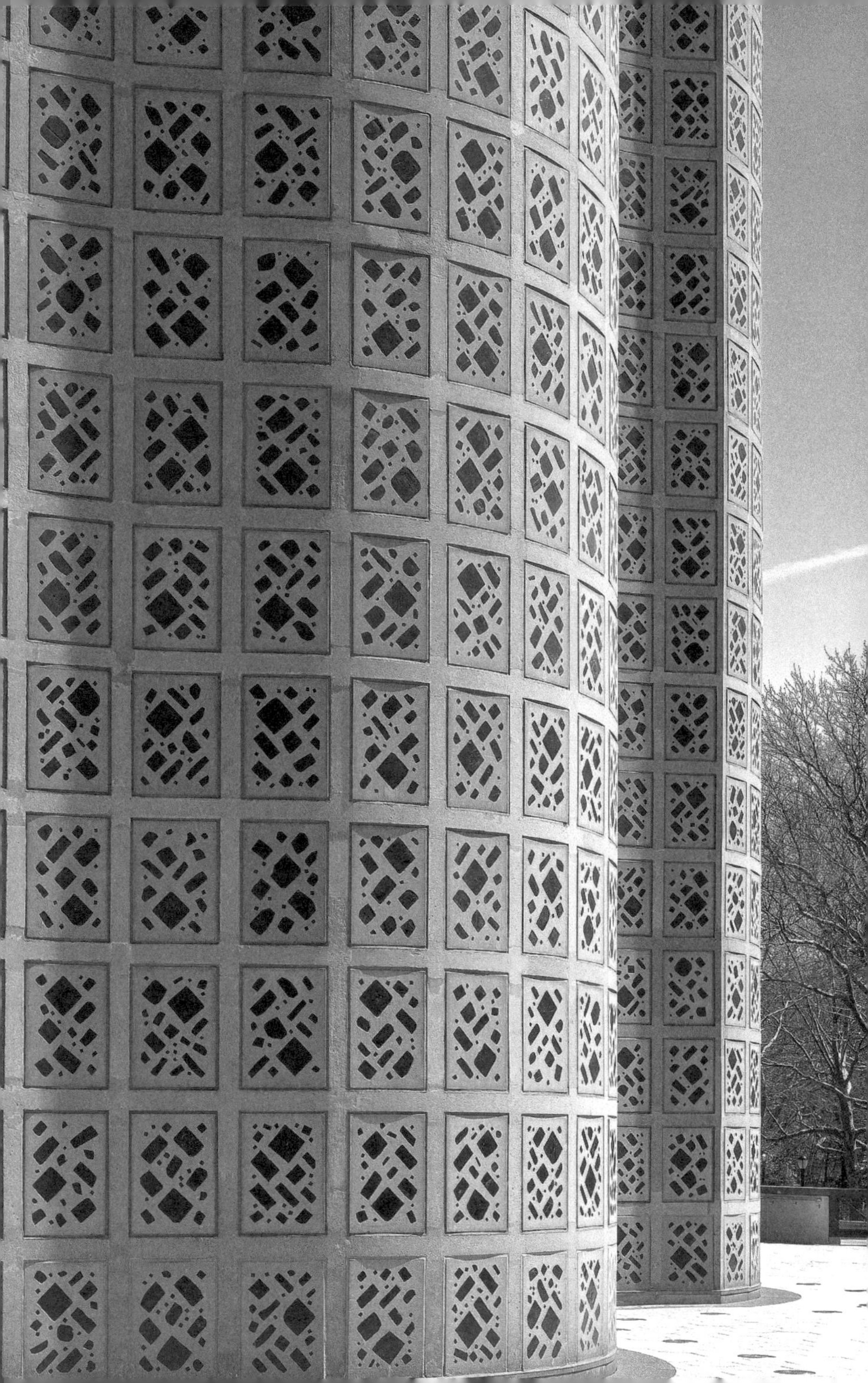

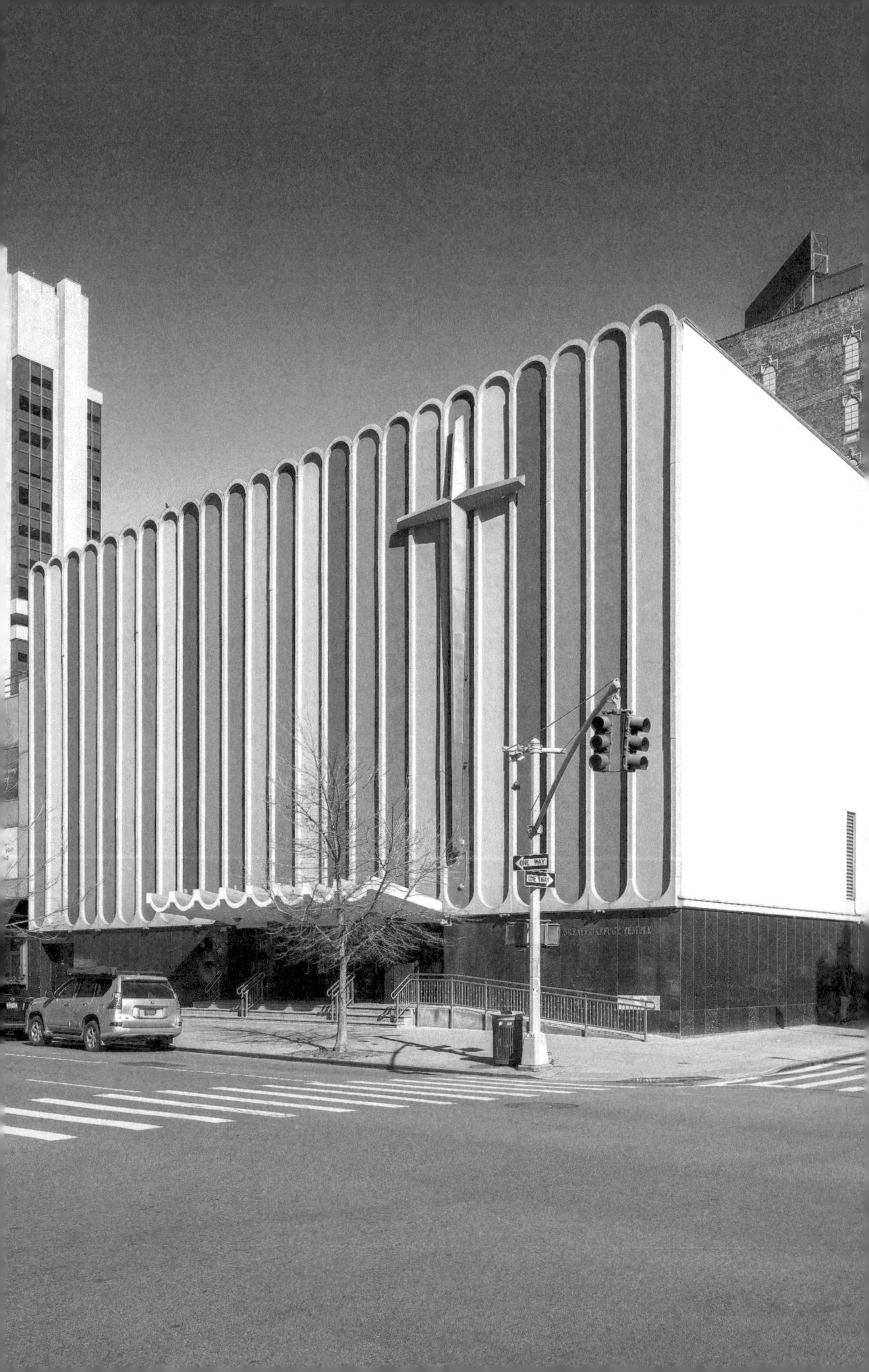
ONE WAY
ONE WAY

25 Greater Refuge Temple

Costas Machlouzarides, 1964–66
2081 Adam Clayton Powell Jr. Boulevard, Manhattan, 10027

This may be Manhattan's most colorful building. Along its façade are 24 stripes in a repeating pattern of blues, oranges, and greens. Each is framed by a long concrete ellipsis, the curved ends echoed in the waves of the concrete canopy that extends above the off-center entrance. Set against this vibrant cadence is a large metal cross, installed on the right side.

Before it was reborn as an exuberant church, this corner building underwent multiple cycles of regeneration. It was the Harlem Casino, built in the 1890s on the foundation of a theater project that went bankrupt not long after laying its cornerstone. In 1910, the music hall was converted into the Loew's Seventh Avenue Theater by architect S. S. Sugar, who worked on a number of the sumptuous Loew movie palaces around the city. It thrived until the Great Depression, and was vacant for several years before being acquired by the Greater Refuge Temple Church in 1945.

Its final (so far) transformation was undertaken by Greek architect Costas Machlouzarides, who moved to New York to study architecture at Columbia University. He also designed Harlem's Church of the Crucifixion [19], although in a more assertively Modernist style strongly reminiscent of Le Corbusier. The old theater was gutted to its frame, with the lobby, second balcony, and boxes all removed. In their place, he added arcing white shapes, crowning the sanctuary with an uplifting 50-foot-high onion dome.

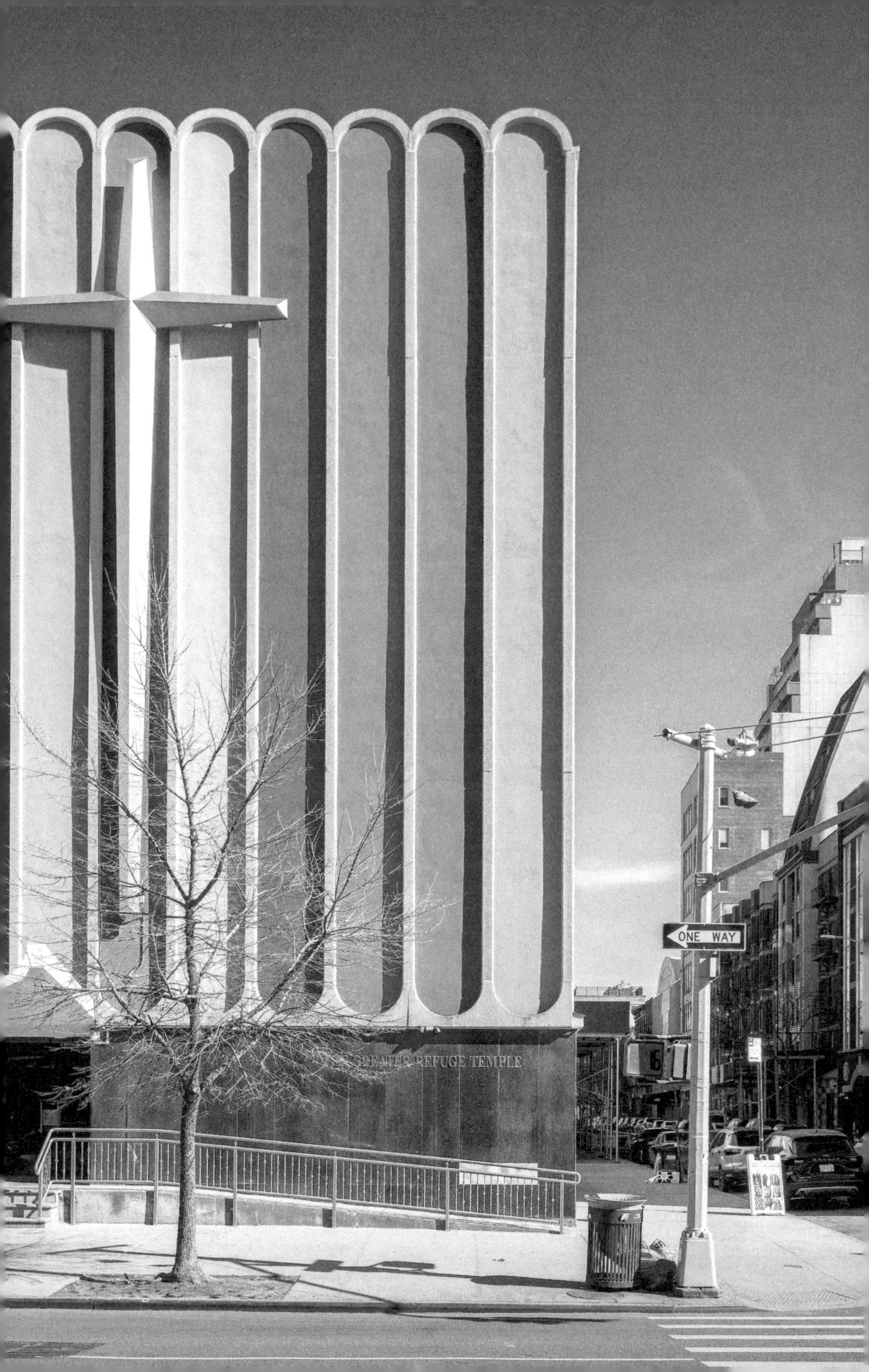
REFUGE TEMPLE
ONE WAY

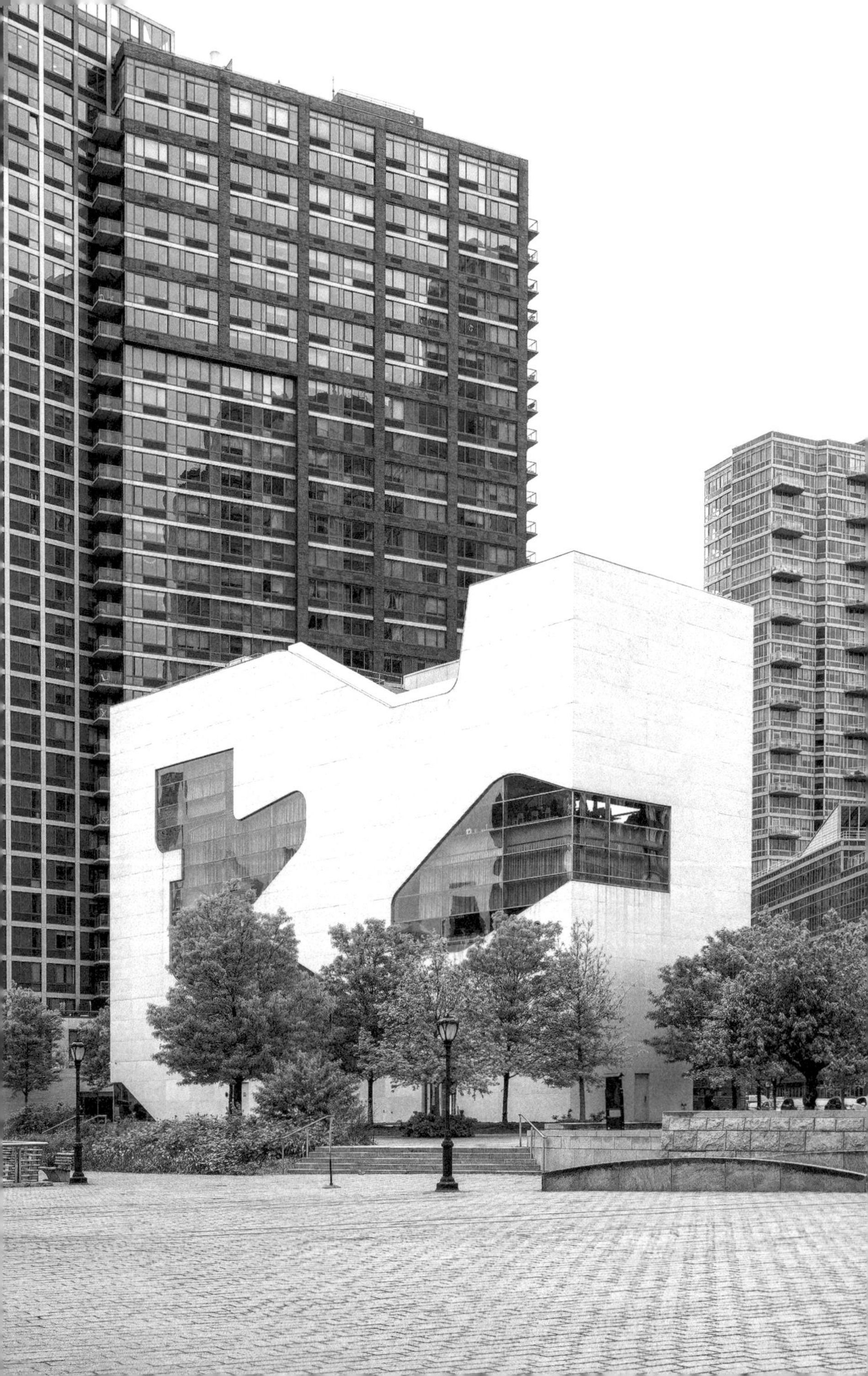

26 Hunters Point Library

Steven Holl Architects, 2010–19
47–40 Center Boulevard, Queens, 11109

The silvery-painted concrete shell of this Queens public library has large windows in amorphous shapes that brush over its sides. These puzzle-like cut-outs have become a hallmark of Steven Holl's work. An early local example is the 1993 Storefront for Art and Architecture in Manhattan, created with Vito Acconci and featuring fold-out panels of a hybrid concrete material. Here, the openings filter in light to an atrium paneled with bamboo, giving it a warm glow. They also offer views out to the surrounding park and Manhattan skyline. The library was constructed on a formerly industrial waterfront of the East River, part of the redevelopment of the area to serve a growing residential community.

The central feature, and one that makes the most of the verticality of the compact 82-foot-high building, is a staircase terraced with bookshelves. While the Hunters Point Library was effusively praised by critics when it opened in September 2019, there was immediate outcry over the accessibility issues of this design, particularly as some of these levels could only be navigated by stairs and thus did not provide an equal experience to all library users. A series of lawsuits were filed to address these complaints, including by the city against the architects for failing to comply with the Americans with Disabilities Act (ADA). A class action lawsuit was settled in 2025, with the remediation of ADA violations planned to take place over the next five years.

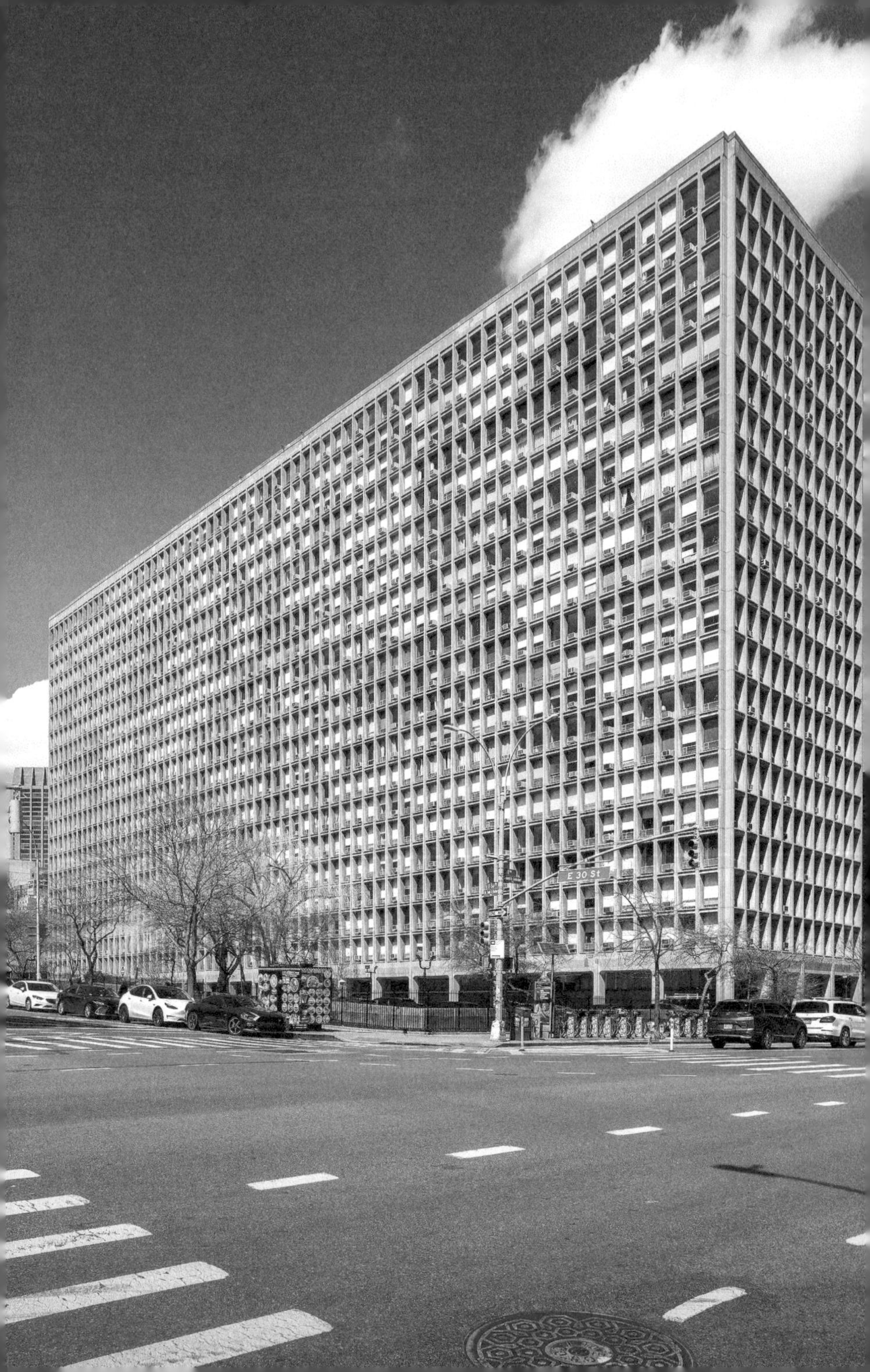
E 30 St

(27)

Kips Bay Plaza

I. M. Pei & Associates, 1957-63
333-343 East 30th Street, Manhattan, 10016

The area of Kips Bay where these towers stand was once filled with tenements. These were razed and their residents displaced in one of the urban renewal projects that aggressively reshaped New York under the powerful planner Robert Moses. A complex planned by Skidmore, Owings & Merrill (SOM) was never realized, and instead, the development company Webb & Knapp took over to create new housing in 1957.

I. M. Pei was soon brought on, and for his first major New York project was inspired by Le Corbusier's Unité d'Habitation in Marseille, France, including its use of concrete. He said in a later *Architectural Record* interview that the developer "was willing to gamble with me on using concrete and not brick for a high-rise apartment building. That was very innovative at the time."

He and James Ingo Freed served as the lead designers, with S. J. Kessler & Sons appointed as structural engineers. It was built as middle-income rental housing, but since the 1980s, it has been condos. The two towers measure 410 feet long and 21 stories high and are oriented along the city grid, perpendicular to the river. Their cast-in-place concrete frames have curved intersections that soften their formidable profiles and shade the floor-to-ceiling windows. Between them is an expansive green plaza. Pei would create a similar pairing of towers and green space with the 1967 Silver Towers [42] in Greenwich Village, there accenting the landscape with art, and here leaving it for the trees.

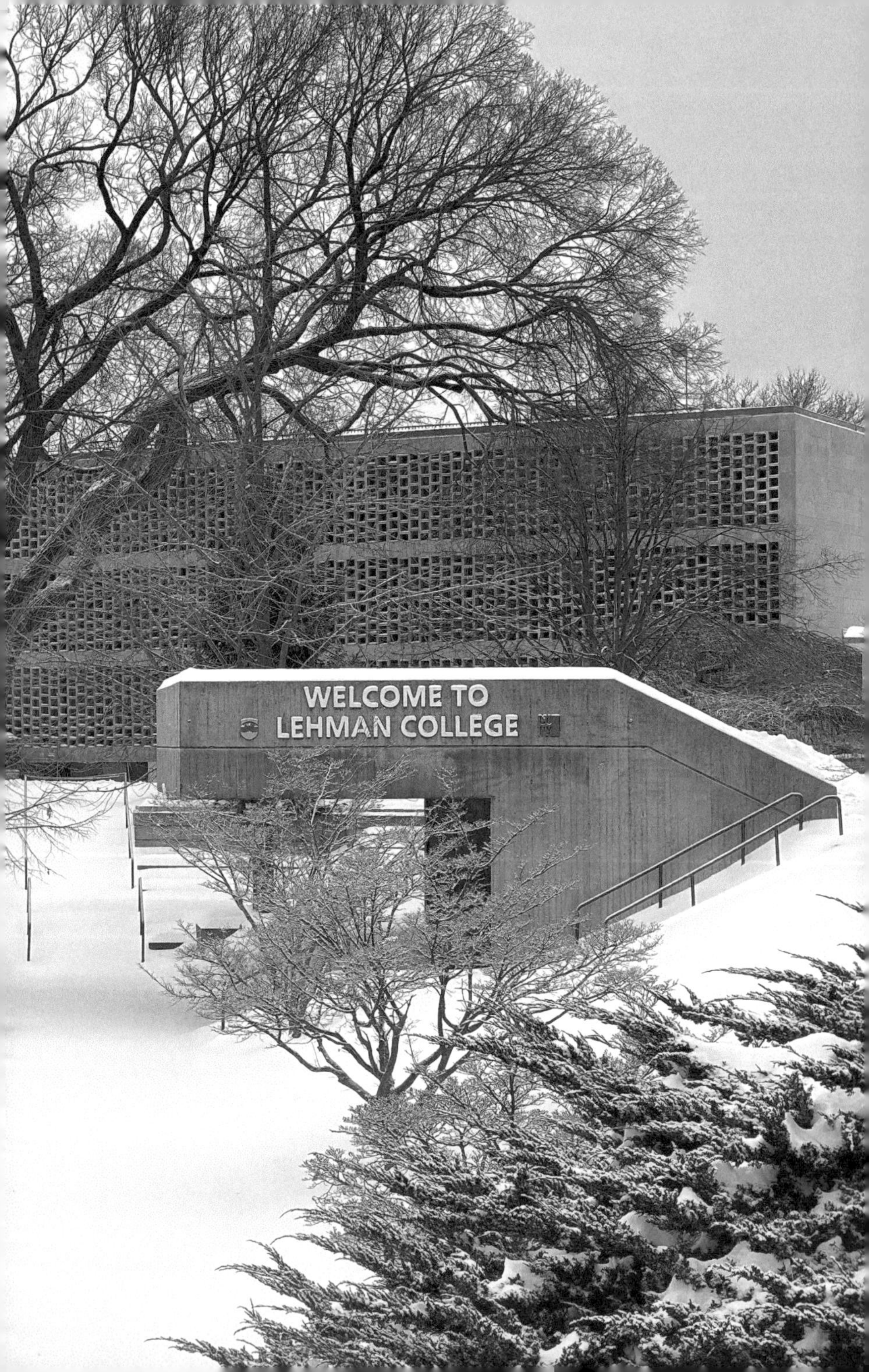
WELCOME TO
LEHMAN COLLEGE

28 Lehman College: Shuster Hall and Fine Arts Building

Marcel Breuer & Associates, 1955–59; 1955–60
Goulden Avenue and Bedford Park Boulevard West, The Bronx, 10468

Marcel Breuer's least-known New York works are arguably these two academic buildings. They were his first permanent structures in the city (he had collaborated with fellow Bauhaus designer Walter Gropius on the Pennsylvania State Exhibition for the 1939 New York World's Fair) and followed his additions to colleges such as Vassar and Sarah Lawrence. Here, he envisioned a library and administration building with Modernist geometries that juxtaposed against the 1930s neo-Gothic architecture on the campus of Hunter College (now Lehman).

The two-story library (now the Fine Arts Building), completed in 1960, has a roof made of six hyperbolic-paraboloid shells of reinforced concrete. Substantial columns descend from their inverted umbrellas into an otherwise unobstructed interior. Glass curtain walls extend around the rectangular building, so from the exterior campus, a viewer can look inside to see these concrete shapes. Breuer worked on the Lehman projects with Robert Gatje and Argentine architect Eduardo Catalano. Catalano had recently completed an audacious 1954 house in North Carolina, nicknamed the "Potato Chip" for its astounding hyperbolic-paraboloid roof.

The library connects to a three-story building for classrooms and administration (now Shuster Hall) completed in 1959. Sunscreens of terra-cotta flue tiles veil its windows from direct sunlight. Architecture critic Ada Louise Huxtable in 1963 called the buildings "novel, daring, and unlike anything the city has built before or since."

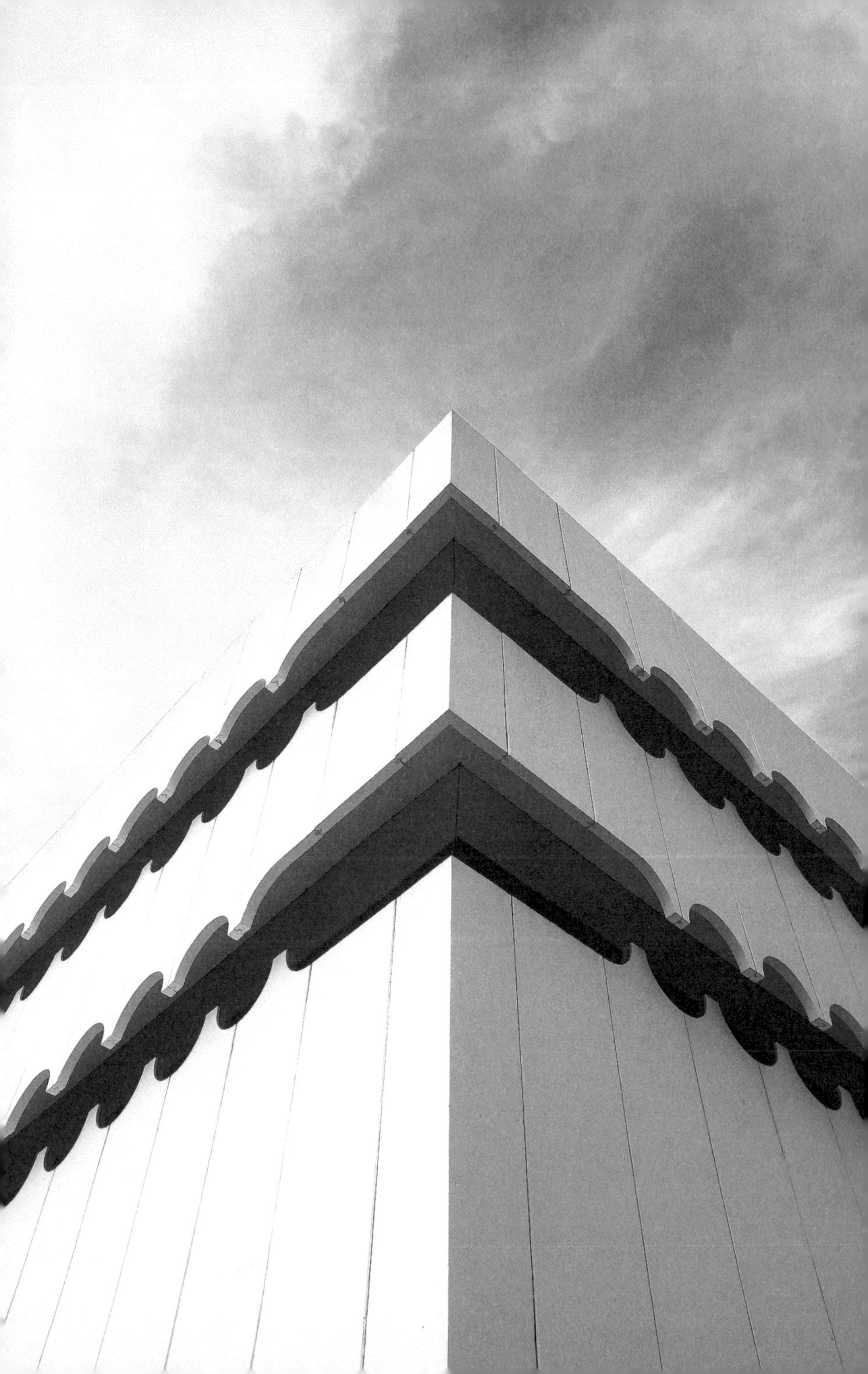

29

Lenox Health Greenwich Village (National Maritime Union)

Albert C. Ledner & Associates, 1964
36 Seventh Avenue, Manhattan, 10011

A student of Frank Lloyd Wright, the New Orleans-based Albert C. Ledner embraced his teacher's approach to architecture that was highly individualistic for each site and client, without mimicking Wright's Prairie School style. His many projects for the National Maritime Union in the 1950s and '60s are particularly fanciful in their Modernism. This six-story former headquarters is the earliest of his three union buildings in Manhattan (another, now the Maritime Hotel [33], is nearby), all of which have a nautical flair. Here, precast concrete panels painted a sparkling white form two rows of portholes, shaped by their sawtooth edges framing the windows. These panels cantilever off a sturdy concrete wall so that the upper levels appear to float. At its dedication in March 1964, Joseph Curran, president of the union, quipped that it was "the box in which the Guggenheim Museum came."

It was acquired by Saint Vincent's Hospital in 1973 and became the O'Toole Medical Services Building. Saint Vincent's received permission to tear it down in 2008 for a new facility. However, the closure of the hospital in 2010 saved it, and it became part of Northwell Health. Diligently restored by architects Perkins Eastman, it opened in 2014 as an emergency care facility. This revival included the removal of tile that had been added to the concrete panels as well as the reconstruction of its gridded concrete platform, returning it closer to Ledner's original vision for a battleship of a building.

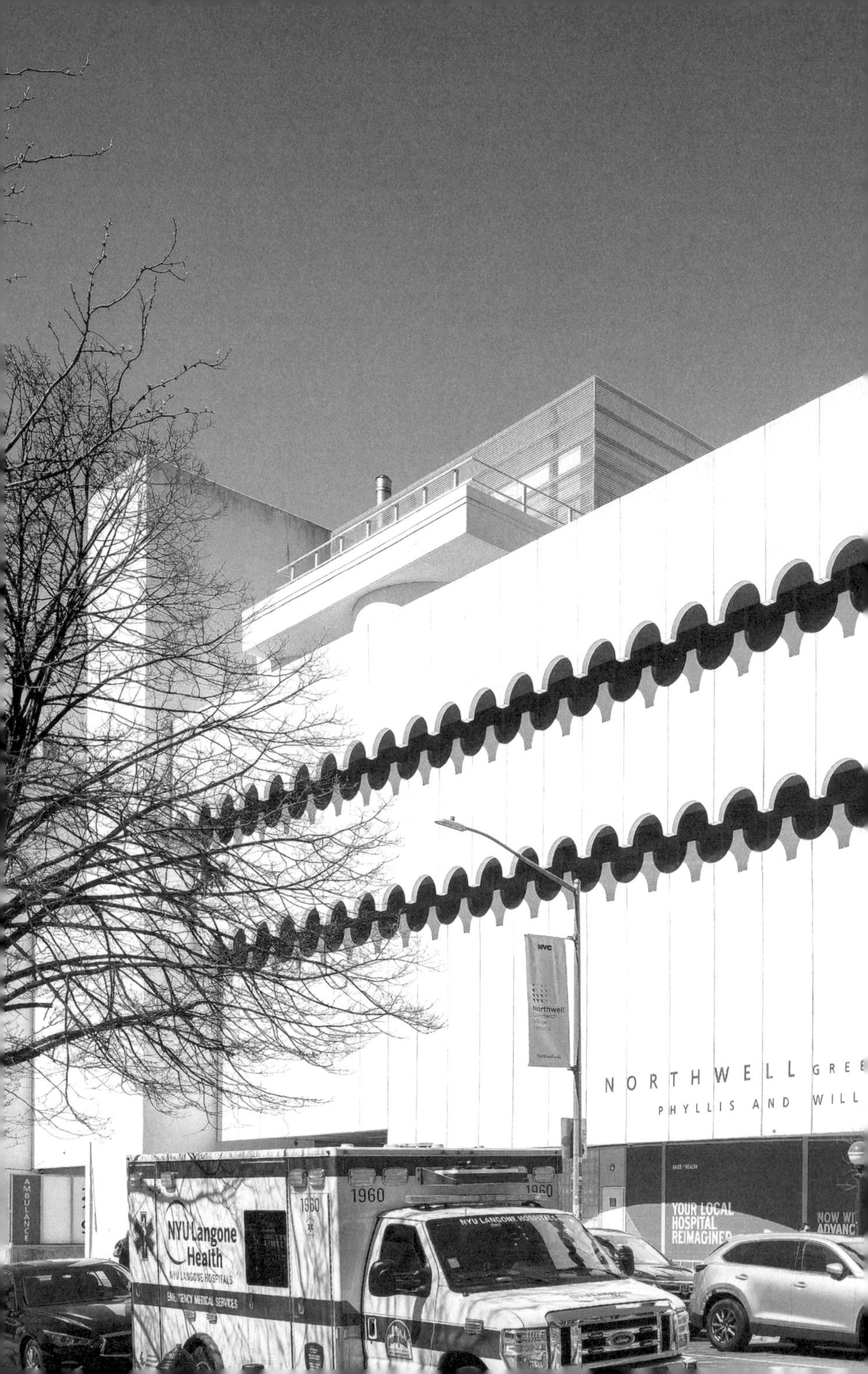
NORTHWELL
AMBULANCE
1960
NYU Langone
Health
NYU LANGONE HOSPITALS
EMERGENCY MEDICAL SERVICES
YOUR LOCAL
HOSPITAL
Northwell

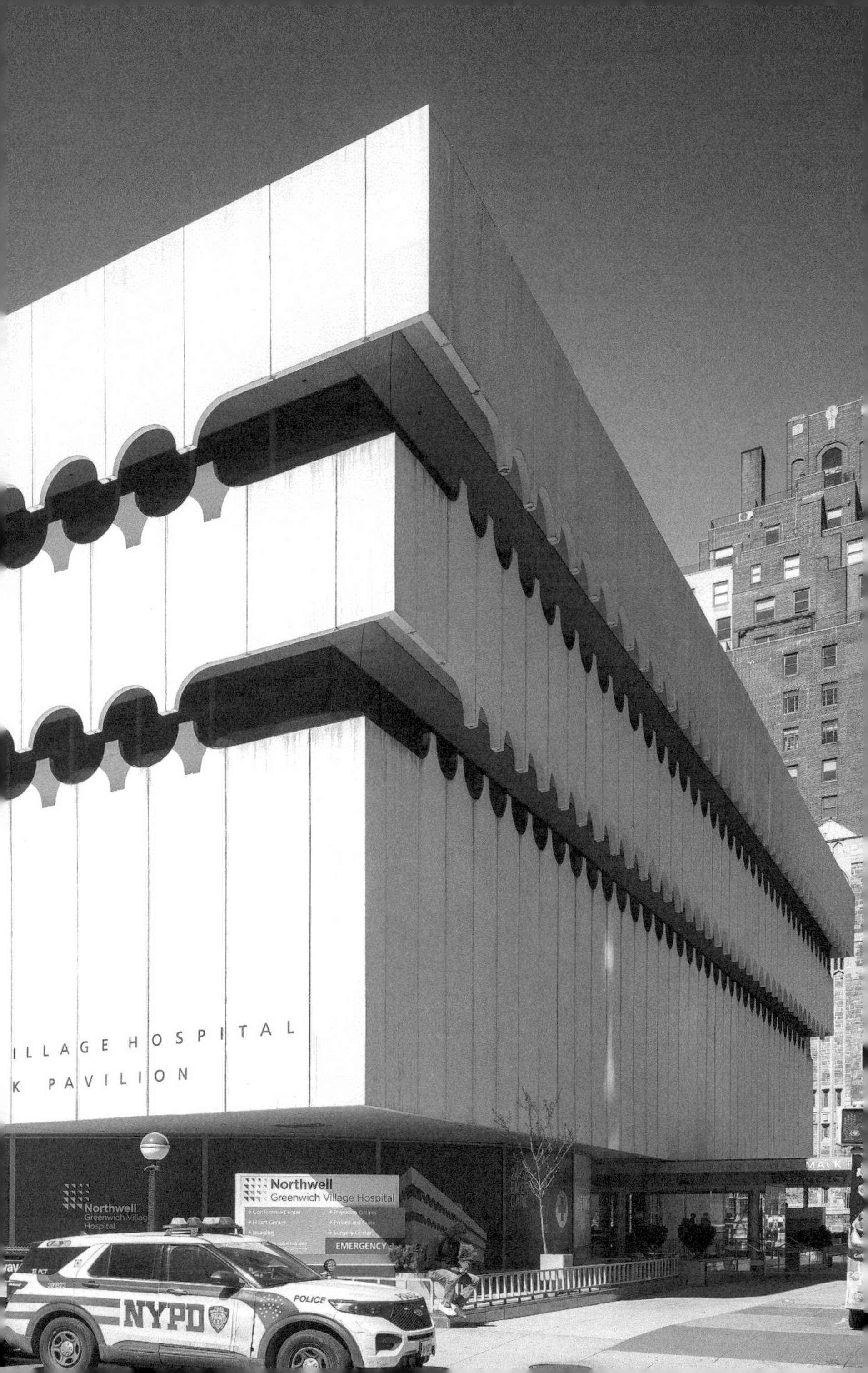
ILLAGE HOSPITAL
K PAVILION
Northwell
Greenwich Village Hospital
Northwell
Greenwich Village
Hospital
EMERGENCY
NYPD
POLICE

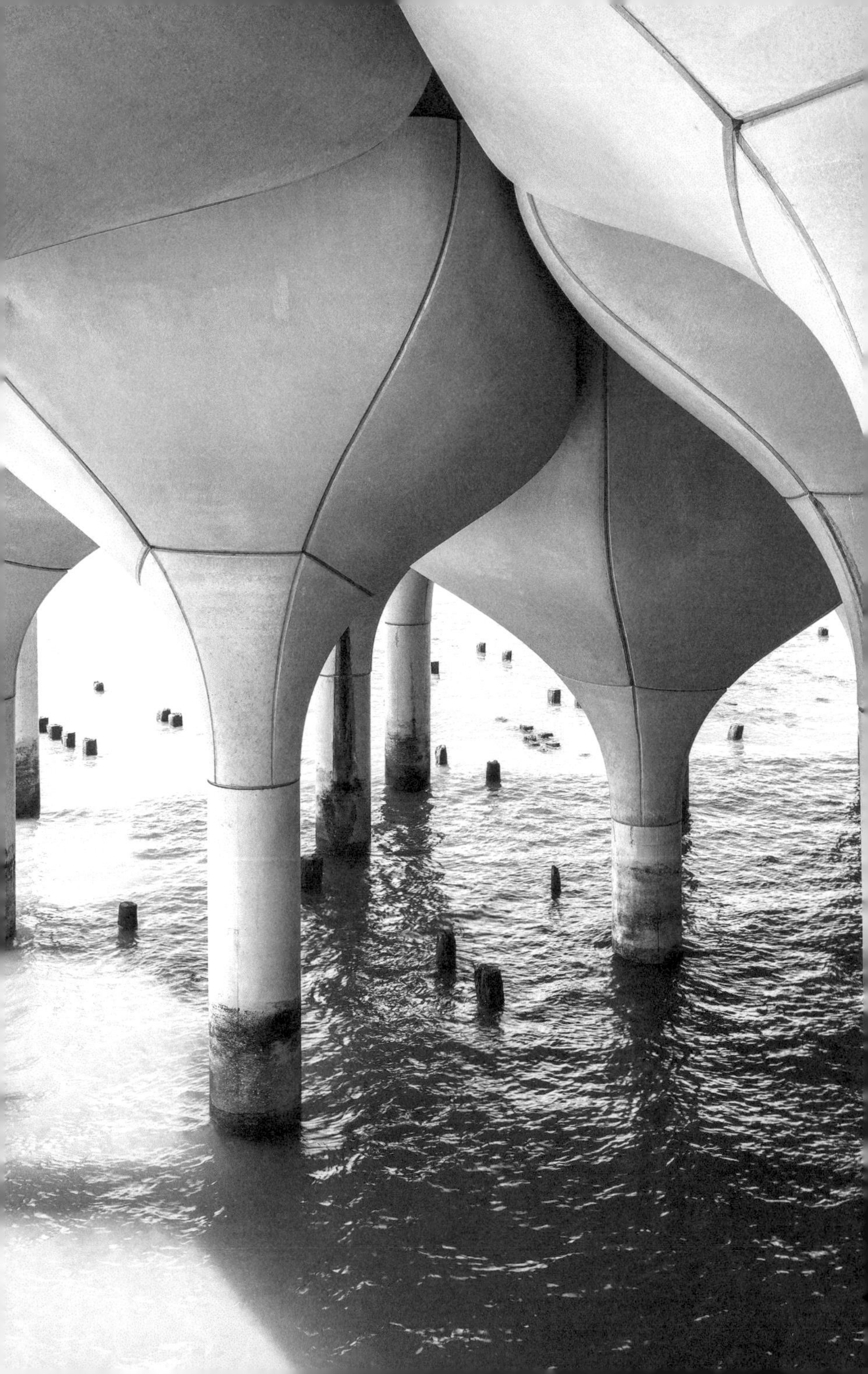

(30) Little Island

Heatherwick Studio, 2014–21
Pier 55, Manhattan, 10014

Some 132 precast concrete columns emerge from the Hudson River to form this 2.5-acre artificial island. Each has petals of concrete that hold soil for the planted landscape, akin to oversized flower pots. Cast-in-place concrete fuses them into a hilly topography, and supportive concrete pilings below are entrenched deep in the riverbed. This is the most successful of British architect Thomas Heatherwick's recent additions to the West Side, succeeding the vacuous Vessel monument of stairs at Hudson Yards and the bulbous Lantern House that crowds next to the High Line. At least here, there is an addition of green space, with hills and paths for wandering that the public can enjoy, something always in short supply in Manhattan.

The irregular elevations of Little Island were achieved with engineering firm Arup, while its diverse ecology on those undulating surfaces was planted in collaboration with Mathews Nielsen Landscape Architects (MNLA). Its concrete construction is best appreciated from the shore or beneath the entry arch on one of the two footbridges, where the use of varying shapes and sizes of those petals can be seen up close. Building a new island for New York took $260 million, primarily funded by media mogul Barry Diller working with the Hudson River Park Trust. Heatherwick Studio has been replicating ideas from Little Island around the world, with plants on concrete appearing on the forthcoming Nodeul Island in Seoul and in a dizzying number at 1,000 Trees in Shanghai.

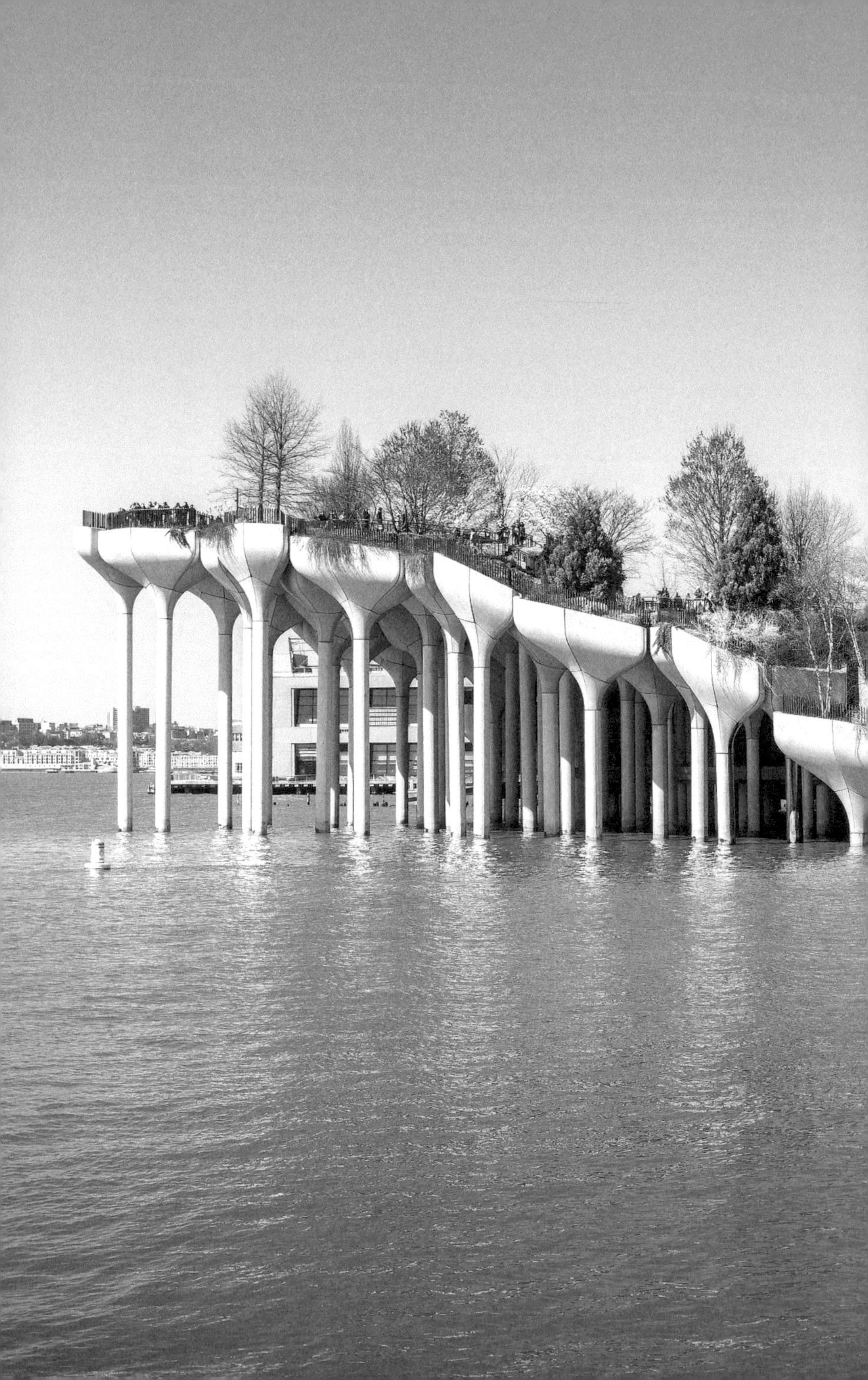

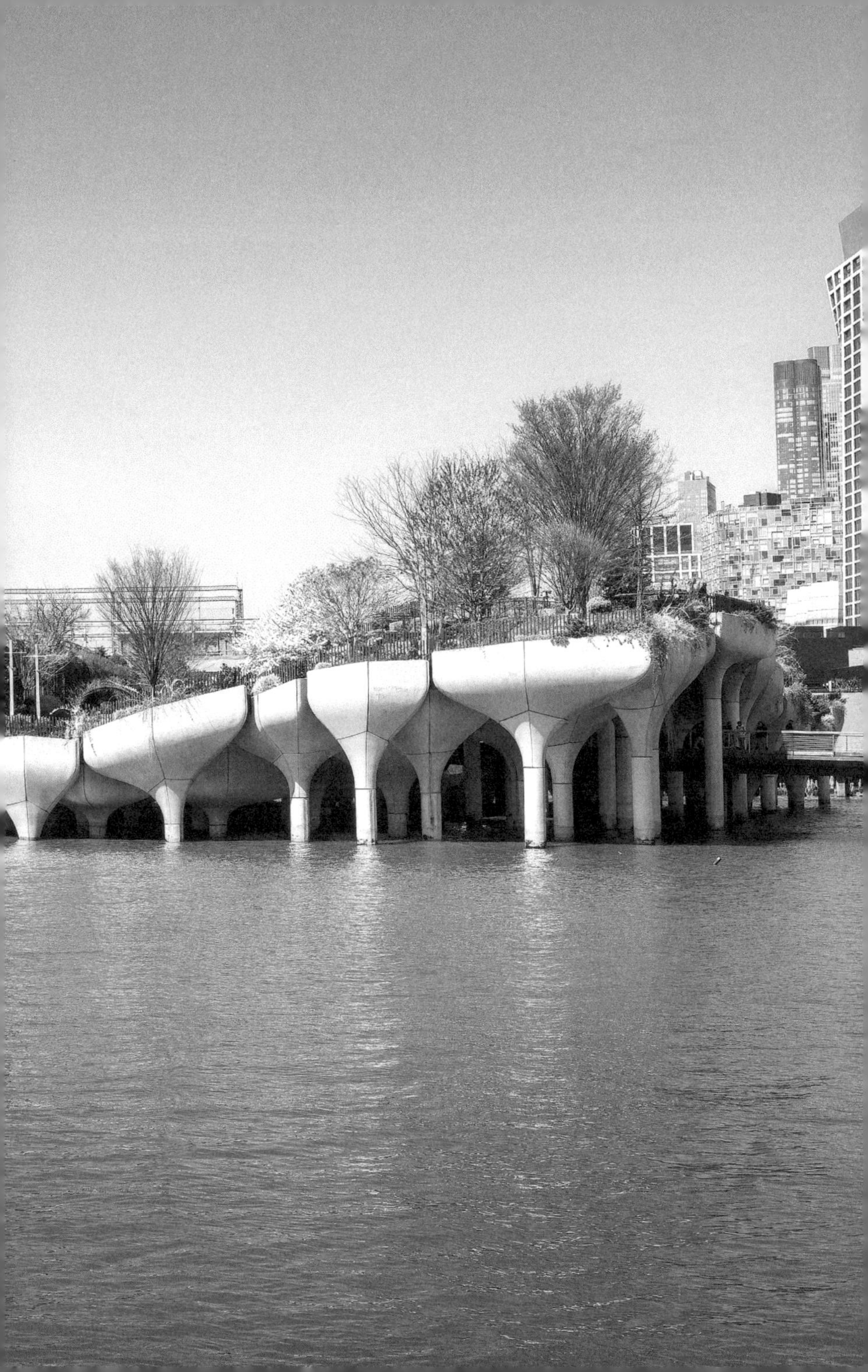

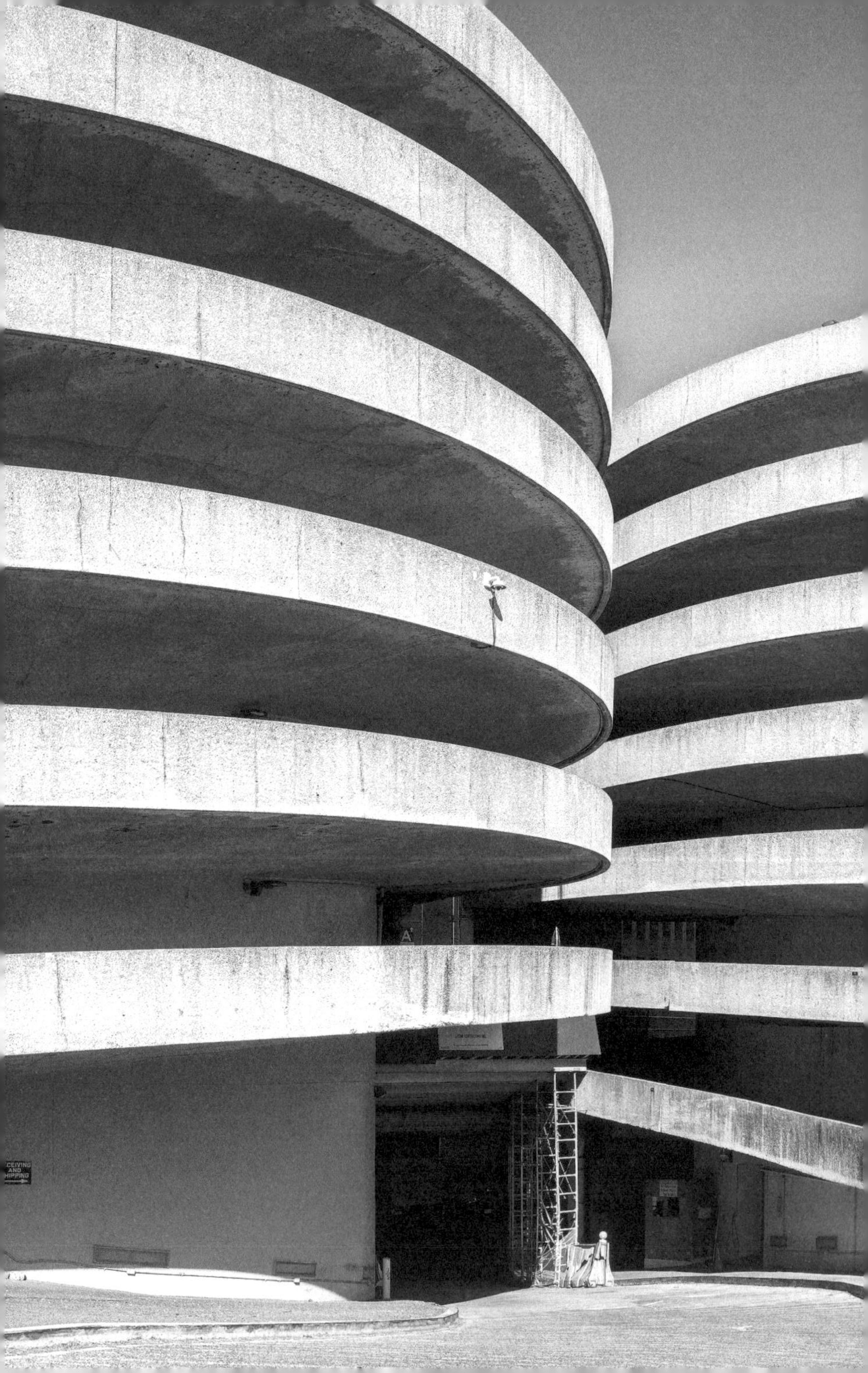

31

Macy's Queens

Skidmore, Owings & Merrill (SOM), 1963-65
88-01 Queens Boulevard, Queens, 11373

The perfect circle of this mall has a notch cut into its western side. The flaw in its symmetry is a reminder of Mary Sondek (spelled Sendek in some sources), who refused to sell her house, where she had lived since 1922, to make way for a colossal development. Instead, the architects had to alter their design to avoid Sondek's land.

Macy's Queens opened in the suburban Elmhurst neighborhood on October 11, 1965. Sondek was still living next door, as she would until she died in 1980. SOM designed the approximately 330,000-square-foot mega-mall for the age of cars. Macy's called it a "store-in-the-round," measuring 426 feet in diameter to allow for maximum floor space. Its grilles of precast concrete that glint with a white quartz aggregate were made to offer ventilation for the covered parking inside the building. On the eastern side are helical concrete parking garage ramps to take drivers on dizzying turns up to its six levels. A cutting-edge computer system directed customers to empty spots.

Progressive Architecture called it in November 1965 "a Queens Coliseum of sorts, sitting amidst the ruins." SOM also designed a 1966 cylindrical bank alongside as a miniature companion, which is still standing as a Citibank on Queens Boulevard. Sondek's house is gone, sold by her children after her death and demolished. A strip mall was built in its place. Macy's moved to the larger Queens Center in the mid-1990s, and the department store's former home is now the Queens Place shopping center.

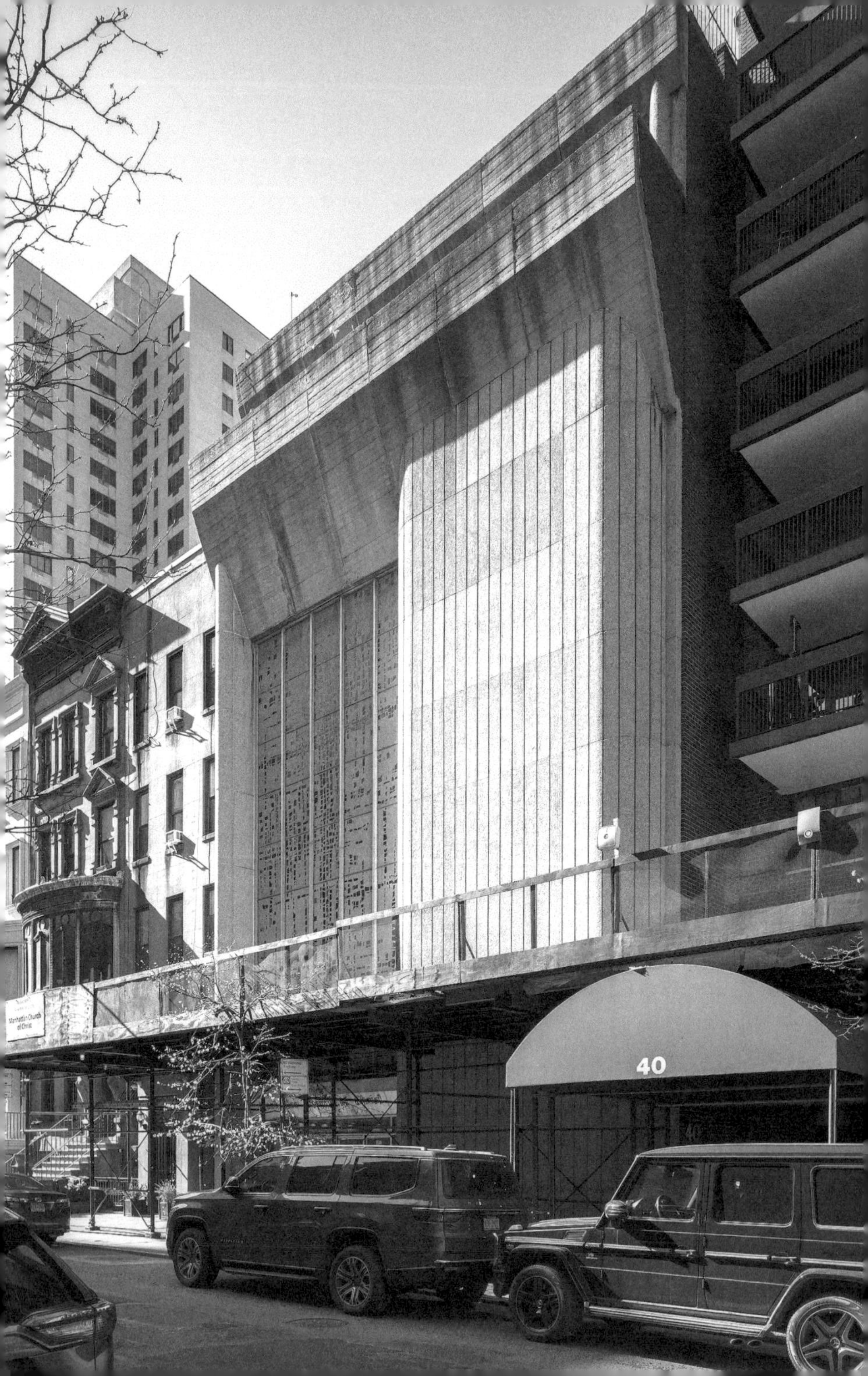
Manhattan Church
of Christ
40

32

Manhattan Church of Christ

Eggers & Higgins, 1966-68
48 East 80th Street, Manhattan, 10075

Stained glass artist Jean-Jacques Duval was an innovator of dazzling abstract compositions made with the *dalle de verre*, or glass slab, technique. It became popular in Modernism as it allowed for glass to be embedded in concrete or epoxy resin, turning entire walls into artistic statements. For this church, he covered the left side of the façade above the recessed entrance with a 38-by-20-foot fractured cross of chipped glass, designed to illuminate from within.

The Brutalist building is in the middle of its Upper East Side block. Horizontal concrete massings at the top contrast with the main curved shape of precast concrete on its front, a motif repeated in the paneling of the minimalist sanctuary inside. Because a cappella singing is central to the congregation's worship, this interior space was designed with resonant acoustics in mind. It was dedicated on June 30, 1968, on the site of the nondenominational Protestant community's former townhouse home. The prolific New York-based Eggers & Higgins firm also worked on the 1964 Holy Trinity Chapel at New York University. It likewise featured reinforced concrete embedded with mosaics of stained glass, although with more symmetry, including a trapezoidal roof. That building was demolished in 2009, with this surviving church preserving their vision of ecclesiastical Modernism. Some have found it fortress-like, others innovative, with architecture critic Paul Goldberger observing that it is "not profound but sensitive."

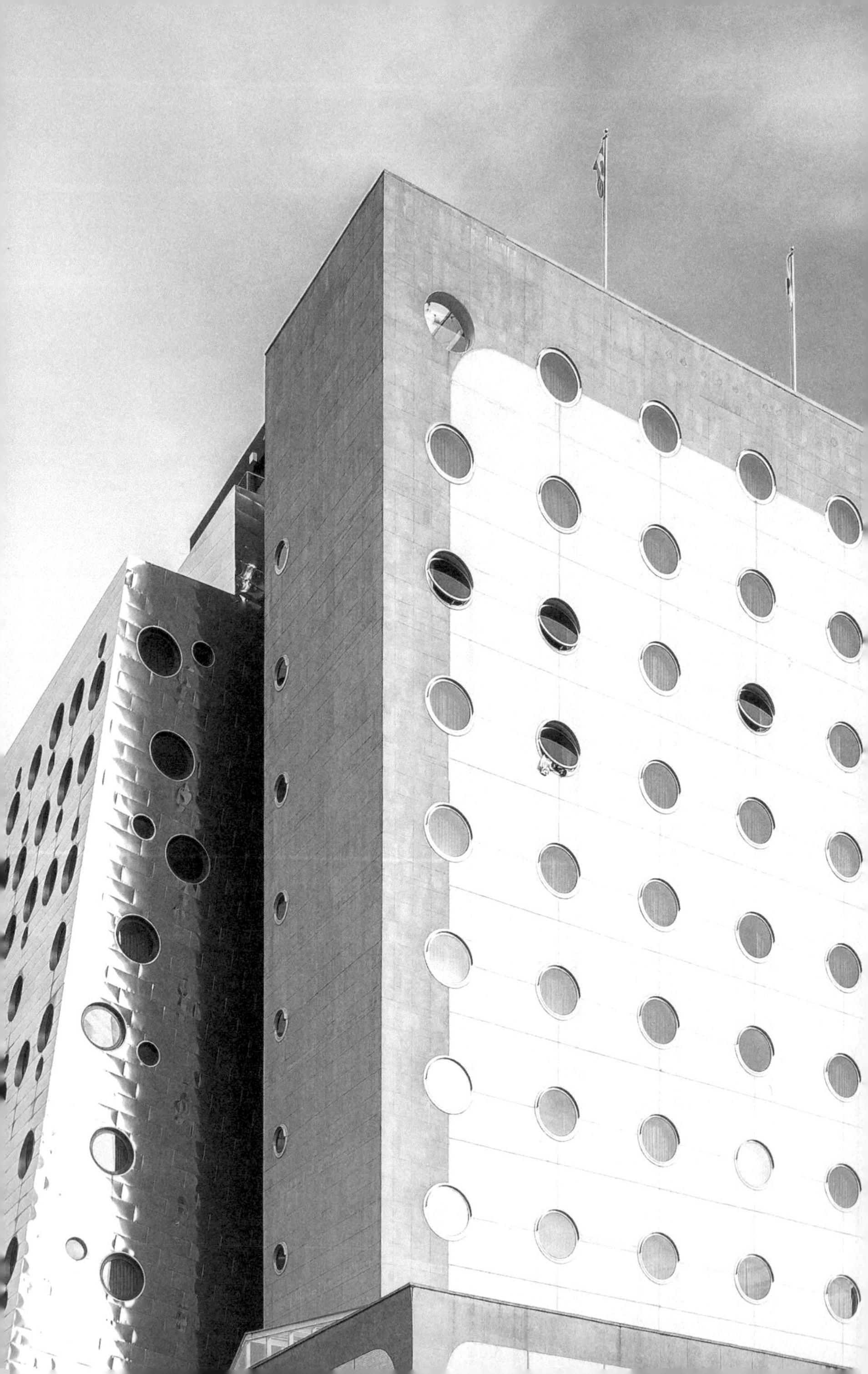

33 Maritime Hotel (National Maritime Union)

Albert C. Ledner & Associates, 1968
363 West 16th Street, Manhattan, 10011

This is the third and final of New Orleans architect Albert C. Ledner's 1960s seafaring-inspired designs for the National Maritime Union in Manhattan. White tile covers much of its 12-story concrete slab, punched through with five-foot-diameter porthole windows facing Ninth Avenue. (Some have compared its tall and narrow shape to a pizza box turned on its side.) Since 2003, it has been the nautically themed Maritime Hotel.

All of the Modernist buildings Ledner designed for the union are delightfully idiosyncratic. They were built to affirm the strength of the organization and its integral place in the thriving port of New York. This 1968 addition to the architectural armada was the Joseph Curran Plaza, built as an extension to the neighboring Joseph Curran Annex, both named for the union's president. The annex is also lined with portholes on a lower, sloped wall that evokes a cresting wave. It once had white tile cladding as well, but is now cloaked in perforated stainless steel from its revamp into the Dream Hotel in 2007.

The waning of the city's seagoing trade led to both the plaza and annex buildings being sold off by the late 1980s. The complex once held offices, a dormitory for hundreds of seamen, a gym, a cafeteria where stewards could get experience, training and medical facilities, a pool, and an auditorium. Both buildings followed a nearby union headquarters that is now Lenox Health Greenwich Village [29], distinctive for its overbite of white serrated portholes.

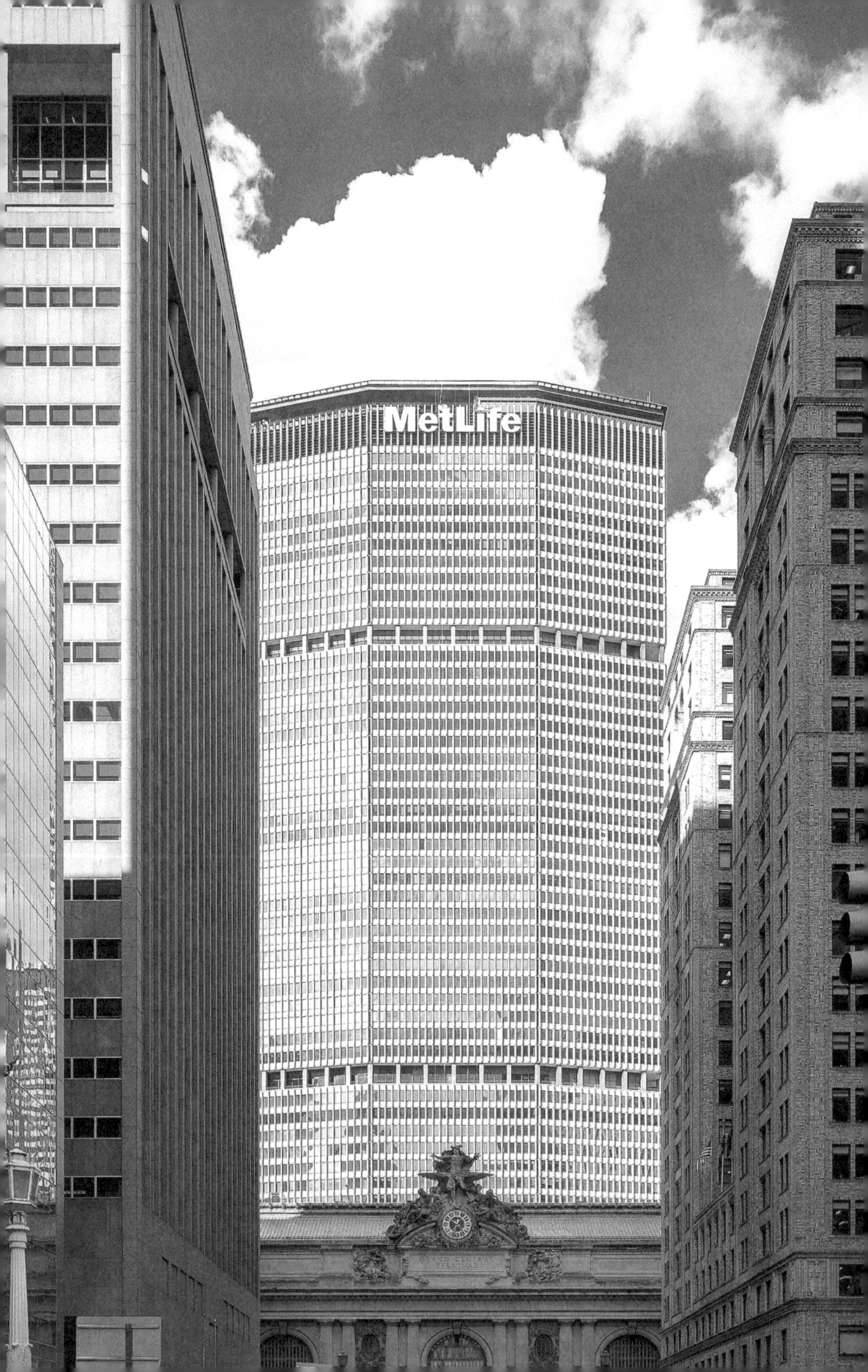
MetLife

(34) MetLife Building (Pan Am Building)

Emery Roth & Sons, Pietro Belluschi,
Walter Gropius, 1959-63
200 Park Avenue, Manhattan, 10017

New Yorkers have both loathed and loved this bulwark of a building since it loomed up over Park Avenue. It is provocatively incongruous with its Beaux-Arts neighbors, Grand Central Terminal and the Helmsley Building, which it overshadows. *The New Republic*'s architecture critic Wolf von Eckardt minced no words in stating that it "is conspicuous for its ugliness and arrogant disregard for its surroundings."

At 2.4 million square feet, it was for a time the largest office building in the world. The 57 stories of its octagonal tower are covered with 9,000 panels of precast concrete, given a glimmer through a quartz aggregate. Emery Roth & Sons initially put forward a design clad in glass and aluminum. It was altered to feature a much more novel exterior of concrete in collaboration with Bauhaus founder Walter Gropius and influential Modernist Pietro Belluschi. It even included a landing pad on the roof for helicopters to take off over the massive logo for the airline Pan Am.

More than a decade after it acquired the building in 1981, MetLife added its neon logo (later changed to LED) to the top of the north and south façades in place of the original Pan Am letters. In recent decades, there has been a reevaluation of the building's design merits, particularly for how it incorporates art into its design. The lobby features an abstract mural (removed in 2001 and replicated in 2019) by Josef Albers with bands of red, black, and white. It is also home to an incredible three-story wire sculpture by Richard Lippold embodying flight in an ascendant form.

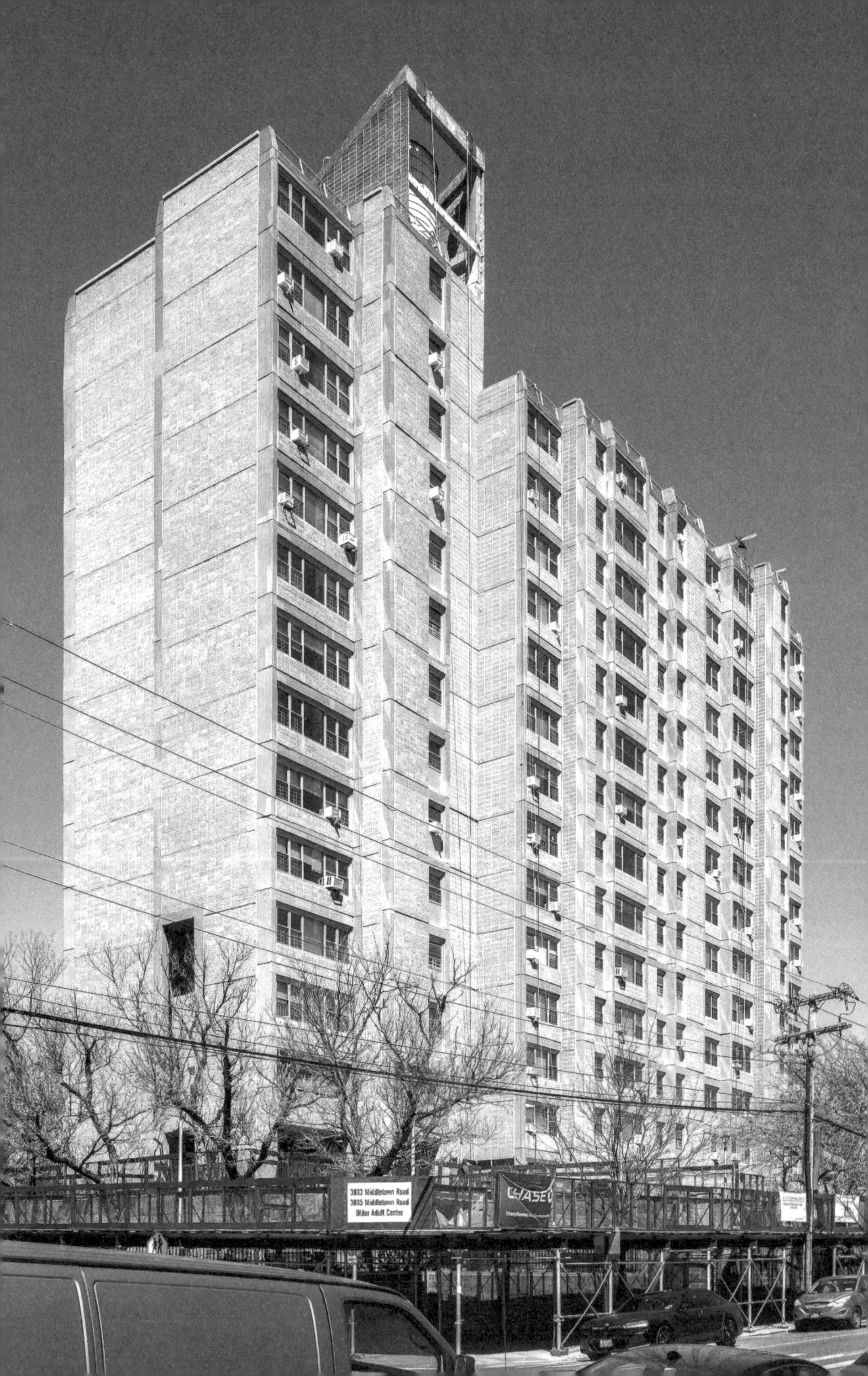
3033 Middletown Road
3035 Middletown Road
Older Adult Center

35

Middletown Plaza

Paul Rudolph, 1967-73
3033 Middletown Road, The Bronx, 10461

The Kentucky-born Paul Rudolph became known in the 1960s for hulking concrete buildings, which were key to bringing Brutalism to the United States. He adapted the exposed materials and simplicity of forms that had emerged in postwar British architecture in a range of civic, residential, and private projects. By 1965, he had his offices in New York, yet only a handful of his designs are in the city. Middletown Plaza, built in Pelham Bay as housing for seniors through the New York City Housing Authority (NYCHA), is one of his more lesser-known projects.

While not as alluring as his curvaceous Tracey Towers [50], also in the Bronx, this 15-story tower embodies his interest in modular components and prefabricated materials. Cast-in-place concrete frames rows of windows and split-ribbed concrete blocks, a Rudolph signature. The 2010 edition of the *AIA Guide to New York City* by Norval White, Elliot Willensky, and Fran Leadon calls it "the late Rudolph's best work in the borough ... One of the Bronx's notable architectural apartment houses."

Since the building was completed in 1973, it has experienced neglectful deterioration, like many NYCHA properties. Its corduroy blocks have collected dirt over the years. Residents have complained about its aging infrastructure and faulty utilities, although there have been recent improvements to address these issues and update the apartments. It was added to the National Register of Historic Places in 2024 as a landmark of public housing design.

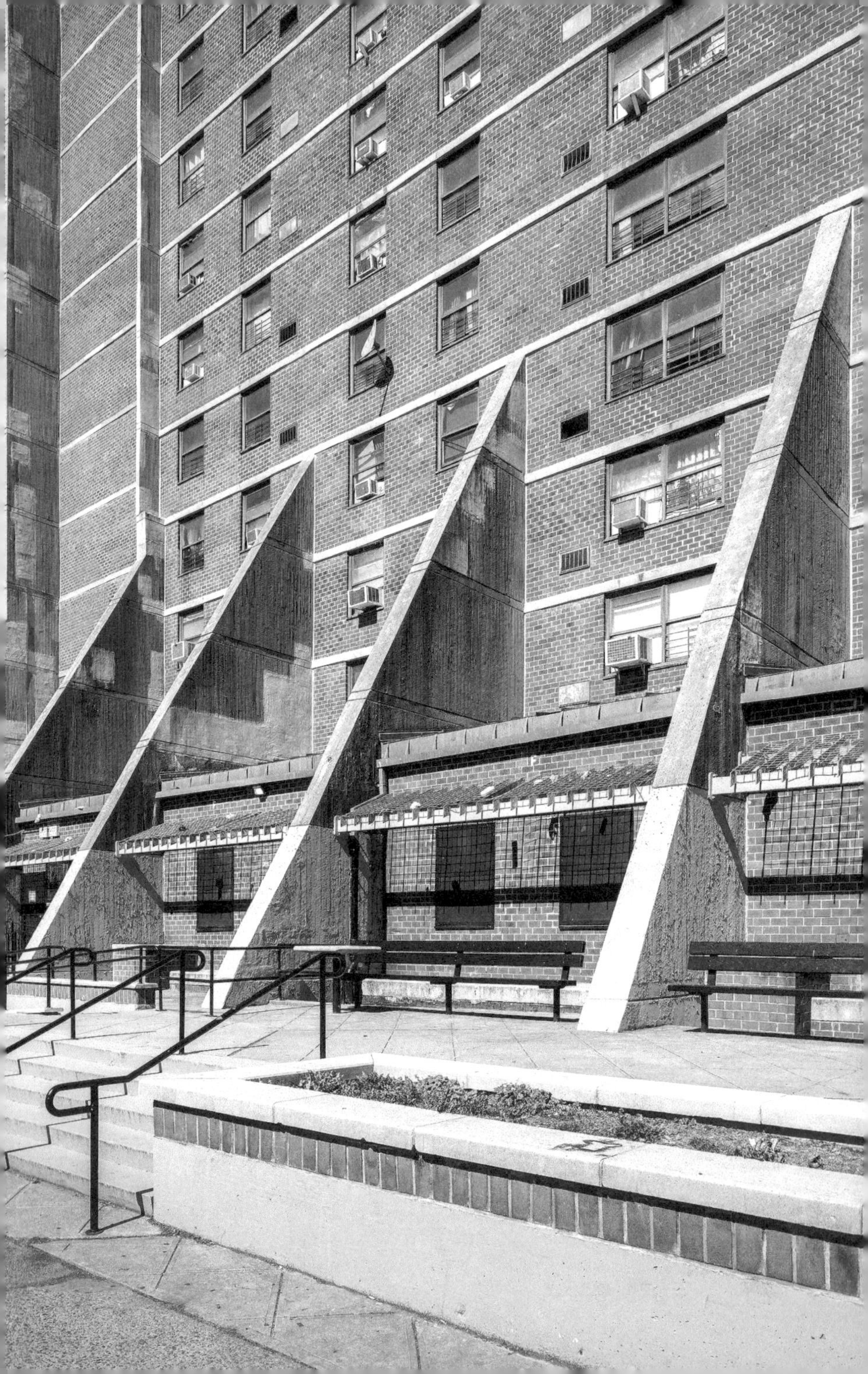

36

Morrisania Air Rights

Jarmul & Brizee, 1977-80
3145 Park Avenue, The Bronx, 10451

You can look down from the end of this gigantic public housing complex to discover how it got its curious name: the Metro-North tracks go right under it. Using acquired air rights, it was built on a platform spanning the railroad cut. It was completed at the end of an era of New York City Housing Authority (NYCHA) projects being dense megastructures. Massive exposed concrete buttresses are its most distinctive design element. They punctuate the sides of three rectangular buildings of varying heights—19, 23, and 29 stories—aligned to the path of the trains below.

The plan to construct public housing here dates to the early 1970s. By the time construction was underway in 1977, its placement over the rail corridor received criticism. *The New York Times* reported that the "proposed site seemed novel, but defensible, seven years ago," yet now "the surrounding neighborhood has been devastated by fires and building abandonments, creating vast stretches of open space."

Instead of rebuilding on these vacant plots, however, city officials cited the complexities of federal housing rules and went forward with using the air rights. When completed, the structures were not only architecturally intimidating, each ending in windowless concrete façades, but also isolated amidst the blight. The concrete fins were easy places for criminals to hide. Although improvements have been made over the years, the design is still more forbidding than friendly, a relic from a period of utopian Modernism that often overlooked the needs of the residents within.

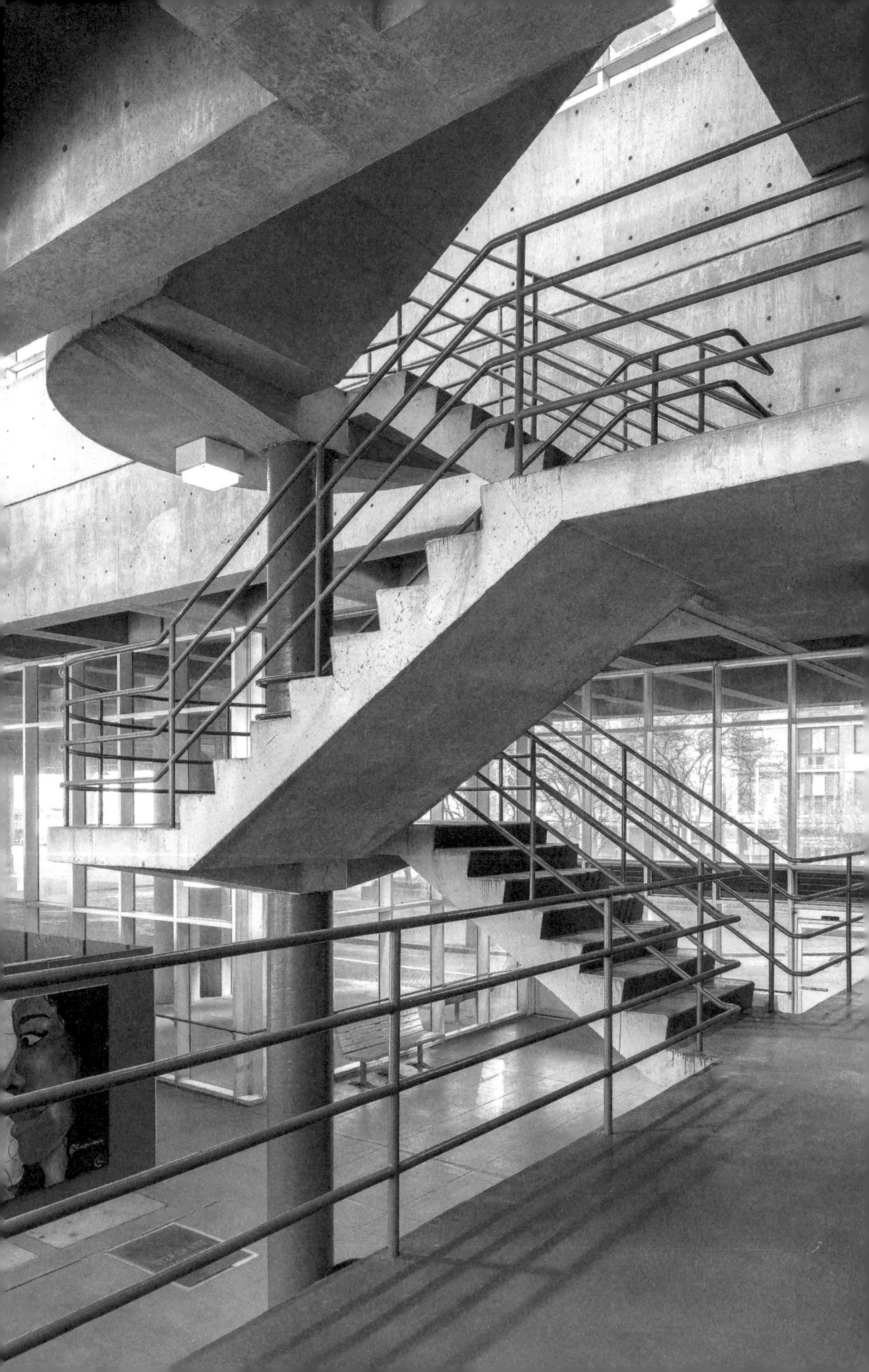

37 Motorgate

Kallmann & McKinnell, 1970–74
688 Main Street, Roosevelt Island, 10044

Unlike the rest of New York City, Roosevelt Island's streets are not clogged with parked cars. Instead, they are warehoused in this enormous garage located where drivers arrive from Queens on the Roosevelt Island Bridge, the island's singular vehicular connection. Informed by their work in concrete on the Brutalist 1968 Boston City Hall, Gerhard Kallmann and Michael McKinnell brought a similar use of detail in the columns and fins of reinforced concrete that animate this utilitarian structure.

Motorgate was a key component of the island's 1970s redevelopment from an isolated place, known for hospitals, asylums, and prisons, into a modern residential neighborhood. (Kallmann & McKinnell also worked on the 1975 collection point of its inventive pneumatic garbage system.) This included its 1973 renaming from Welfare Island to Roosevelt Island. Philip Johnson and John Burgee created its master plan in 1969. One of the objectives was that it would be a traffic-free community.

Motorgate was intended to be where all cars parked, and people then caught electric minibuses to the rest of the island. Playful red accents on the railings and support bars as well as dramatic signage—like the painted "Parking Motorgate" sans serif letters that descend from a vertical concrete volume—keep the expanses of exposed concrete from appearing drab. The glass-enclosed pedestrian entrance on the south side has an eye-catching triangular angle as it extends from the main complex, leading to a warren of looping concrete staircases within.

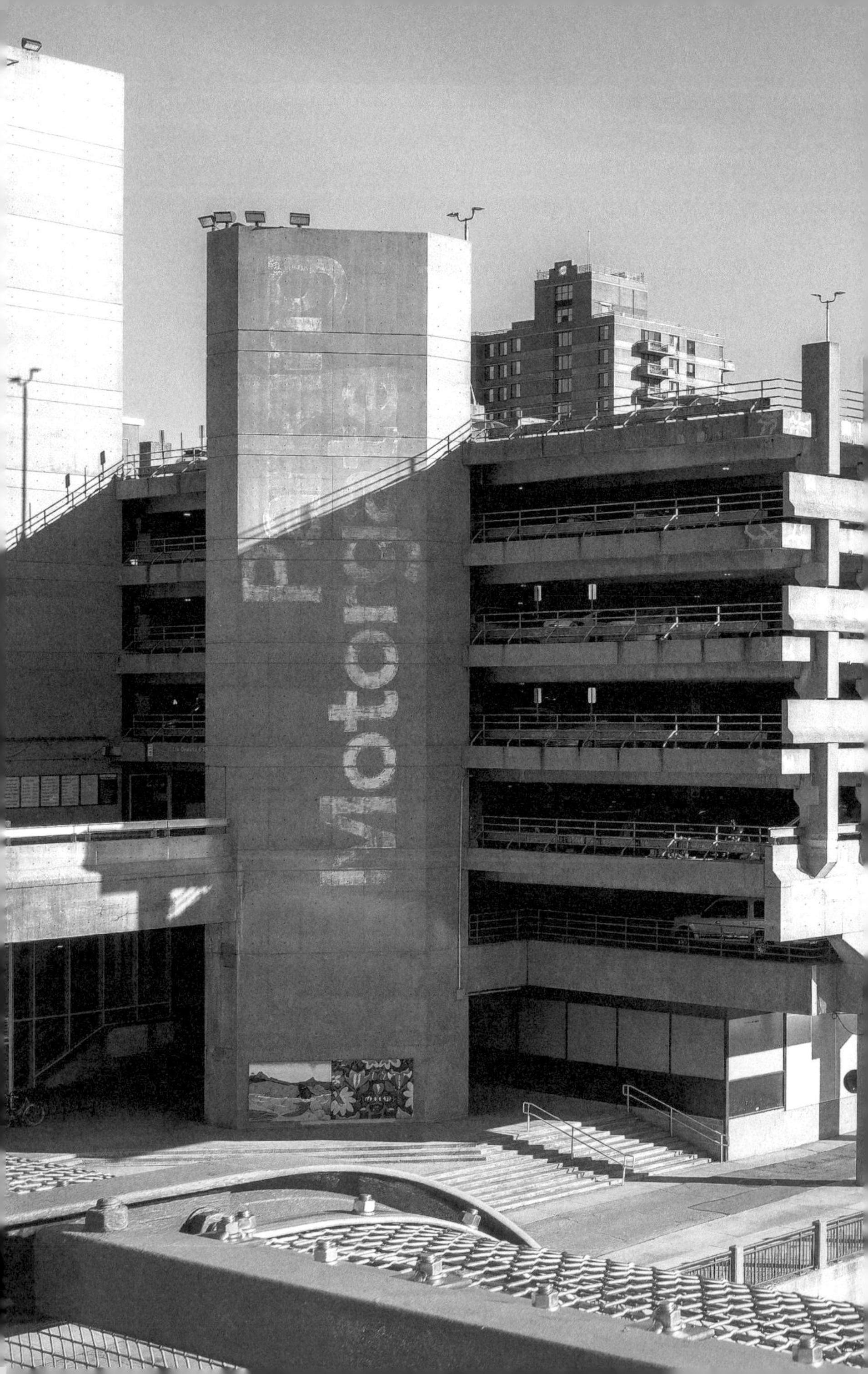

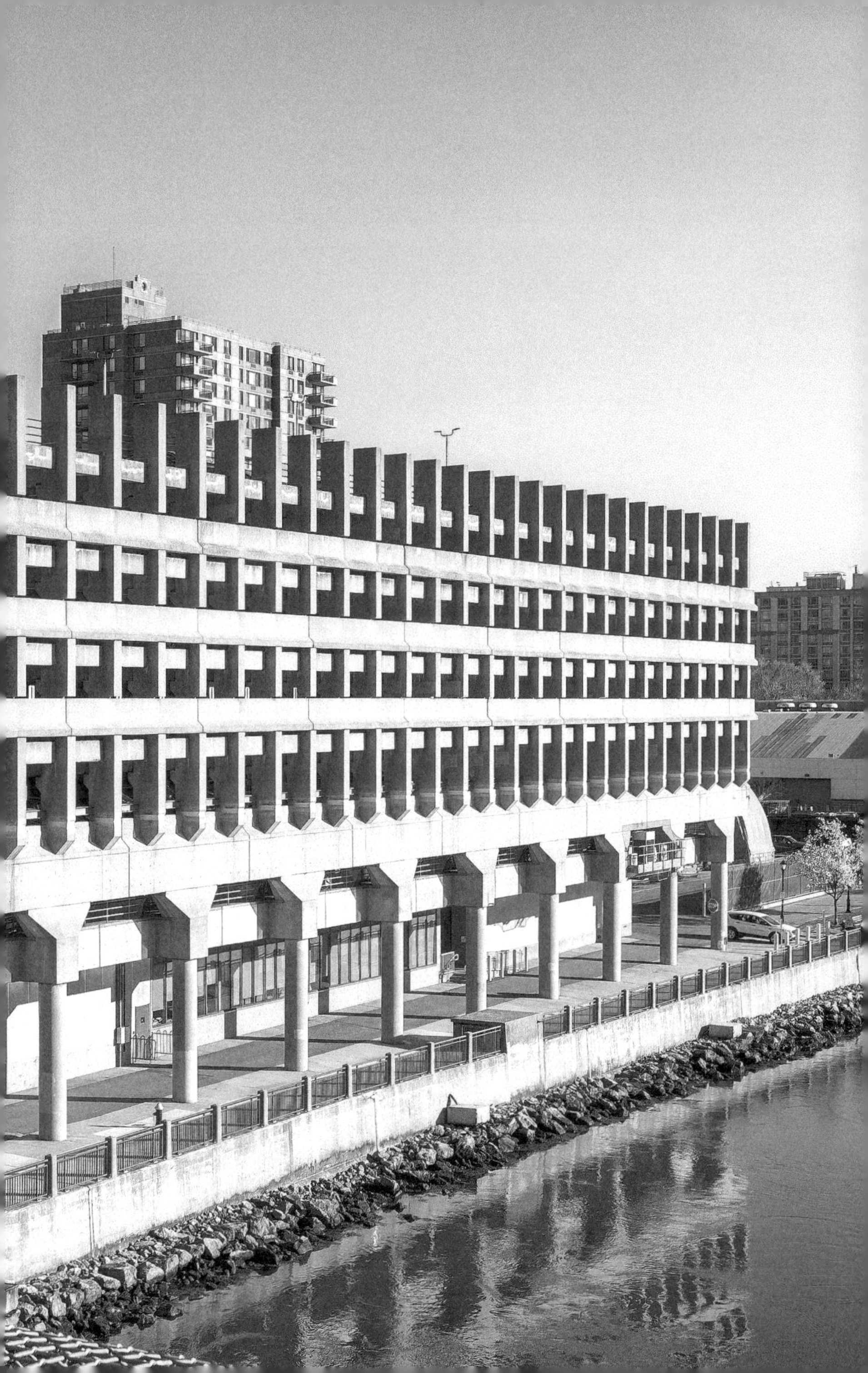

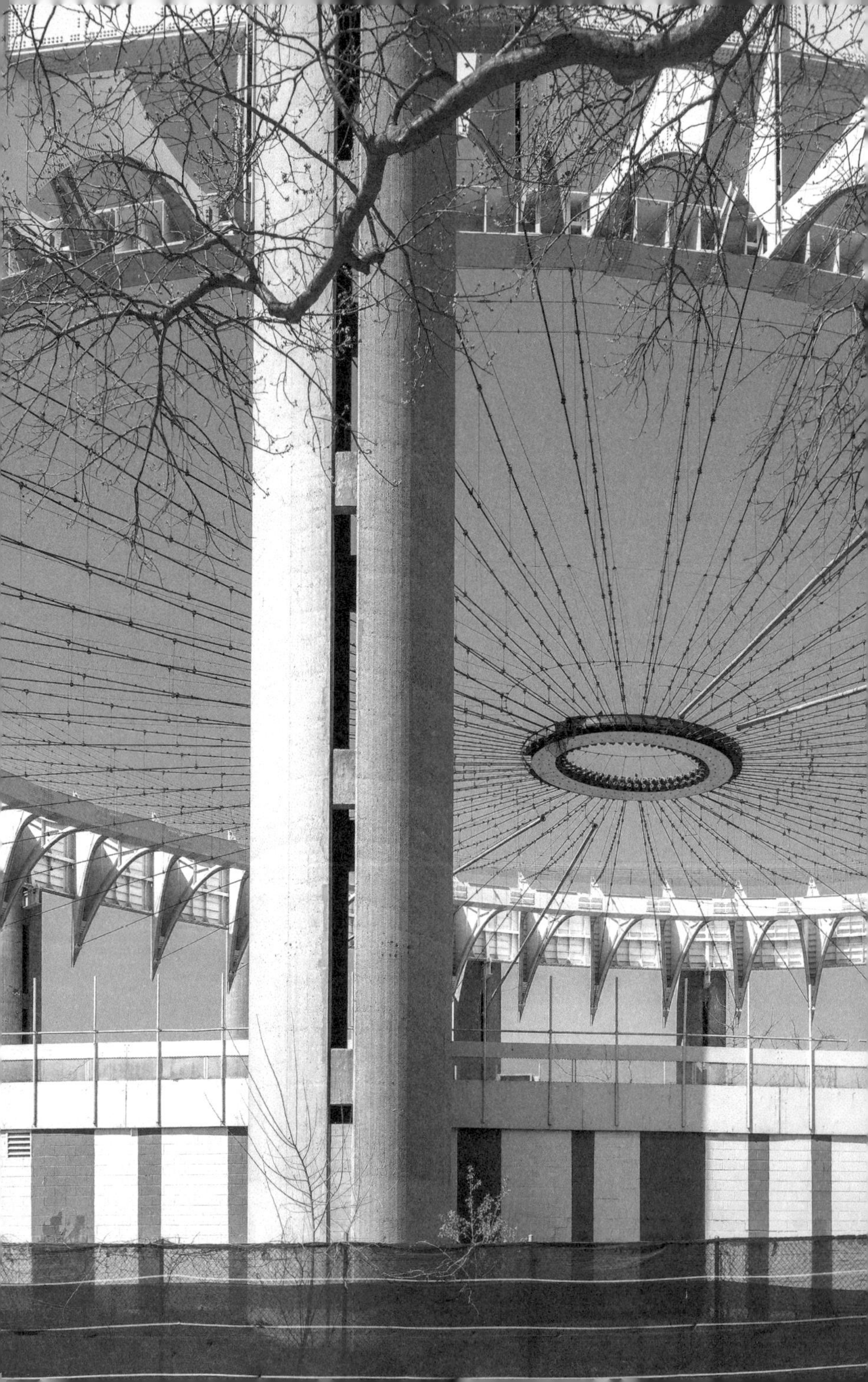

38 New York State Pavilion

Philip Johnson, Richard Foster, Lev Zetlin, 1962–64
Flushing Meadows-Corona Park, Queens, 11368

A "County Fair of the Future" was the New York State Pavilion's theme for the 1964–65 World's Fair. Architect Philip Johnson attacked this prompt with zeal, erecting a lively Modernist carnival. A large open-air elliptical "Tent of Tomorrow" has a ring of 16 slip-formed concrete columns supporting a 100-foot-high suspension roof reminiscent of a bicycle wheel. Alongside are three "Astro-View" observation decks, their flying saucer discs supported on concrete towers, the tallest rising to 226 feet. The adjacent cylindrical reinforced concrete Theaterama (now the Queens Theatre) was designed for screening 360-degree movies.

Unlike the fair's Terrace on the Park [49] and Great Hall of the New York Hall of Science [24], the pavilion has struggled to find a second life. It was briefly a concert venue and a roller rink until, aside from Theaterama, the complex was abandoned. The kaleidoscopic plastic tiles that covered the tent's roof were removed in 1976, and weeds sprouted through the exposed terrazzo Texaco road map on its floor. Its joyous red and white stripes faded; the sunny yellow of its painted steel rusted.

Ultimately, in the 2010s, a grassroots effort combined with interest from city officials turned things around from certain doom. The stripes were repainted, and, finally, the first phase of stabilization work was completed in 2023. Nighttime illumination was also returned to the Tent of Tomorrow, making it more visible, so it no longer appears like a forgotten ghost of the past.

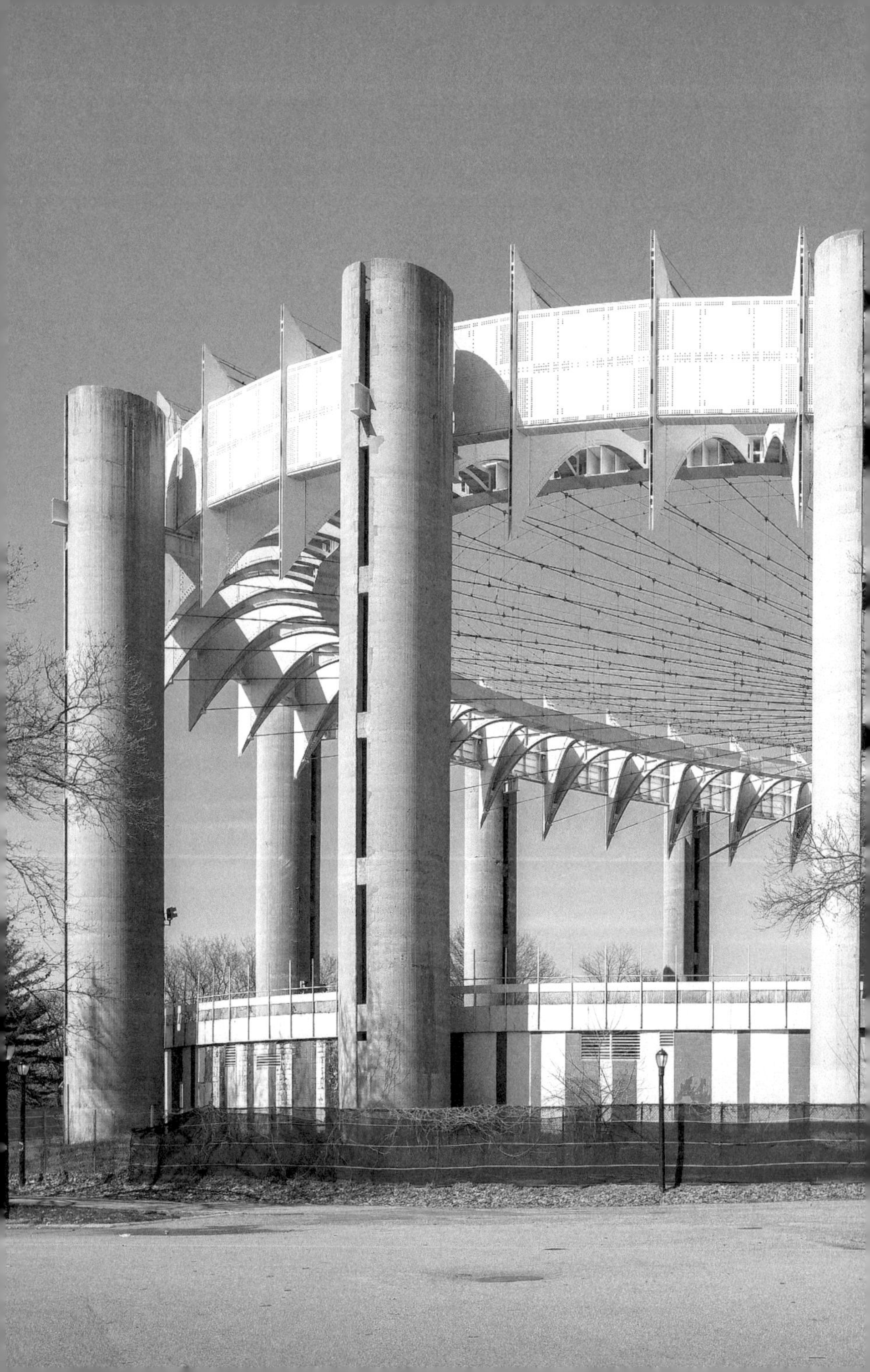

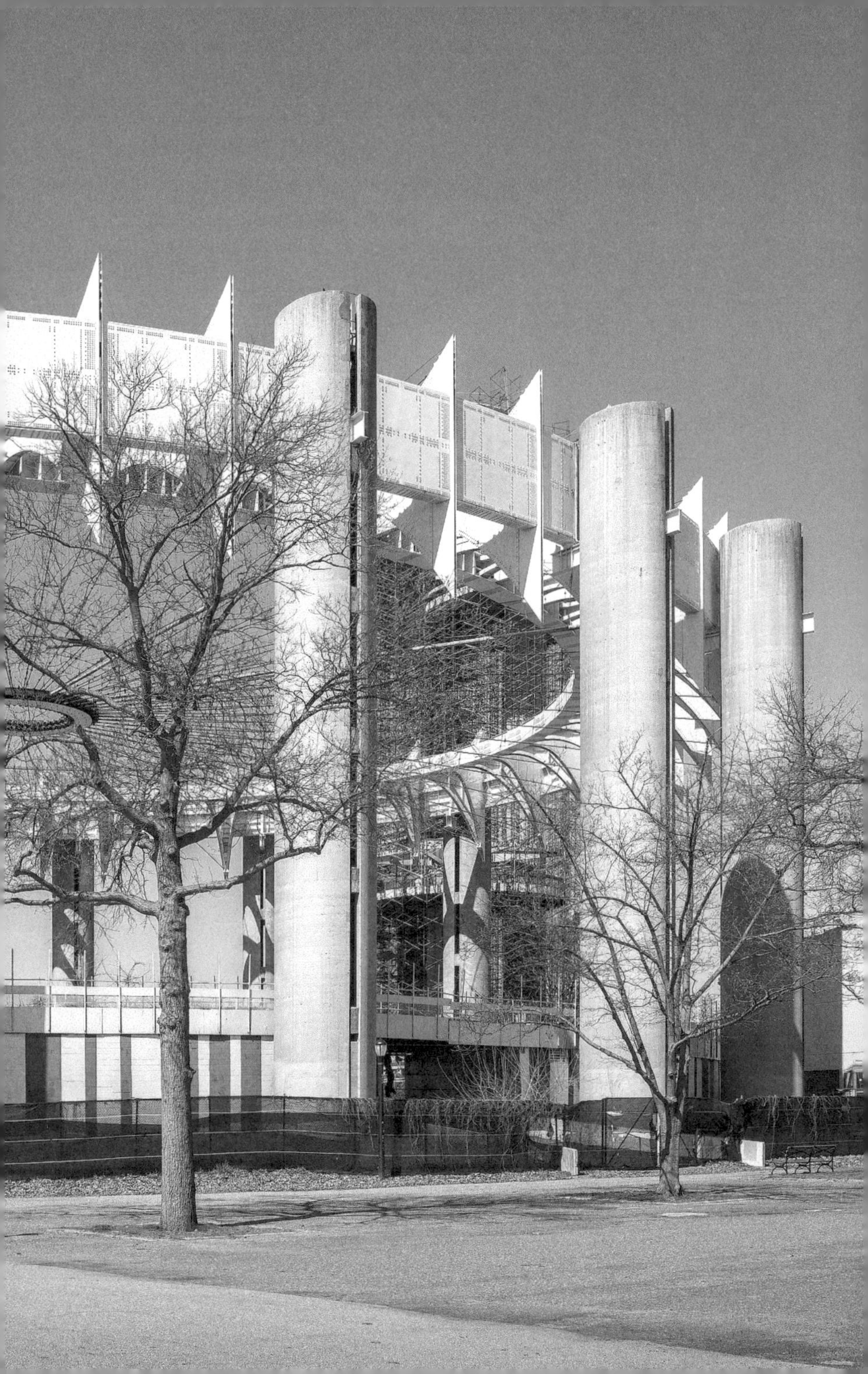

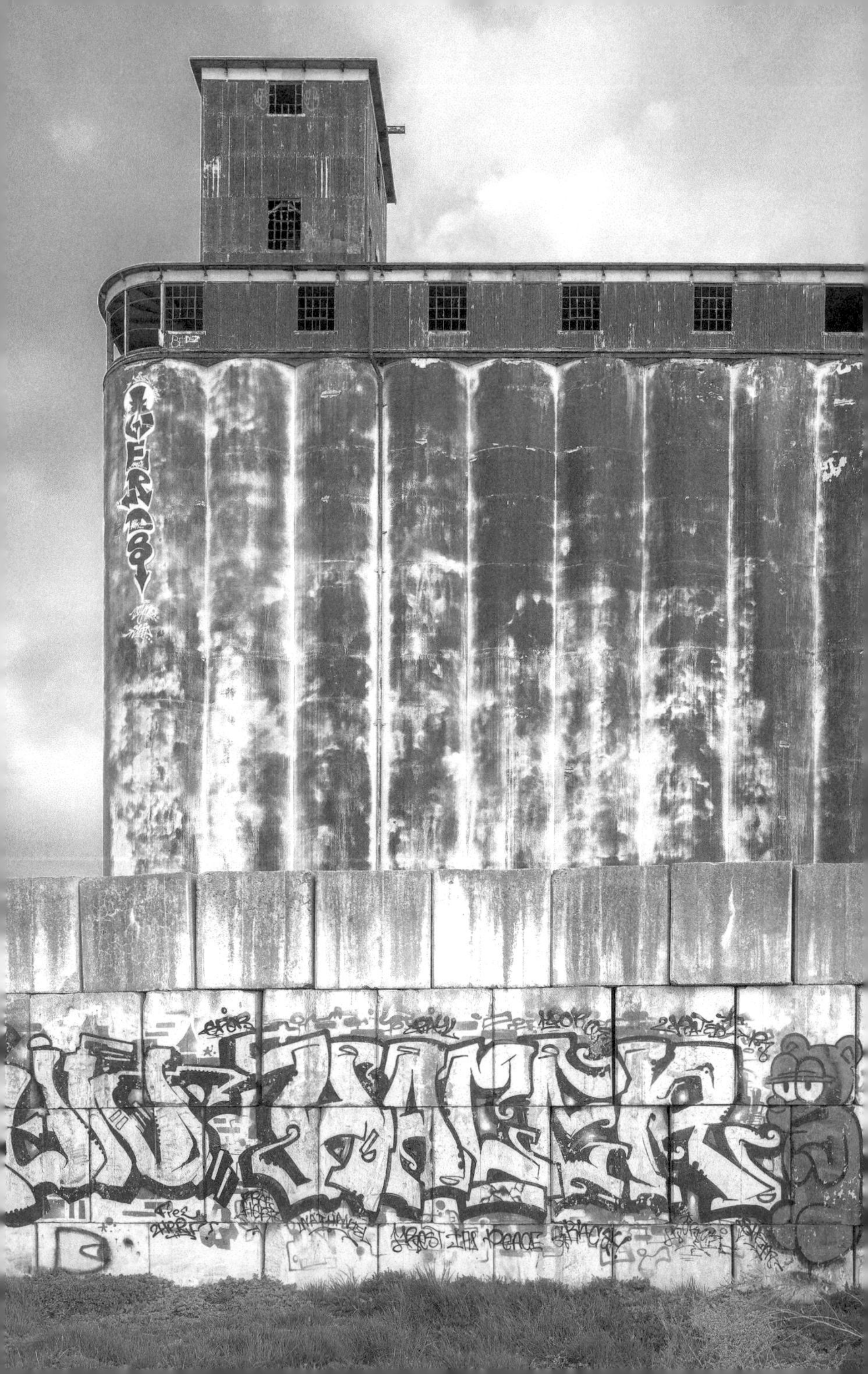

39

Red Hook Grain Terminal

Office of the State Engineer, 1922
Between Columbia Street and Henry Street Basin, Brooklyn, 11231

This concrete leviathan recalls when the waterways were central to New York's industry. Yet even when it opened, this era was giving way to the railroads. It's similar to other 1920s grain elevators constructed in the United States; their exposed concrete helped shape the style of Brutalism. (Le Corbusier called them "the first fruits of the New Age.") This 429-foot-long grain elevator with 54 circular storage structures made from reinforced concrete could hold two million bushels. Positioned where the mouth of the Gowanus Canal meets the Erie Basin, it was part of the New York State Barge Canal System, which aimed to support shipping across the state with a new series of routes expanding from the Erie Canal. Despite its prodigious size, the elevator was built over 16 months, with the concrete for its 90-foot-high silos poured in just 13 days.

It was never profitable and was deeded by the state to the Port Authority of New York and New Jersey in 1944. Usage continued to decline, so that it was decommissioned in 1965. In 1987, its conveyor and loading pier for docking freighters were destroyed. Over time, its concrete became darkly blotched and stained.

It's still the tallest structure in this part of Brooklyn. Although redevelopment has touched much of Red Hook's industrial waterfront, the grain terminal remains vacant. It has served as the background for music festivals and performances, but its stunning interior rows of concrete silos are off-limits, making it something of a holy grail for urban explorers.

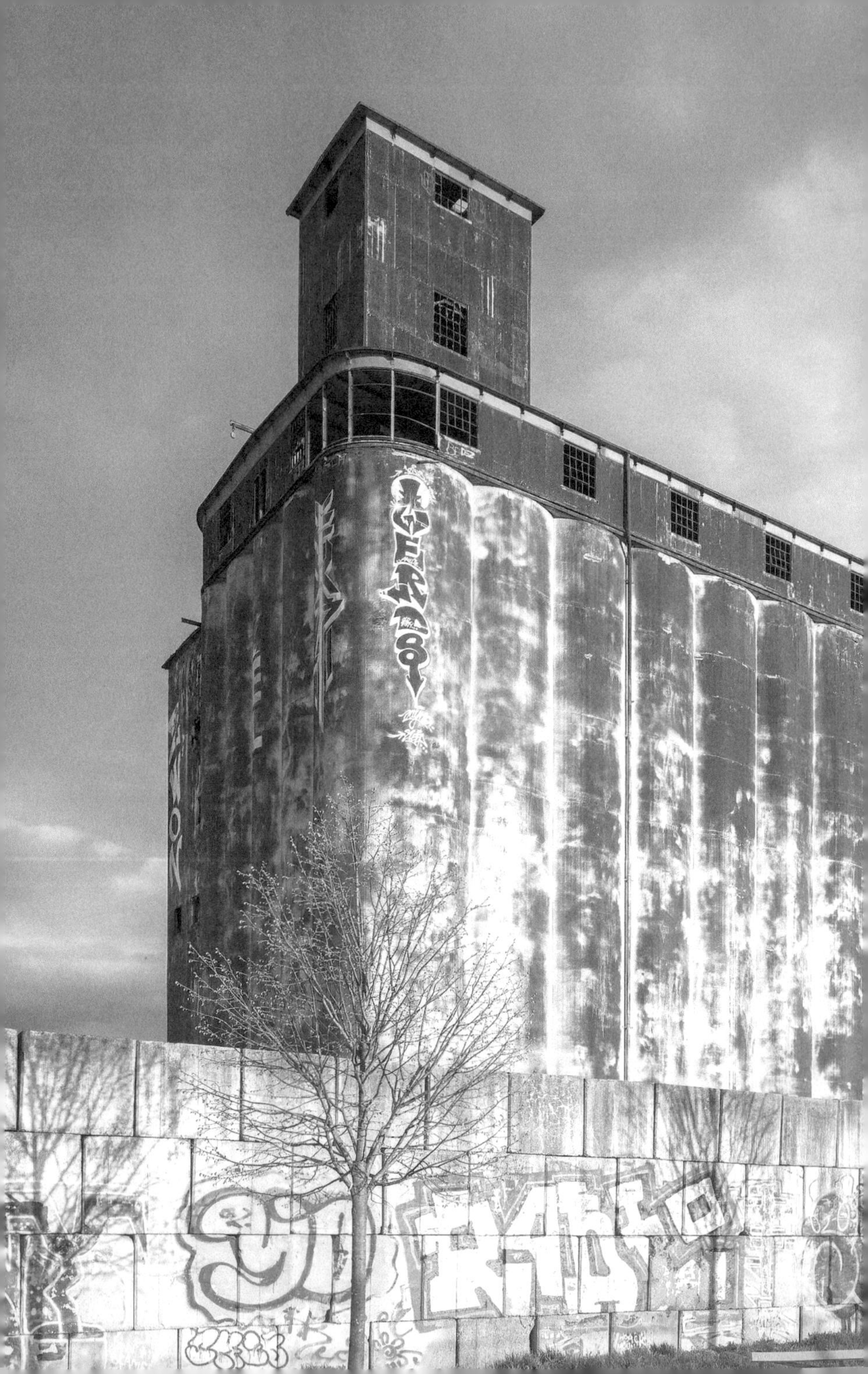

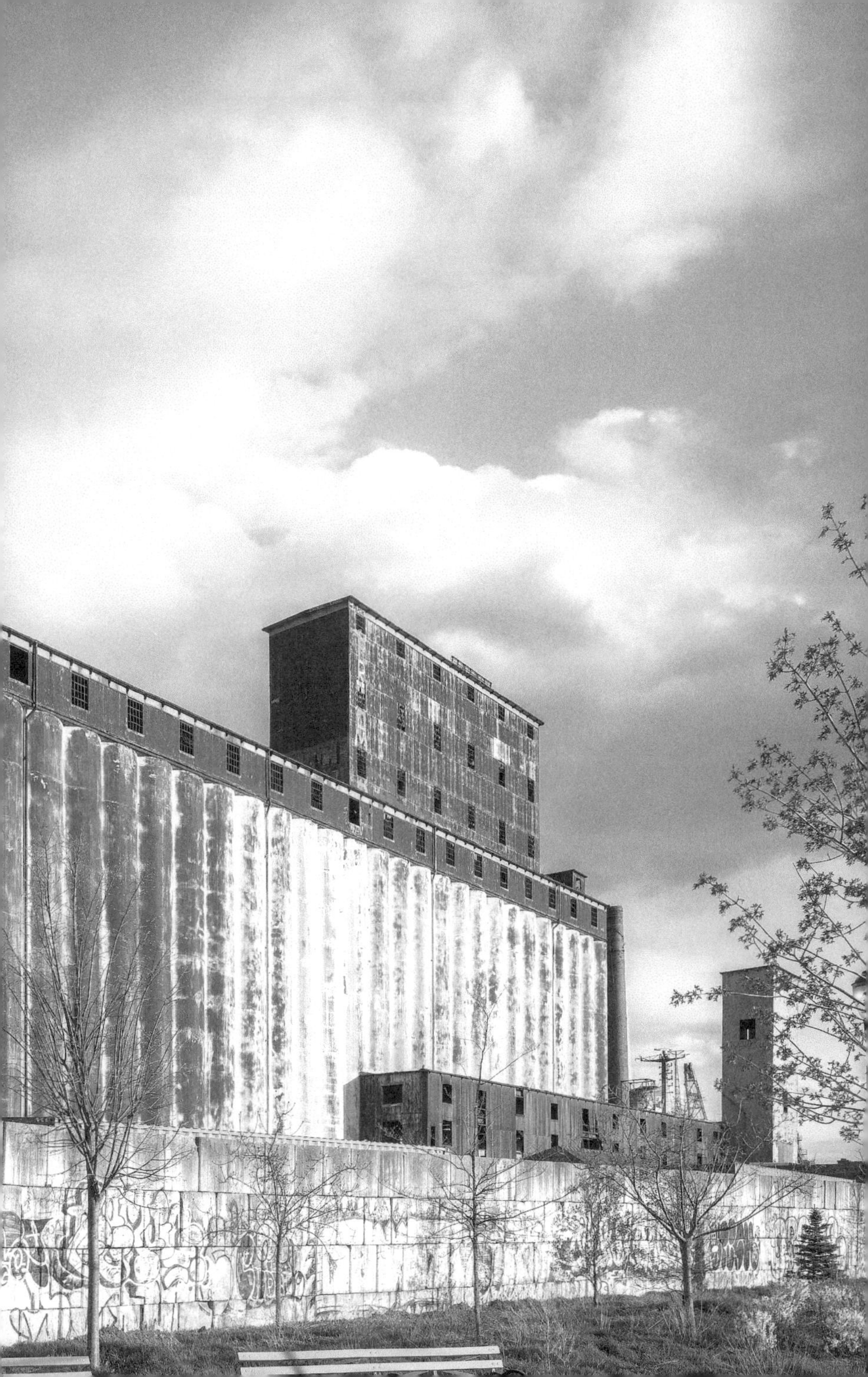

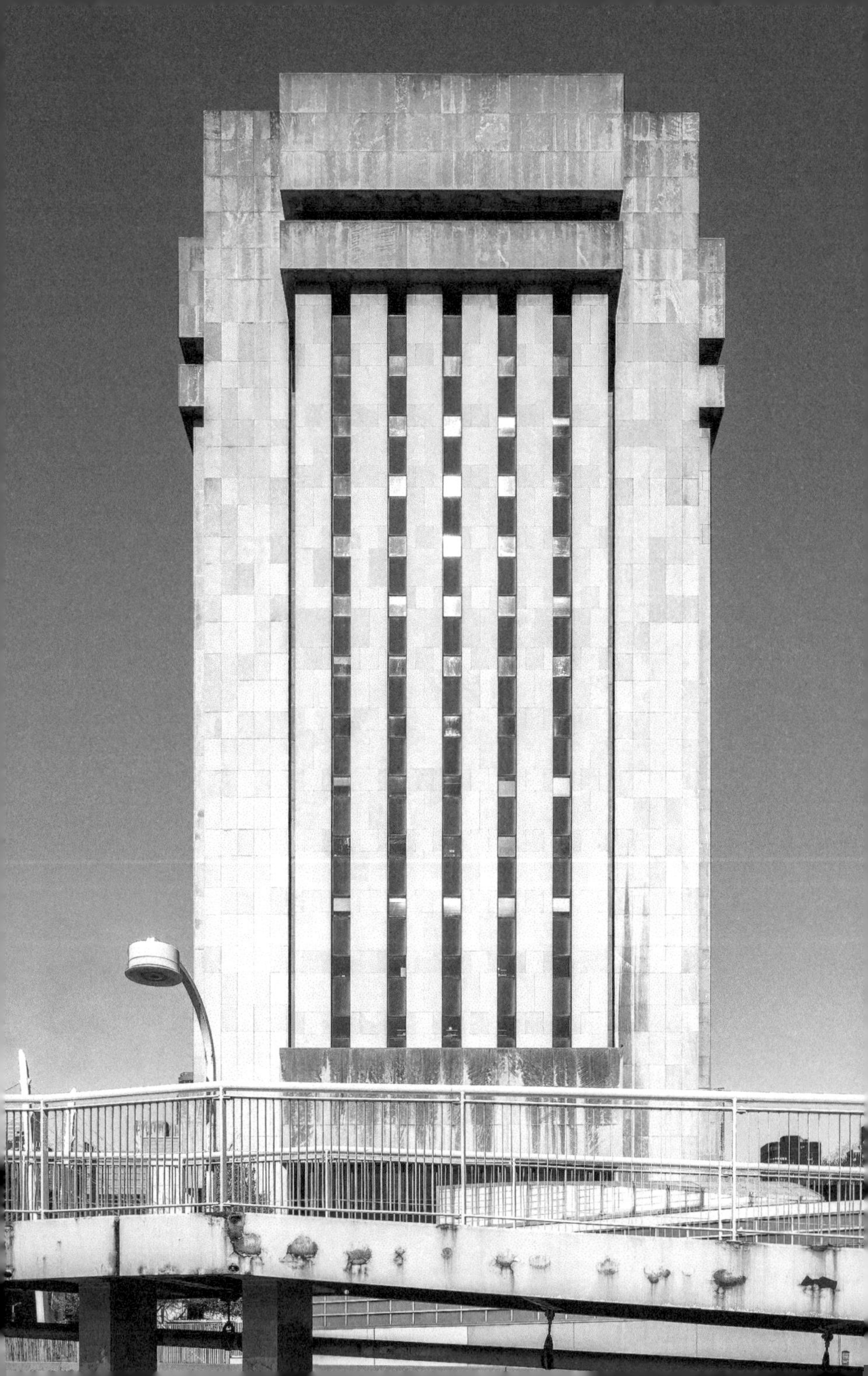

40 Rockefeller University: Benjamin and Irma G. Weiss Research Building

Campbell, Aldrich and Nulty, 1967-71
East 63rd Street and York Avenue, Manhattan, 10065

Approximately 14,700 cubic yards of concrete were poured into plywood forms for this 280-foot-tall, 17-story tower at Rockefeller University. Its robust silhouette, clad with limestone, almost hides its ribbon windows within extended vertical columns. It was one of the first building projects in the city to involve the post-tension technique, with steel cables lodged in the concrete on the third and seventeenth floors, supporting and suspending the building's perimeter load between them.

This accommodated a larger floor space without interior columns, ideal for the campus's laboratories. Architect Nelson W. Aldrich of the Boston-based Campbell, Aldrich and Nulty said in a 1980s interview for the Archives of American Art that it "was one of the very first science buildings, I believe, that was designed to go into a high-rise building. And the design concept there was to have all of the scientific and building services ... clean air and gases and all the things that were needed for a medical research building would be in these corner elements with the laboratories in between them."

When it opened on July 1, 1971, it was known as the Tower Building and held conference rooms, lecture halls, and laboratories for subjects ranging from chemical biology to experimental physics. In 1995, it was renamed the Benjamin and Irma G. Weiss Research Building following a bequest from investor Benjamin Weiss. Its lobby was refurbished alongside this rededication, including the filling in of its sunken seating pits.

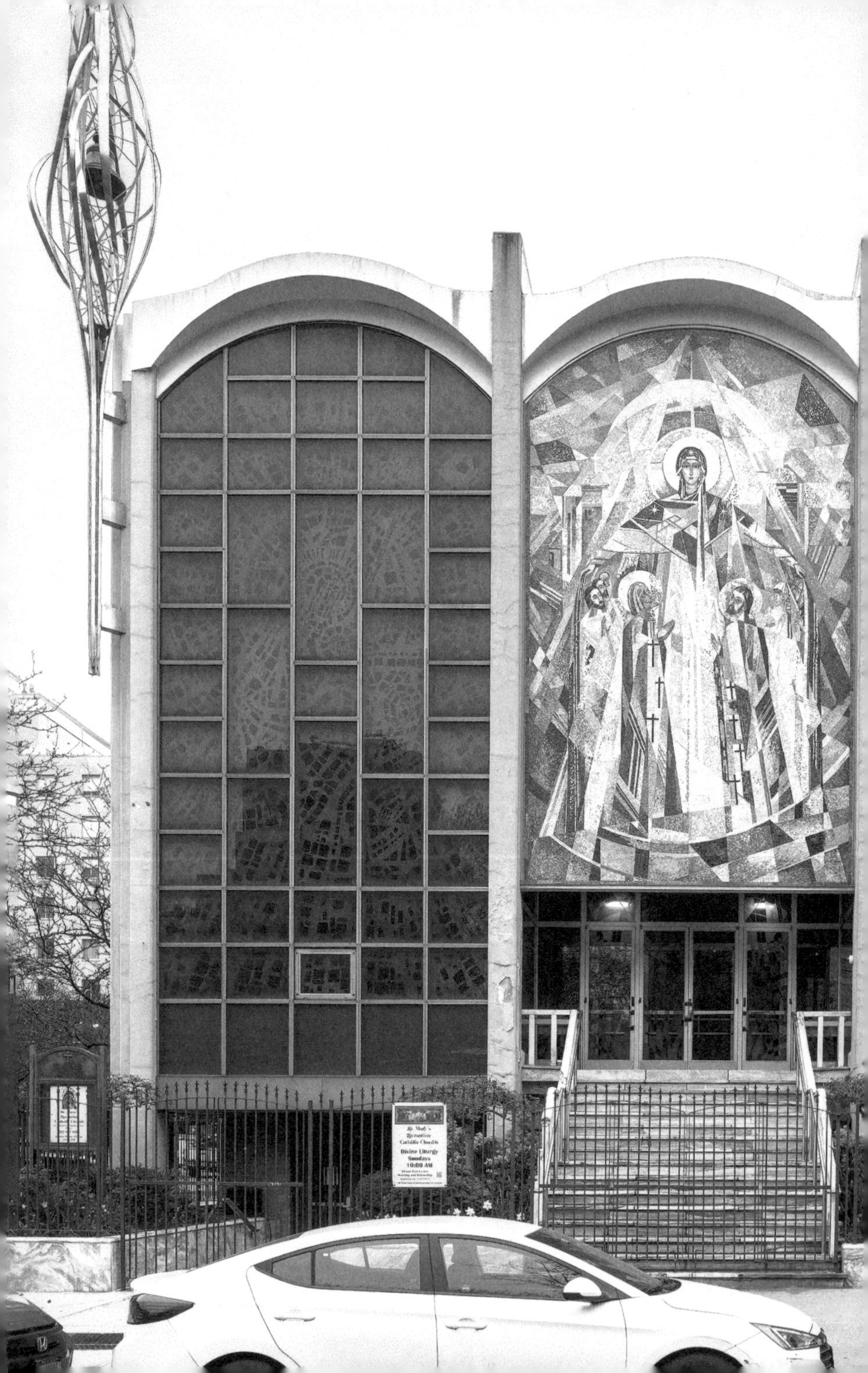
Divine Liturgy
Sundays
10:00 AM

41

St. Mary's Catholic Church of the Byzantine Rite

Brother Cajetan J. B. Baumann, 1963
246 East 15th Street, Manhattan, 10003

The predominantly Slavic congregation of this church marked its dedication in 1963 with a procession. *The New York Times* reported that they began at "225 East 13th Street, where they had worshipped for 50 years." They walked with crosses aloft to this new home, where a bishop "sprinkled the glass and cement façade with holy water and then celebrated the dedicatory mass and preached." Instead of the Latin Catholic rite, the mass was in Old Church Slavonic.

Despite this honoring of the past, the new St. Mary's Catholic Church of the Byzantine Rite was resolutely modern. It was designed by Brother Cajetan J. B. Baumann, a Franciscan friar and architect who led the New York-based Office of Franciscan Art and Architecture. Both sides of the corner lot building are almost completely covered with *dalle de verre* glass, with shards embedded in resin. It holds a sanctuary, rectory, and community center. A 50-foot spire by artist Jan Peter Stern wraps the old church's bronze bell in steel reminiscent of an onion dome.

Over the entrance is a vibrant mosaic of Mary by Felix Senger. When the interior is illuminated at night, she is surrounded by glittering color. Brother Cajetan stated in the dedication booklet: "Sacred Scripture applies the words of the Psalmist to Our Lady: 'All the beauty of the King's daughter is from within.' Taking this text as the basis of the design for this church, we tried to focus all the glory and beauty of this edifice within this sacred enclosure."

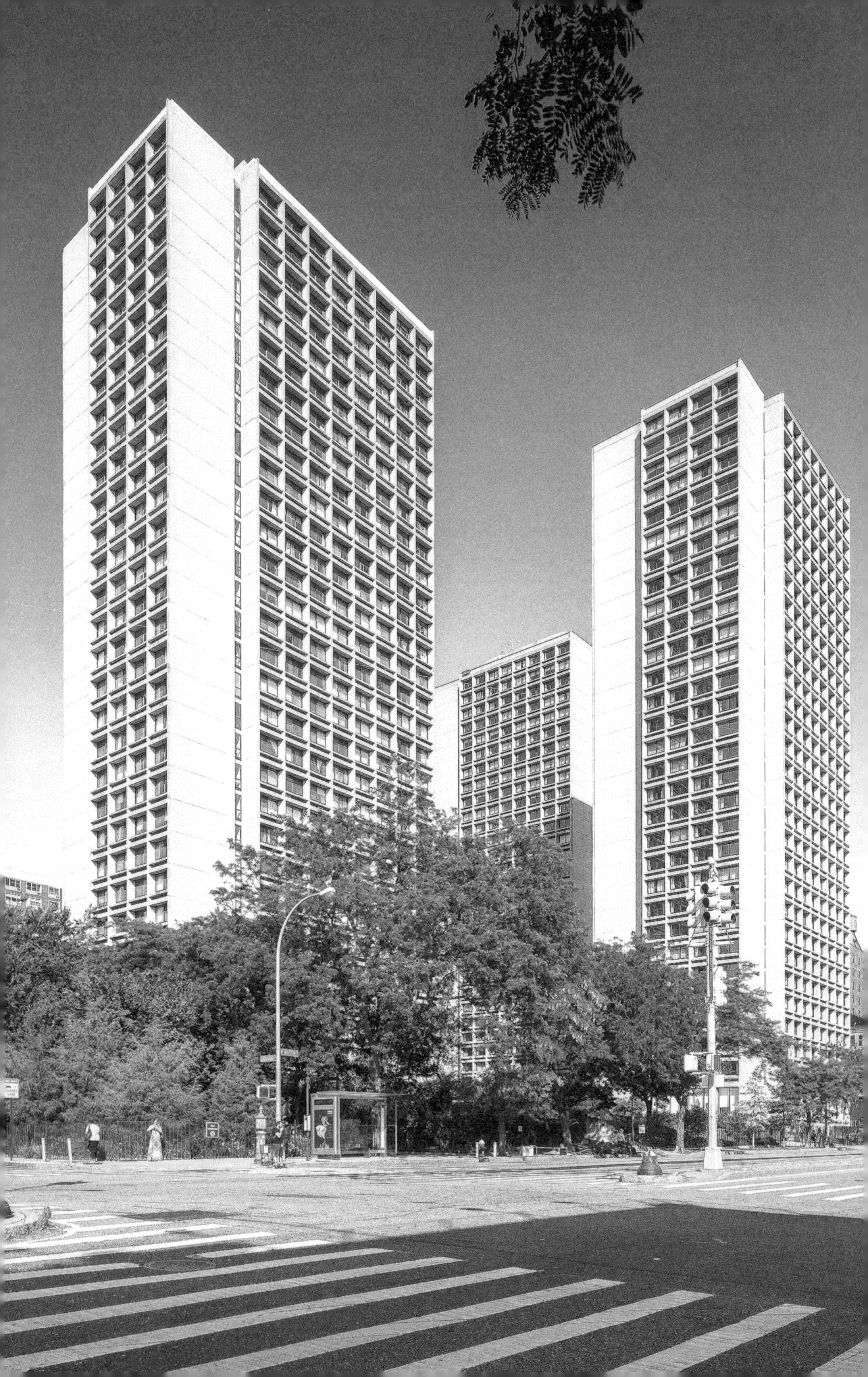

42 Silver Towers (University Village)

I. M. Pei & Associates, 1964-67
100 and 110 Bleecker Street, Manhattan, 10012

Each of the three concrete towers in this superblock is set at a different angle as they pinwheel around a wide lawn. The 100-foot-square green space is accented by the 36-foot-tall, 60-ton sandblasted Cubist concrete sculpture *Bust of Sylvette*, designed by Pablo Picasso and executed by Carl Nësjar. University Village, renamed Silver Towers in 1974, is one of the city's more successful housing developments to come out of the aggressive urban renewal of the 1960s in the name of "slum clearance." Superblocks like this were made from tearing down numerous blocks and combining them into huge complexes that prioritized pedestrian space.

Influenced by Le Corbusier's economical use of exposed concrete and the postwar tower-in-the-park Modernist model, I. M. Pei was already working on another superblock location in Manhattan, Kips Bay Plaza [27]. James Ingo Freed was the lead architect for University Village, a five-and-a-half-acre site that was built for New York University (NYU) housing, with a third of it reserved for affordable apartments. All three towers have gridded light brownish concrete, made with fiberglass molds, around deep-set windows. Flat concrete walls are at the towers' corners.

The Silver Towers were designated a New York City landmark in 2008. NYU floated plans to expand the complex, but these were met with local opposition. One of the supporters for preserving Silver Towers was Sylvette David (now known as Lydia Corbett), who modeled for the folded-metal sculpture by Picasso that formed the basis of the concrete work.

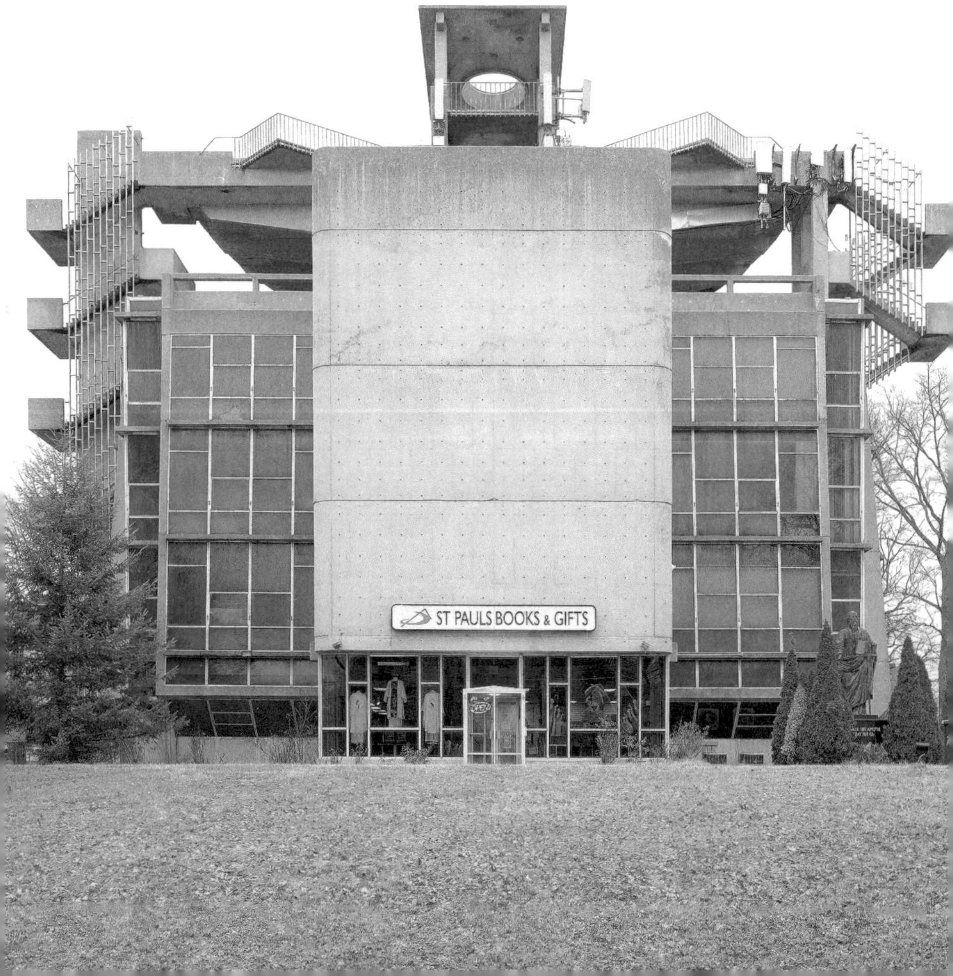
ST PAULS BOOKS & GIFTS

43 Society of St. Paul (Alba House)

Silverman & Cika, 1966–69
2187 Victory Boulevard, Staten Island, 10314

Many passersby have been perplexed by the wild concrete angles and protrusions of this Staten Island building. It was constructed as the publishing house of the Society of St. Paul, an international Catholic congregation. Its members, the Paulines, have as their mission the use of all available technology to evangelize Christian messages. Books are key to that charge, so the structure is a huge part of their complex, which also includes a popular shrine and dormitories, connected to the publishing house by a covered bridge.

Silverman and Cika was led by Gerard Silverman and Robert Cika, who studied with Frank Lloyd Wright. The firm's best-known projects are the glass-and-concrete 1979 Taino Towers in East Harlem and a 1959 UFO-shaped house designed for Jackie Gleason in the Hudson Valley. The needs of constructing a building that would house a printing press as well as offices, a bindery, spaces for worship, and a bookstore informed the seemingly strange choices for this design. External staircases, something more common in a factory, fly around each floor. Ample windows provided ventilation for the printing presses and other machines. A concrete volume in the center holds a freight elevator for hoisting books. At the top is a platform for a rarely used open-air chapel with a concrete altar and canopy.

Production of books has largely ended in the building, although the first-floor bookstore is still an active part of the Society of St. Paul's publishing efforts.

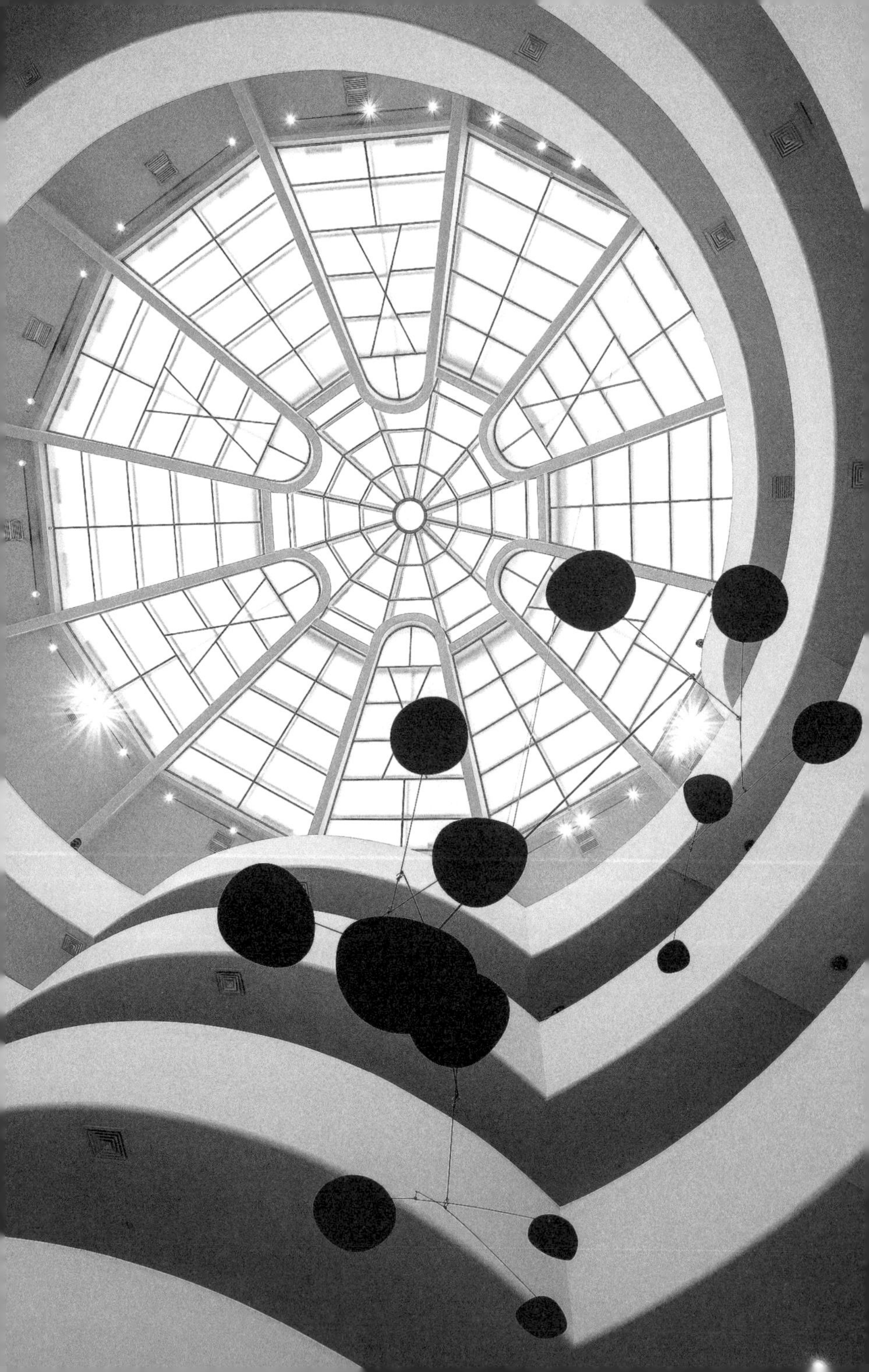

44 Solomon R. Guggenheim Museum

Frank Lloyd Wright, 1943-59
1071 Fifth Avenue, Manhattan, 10128

Frank Lloyd Wright was no fan of Manhattan, which he considered crowded with architecture that had no cohesive planning behind it. Still, he took the 1943 commission to build, per its patron Solomon R. Guggenheim, a building "unlike any other museum in the world." The project took years of navigating regulations and budgets, not breaking ground until 1956. The famously caustic Wright wrote in 1949, "I can think of several more desirable places in the world to build his great museum, but we will have to try New York."

It may not have been his ideal locale, yet somehow the highly unconventional Guggenheim Museum fits into its corner on the Upper East Side. Its inverted white ziggurat of concrete plays off the canopies of the trees across the street in Central Park, while its curves challenge the angles of the stately homes on the surrounding blocks. Inside, its concrete spiral remains a destination, even if generations of curators have now struggled, and often failed, to tackle this unconventional exhibition space.

Wright died six months before it was completed. On the exterior, his name is joined in metal by that of George N. Cohen, the general contractor. A concrete expert, he was key to realizing its sculptural shape through the innovative use of "gunite," in which concrete is sprayed onto plywood forms. Wright was unhappy with the impressions from these molds. Cohen advised that it gave the design "honesty" in not hiding its construction that took so many human hands. "Perfection," he said, "is not in the nature of the material we are working with. Perfection is for stone or marble or metal."

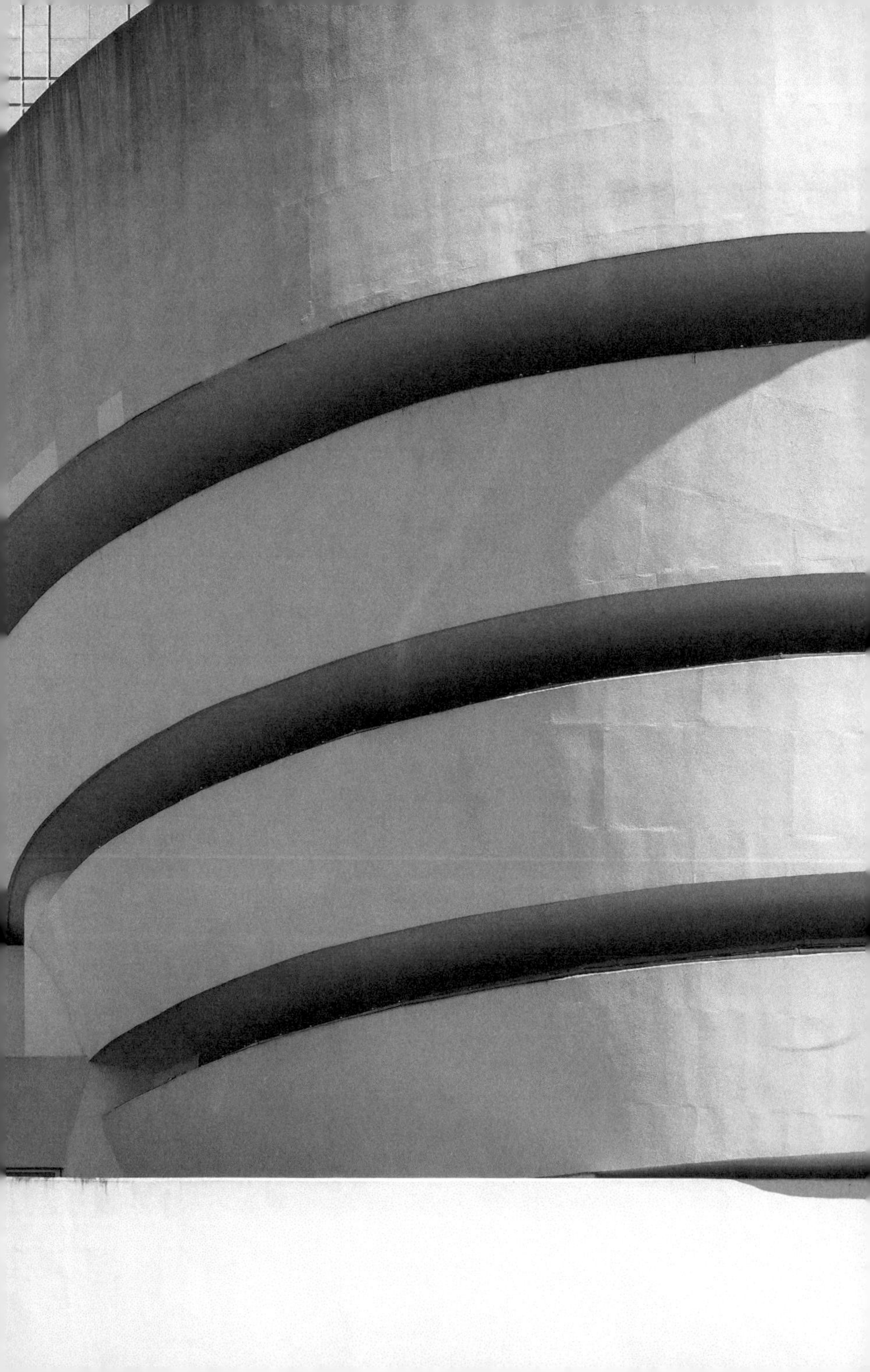

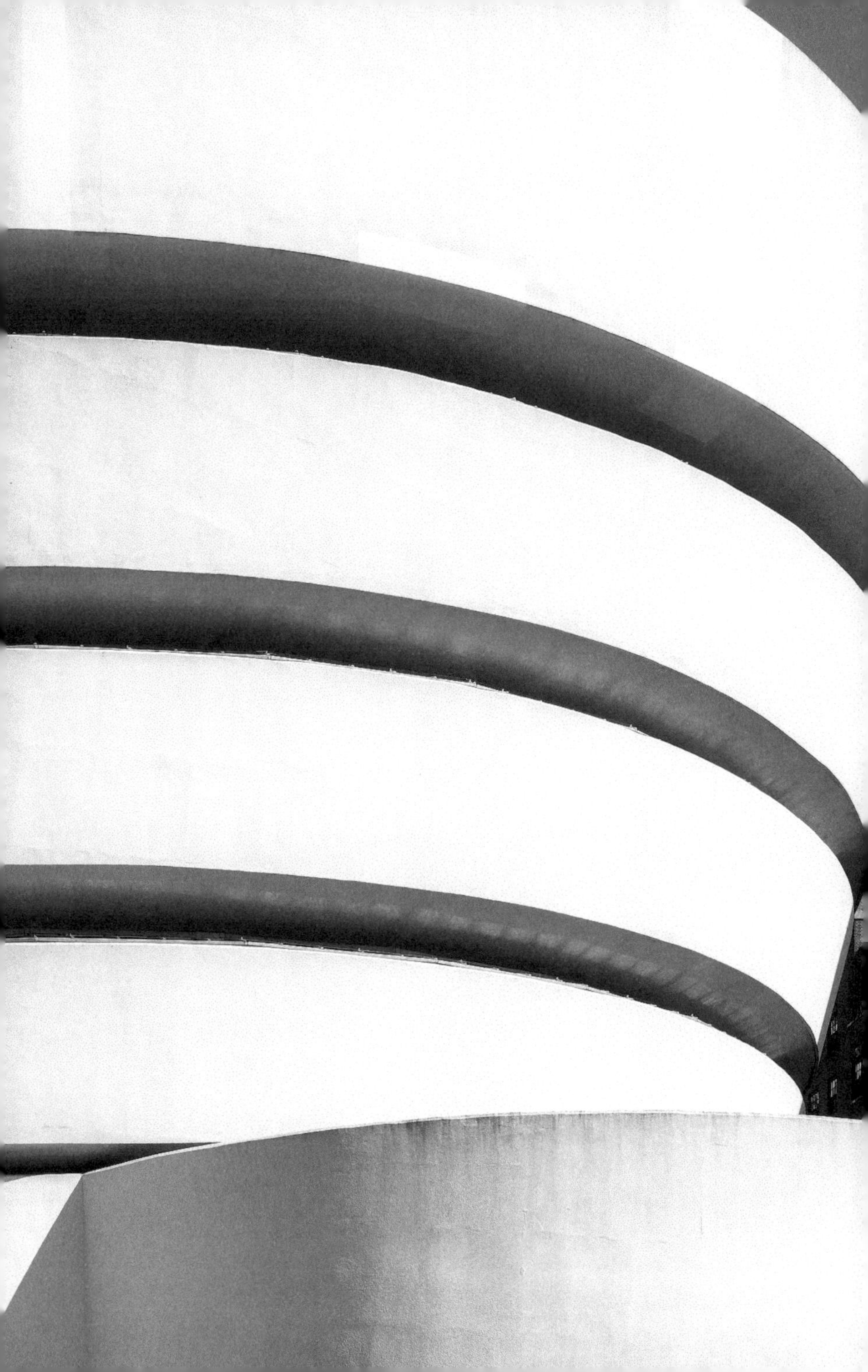

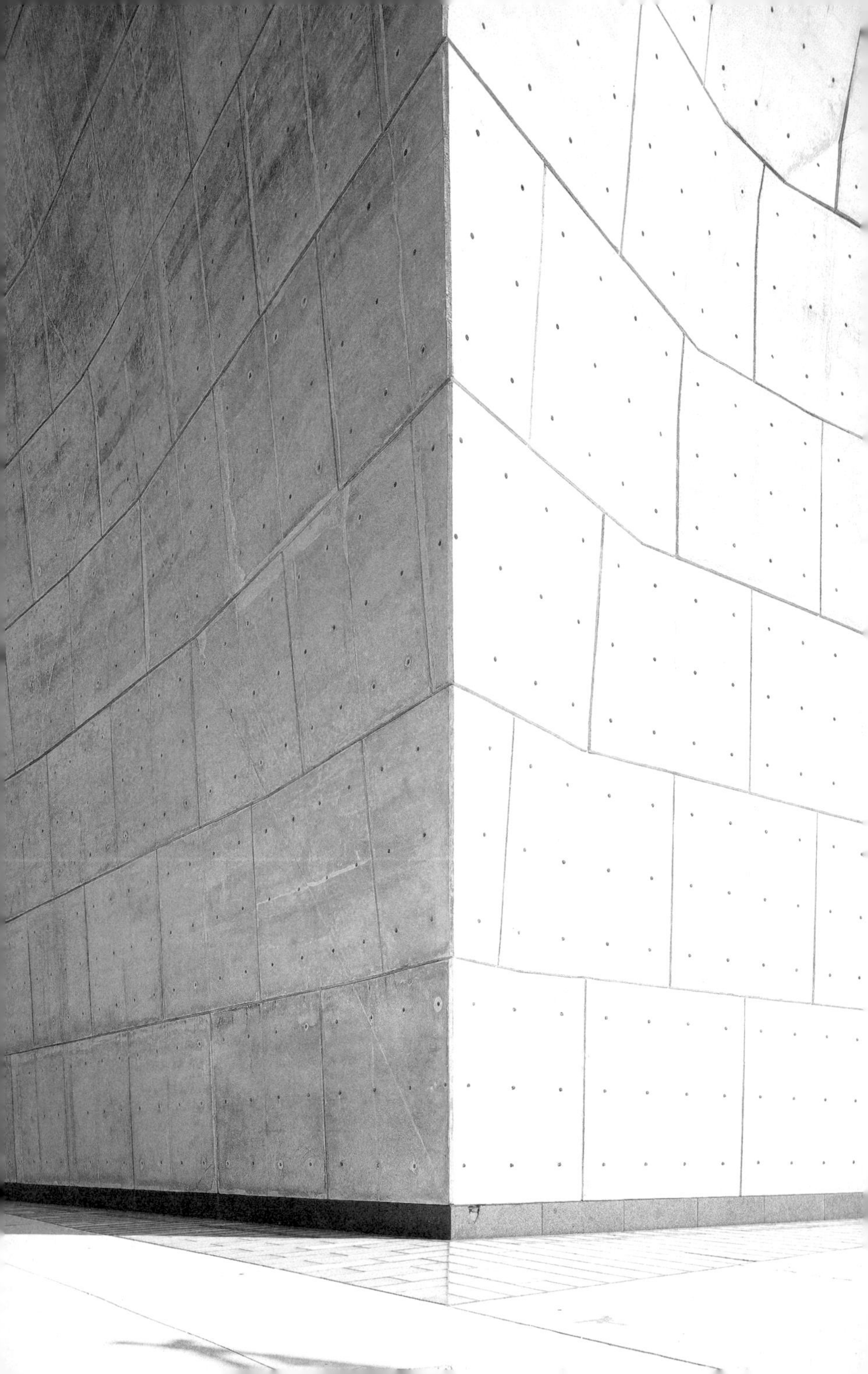

45 Spring Street Salt Shed

Dattner Architects with WXY Architecture + Urban Design, 2010–15
336 Spring Street, Manhattan, 10013

Inspired by what it was designed to hold, this is an impressive example of civic architecture as art. Its cast-in-place concrete walls measure up to six feet thick and are lined with steel plating to withstand the elements alongside the Hudson River. Their faceted planes that taper toward the bottom are reminiscent of the organic shapes of salt grains. One side rises 70 feet, the asymmetry accommodating the natural slant of the salt's "angle of repose" that it assumes when piled inside. Salt sheds dot the city, holding tens of thousands of tons of salt used each year to clear the roads of ice and snow, but none before have so honored this crucial winter resource in their forms.

It complements the Department of Sanitation garage across the street, a building likewise nuanced to its purpose and sustainability, from the rainwater collected to wash trucks to its color-coded floors visible through perforated metal fins that shield it from the sun. These dual projects were contentious in their development, with celebrity neighbors voicing concerns about the salt dust. In response, the architects concentrated on producing a fully enclosed salt shed that would beautify its surroundings. It has won over critics with its thoughtful form and attention to creating pedestrian space around it, and it has become a destination for photoshoots against the distinctive concrete walls. These have already aged gracefully, starting as a glacial-blue from the slag mixed into the material and fading into a radiant white, even more closely resembling a magnified salt crystal.

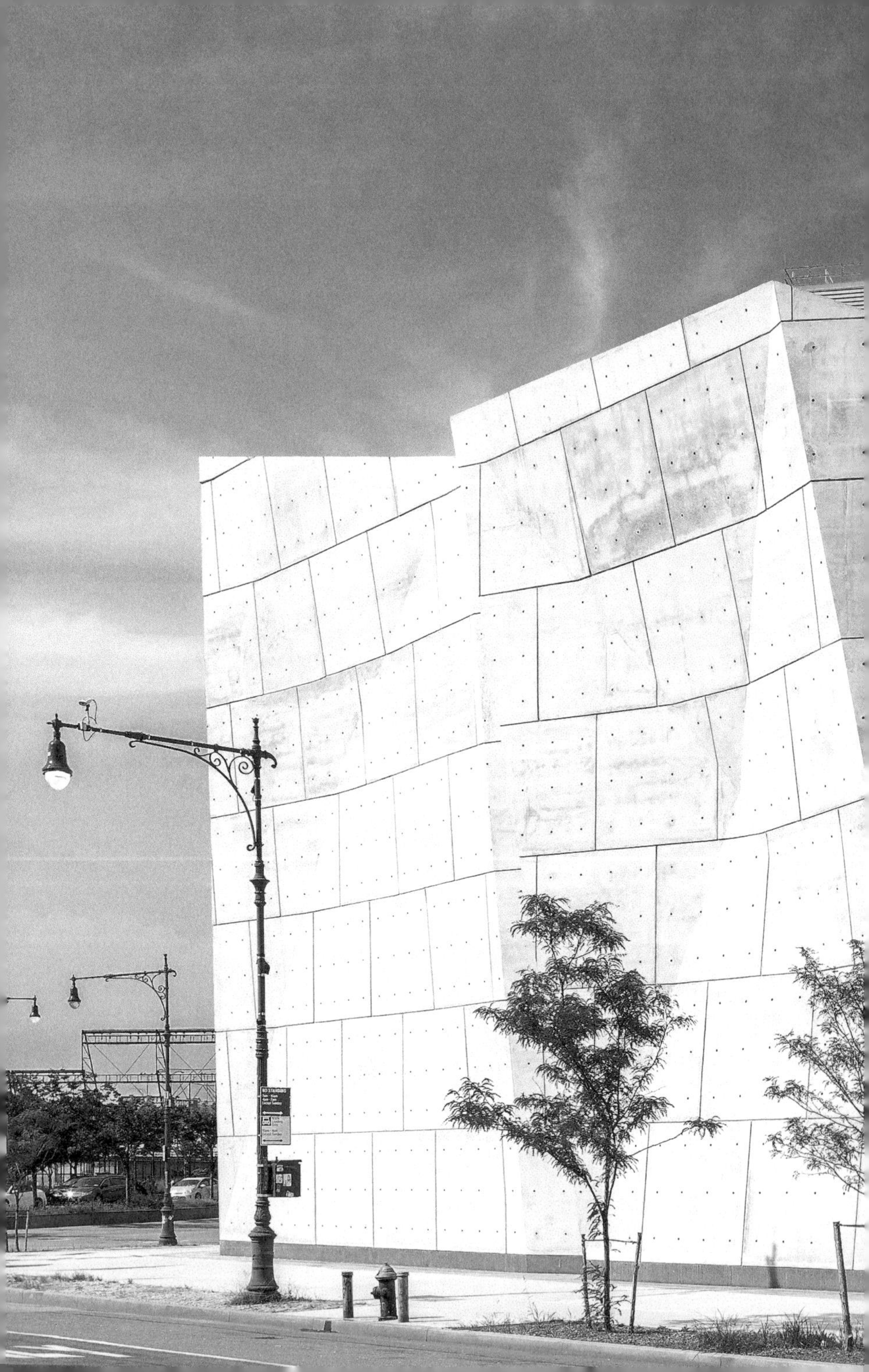

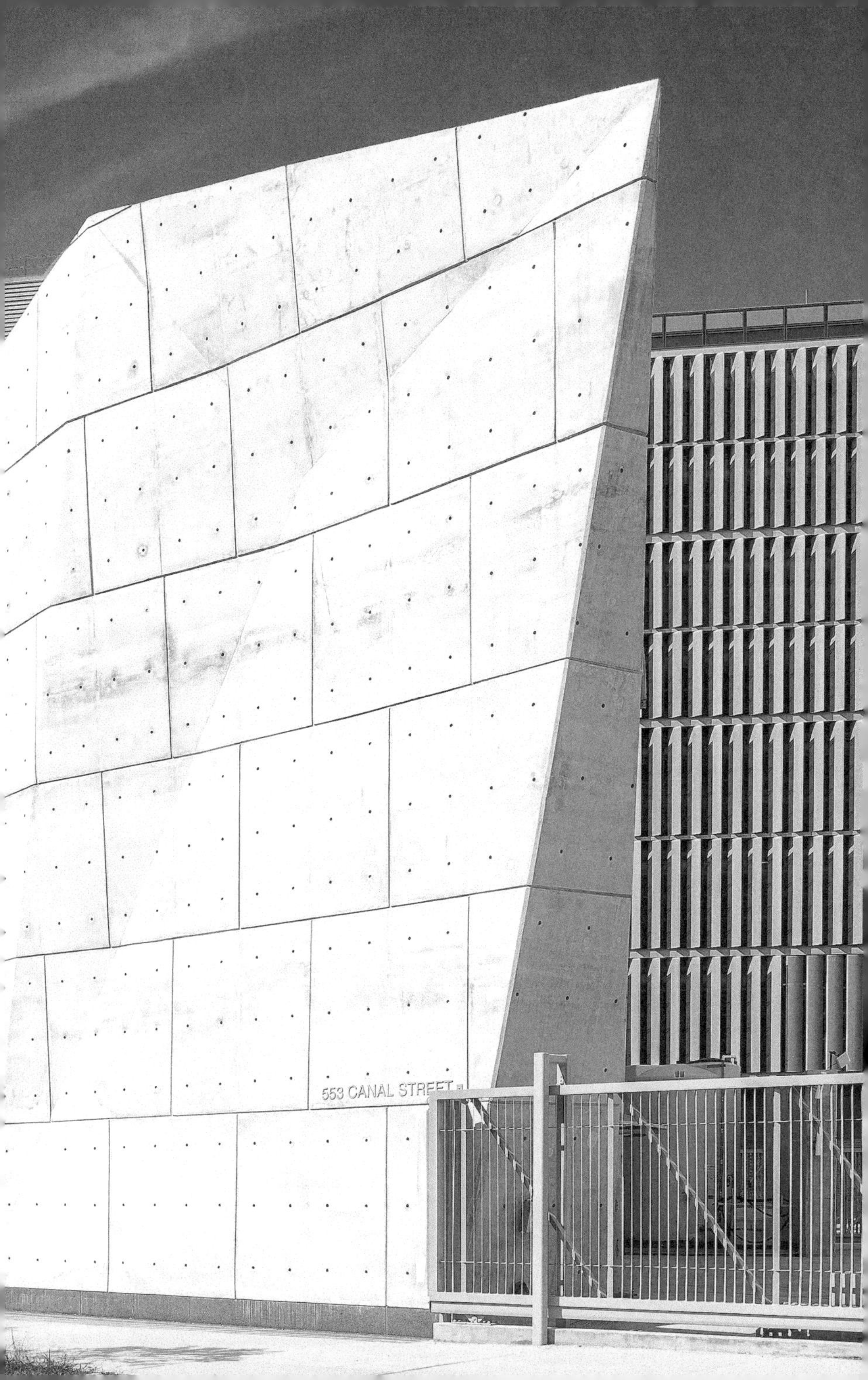
553 CANAL STREET

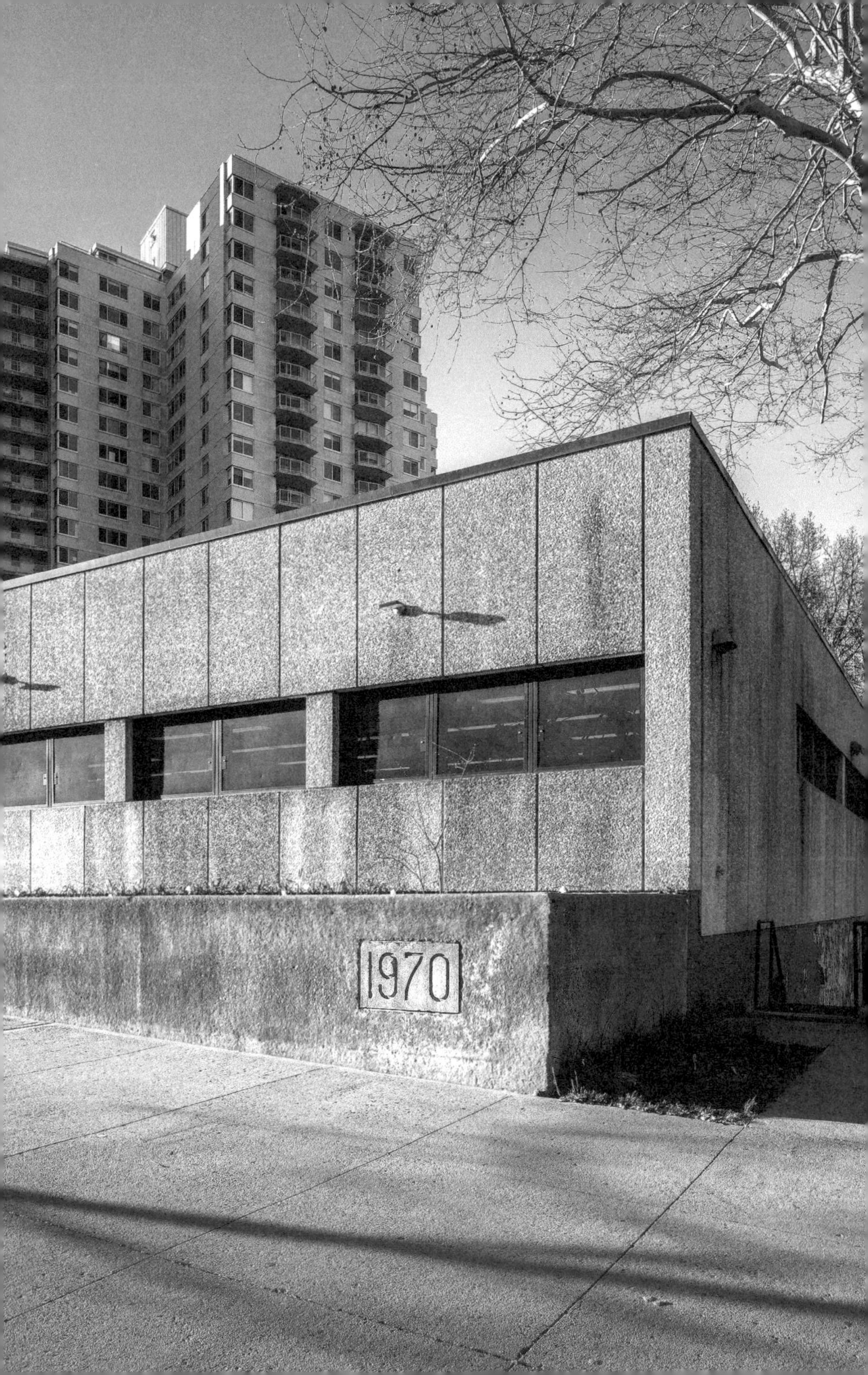
1970

(46) Spuyten Duyvil Library

Giorgio Cavaglieri, 1970–71
650 West 235th Street, The Bronx, 10463

As the aesthetics of Brutalism spread from Europe to the United States in the 1950s to '70s, the severe geometric forms, monochrome colors, and functional building materials made their way into vernacular neighborhood architecture. This included something as humble as a branch library, as seen with this one-story building by Giorgio Cavaglieri. It opened in August 1971 in Riverdale, in the northwest portion of the Bronx. Its 1970 cornerstone is embedded in a front wall of concrete, and its textured surfaces and block-like façade further mark it as part of this era.

Long, narrow windows cut through the rectilinear fronts of the library. Inside, it is much less stern and surprisingly luminous, with a hexagonal opening letting in natural light. Around the same time, Cavaglieri designed another New York Public Library (NYPL) building, the Kips Bay Branch, which opened in March 1972. It is likewise Modernist in its angular two-story masonry structure. As one of the first branches built for accessibility for patrons who use wheelchairs, it has no entry stairs and doors that are extra-wide for ease of mobility.

The Venice-born Cavaglieri studied architecture in Italy before fleeing the rise of fascism in 1938. He set up his practice in New York in 1946. In the city, he became a major historic preservation advocate and was especially known for trailblazing the adaptive reuse of 19th-century architecture. One of his biggest projects was the 1960s transformation of the Jefferson Market Courthouse into an NYPL branch.

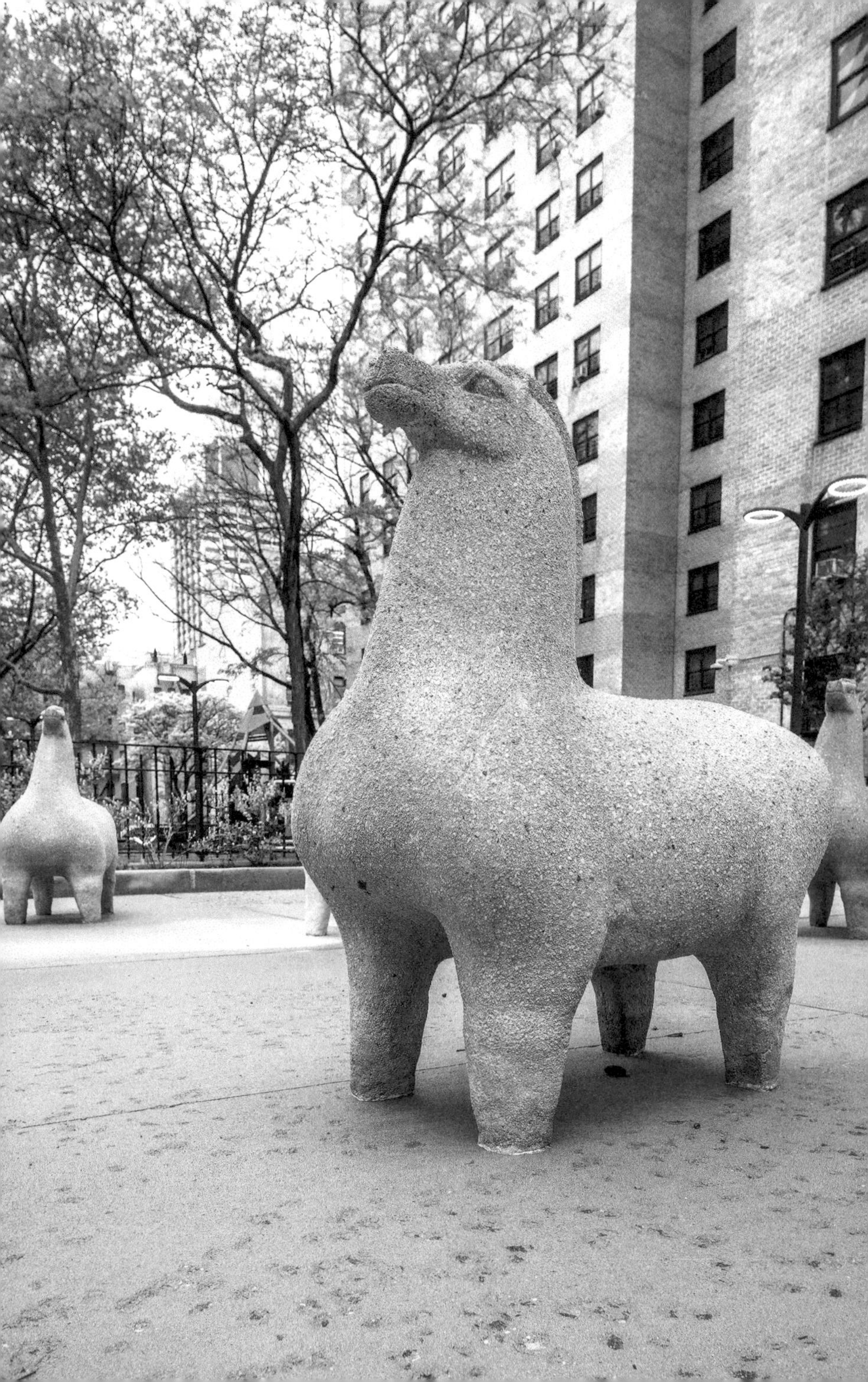

(47) Stephen Wise Towers Playground Horses

Costantino Nivola, 1964
109-17 West 90th Street, Manhattan, 10024

A herd of portly concrete horses stands proudly on the Upper West Side. Costantino Nivola sculpted them as part of a playground for the Stephen Wise Towers. Just recently, their future was uncertain. After decades of play and vandalism, their muzzles were broken. Then in 2021, they were cut off at the knees and removed for a water main repair. Only their hooves remained. But in January 2024, all 18 were reinstalled.

Their restoration by Jablonski Building Conservation was meticulous, using a mold from 1970s fiberglass versions made for an Indiana school. Born in Sardinia, Nivola fled Italy during the rise of fascism and arrived in New York in 1939. He cared about the accessibility of art and how it could engage with architecture. He often worked with concrete, molding it into forms or carving it into murals. His work in New York City spans decades, from a 1958 education-themed sand-cast bas relief on the façade of Coney Island's William E. Grady High School to 1980s bronze statuettes at the 19th Precinct Combined Police and Fire Facilities on the Upper East Side.

At the Wise Towers, built as public housing in the 1960s, he created several plaza works along with the horses. Each encourages a different kind of recreation, whether relaxation or play. Two concrete polygons were built as a fountain; an abstract humanist concrete sculpture, which *Time* magazine called "a sort of guardian nanny" in 1965, presides over the space. An expressive mural was also made with the sgraffito technique of scratching away to reveal the color underneath.

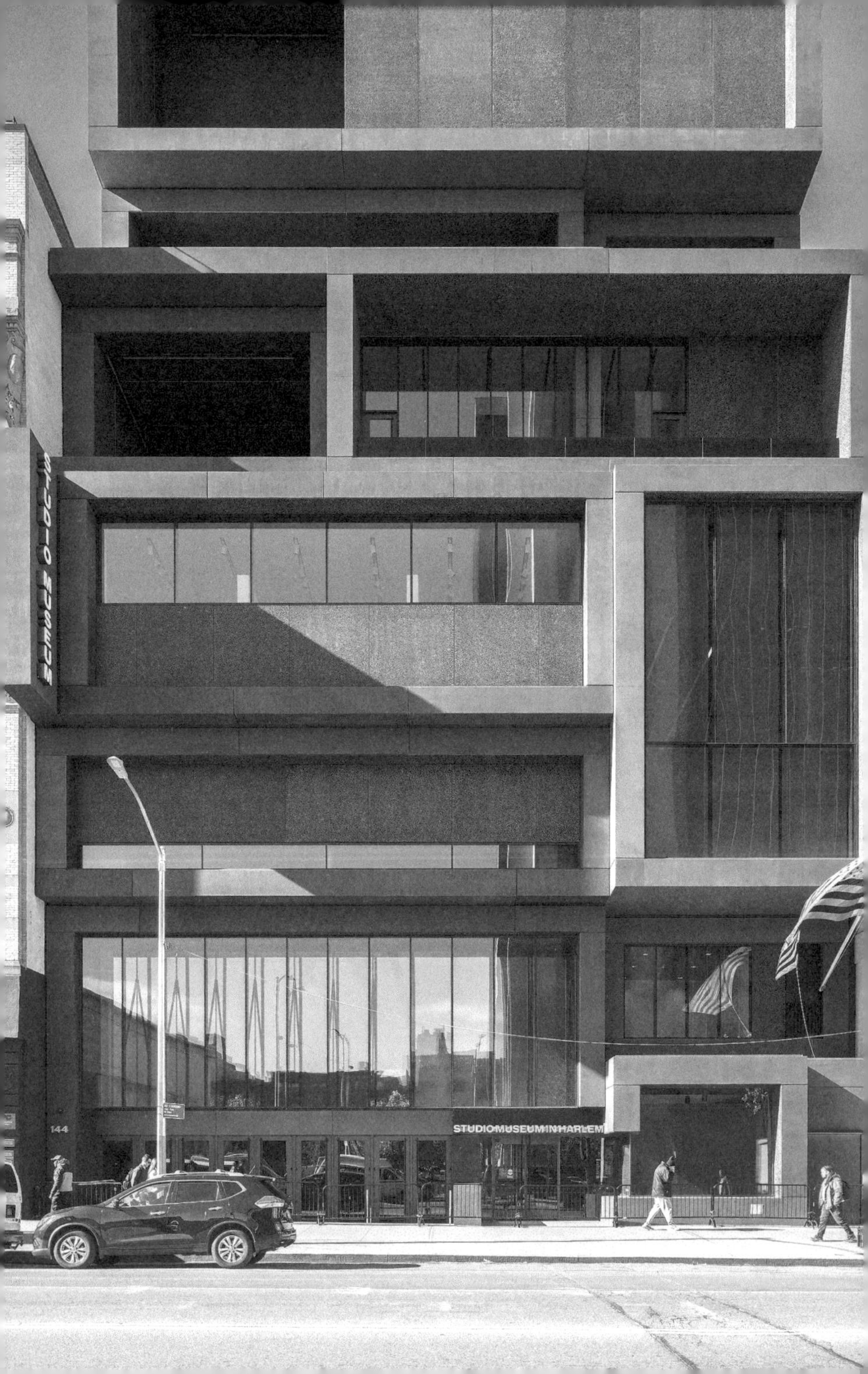
STUDIO MUSEUM
144
STUDIO MUSEUM IN HARLEM

48 Studio Museum in Harlem

Adjaye Associates with Cooper Robertson, 2017-25
144 West 125th Street, Manhattan, 10027

The gray concrete of this museum's stacked volumes shift in tone with the changing light and weather. The mix of matte and polished surfaces, and variations in the dark color, gives it a range of tones from light graphite to rich charcoal. Wide recessed windows are framed by the hard edges of the material, offering inviting views from the street. Inside the lobby are bleacher seats, a sophisticated take on the New York City stoop, and, to the back, a terrazzo-covered staircase that leads up to the galleries.

The Studio Museum in Harlem opened in 2025 following Adjaye Associates' work in Manhattan on the Sugar Hill Development and 130 William [4]. Both projects also feature textural gray concrete, with this design completed in collaboration with Cooper Robertson.

This stretch of 125th Street has changed significantly since the museum arrived in 1982, with the encroachment of gentrification. Its previous home was a repurposed bank, and this new 82,000-square-foot building doubles the exhibition space. It has studios for residents, a library, and a roof garden. It's located directly across the street from the burly Adam Clayton Powell, Jr. State Office Building [9]. While that project was controversial for the state government imposing its will on Harlem, here the country's leading museum devoted to Black art has affirmed the neighborhood's cultural importance. From its concrete façade flies an American flag overlaid by artist David Hammons with black, red, and green, referencing Marcus Garvey's 1920s Pan-African flag.

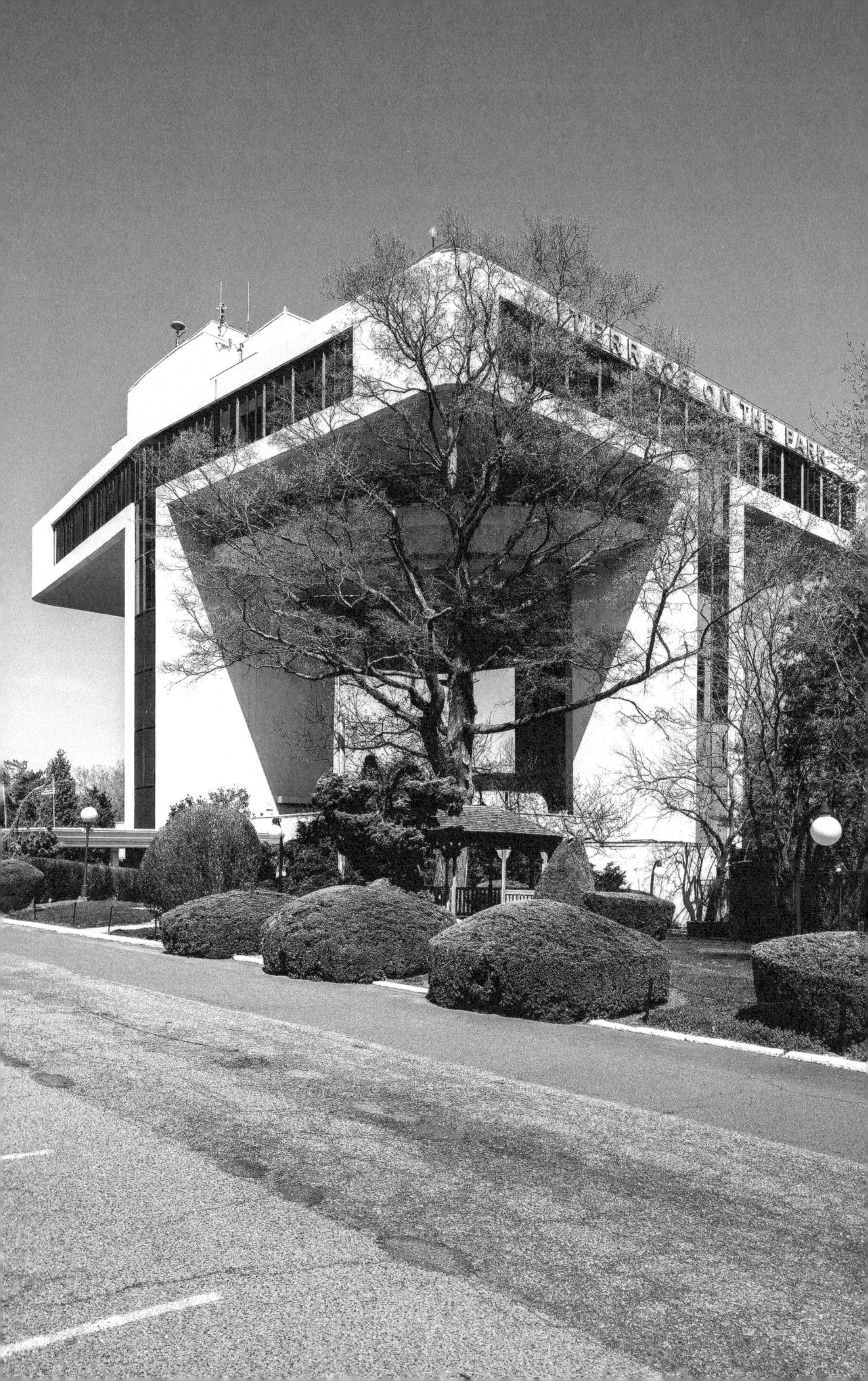
ON THE PARK

49 Terrace on the Park (Port Authority Heliport)

Port Authority of New York with Allan Gordon Lorimer as chief architect, engineers John Kyle and Ray Monte, and planning chief E. Donald Mills, 1962-63
52-11 111th Street, Queens, 11368

The 120-foot-tall conjoined stilts that support this Brutalist behemoth create a "T" on each side for "transportation," emphasized by the lines of horizontal and vertical windows. It was originally built as a heliport for the 1964–65 New York World's Fair. While its fellow fair remnant the New York State Pavilion [38] remains vacant, the former heliport has become an in-demand wedding venue. Renamed Terrace on the Park, its panoramic vistas are as much a draw as they were when it was the first building completed for the international event.

Then called the Port Authority Heliport and Exhibit Building, the concrete and steel structure lofted a 1,100-seat restaurant and a "Drinks Around the World" cocktail lounge above the fairgrounds. Its exhibitions included a 360-degree film in a circular theater telling the story of transit in New York City. With a landing helipad measuring 175 feet by 200 feet, it was intended as an aerial gateway to the fair, also offering a takeoff point for helicopter sightseeing tours. Heliports were then envisioned as a way to quickly leapfrog across the city; another topped the recently completed Pan Am Building [34] in Manhattan. The Beatles famously landed here in August 1965 as they made their way to a Shea Stadium concert. A restoration completed in 2017 revitalized the building with new roof pavers, paint, and lighting, ensuring it continues to be one of Queens's gargantuan icons.

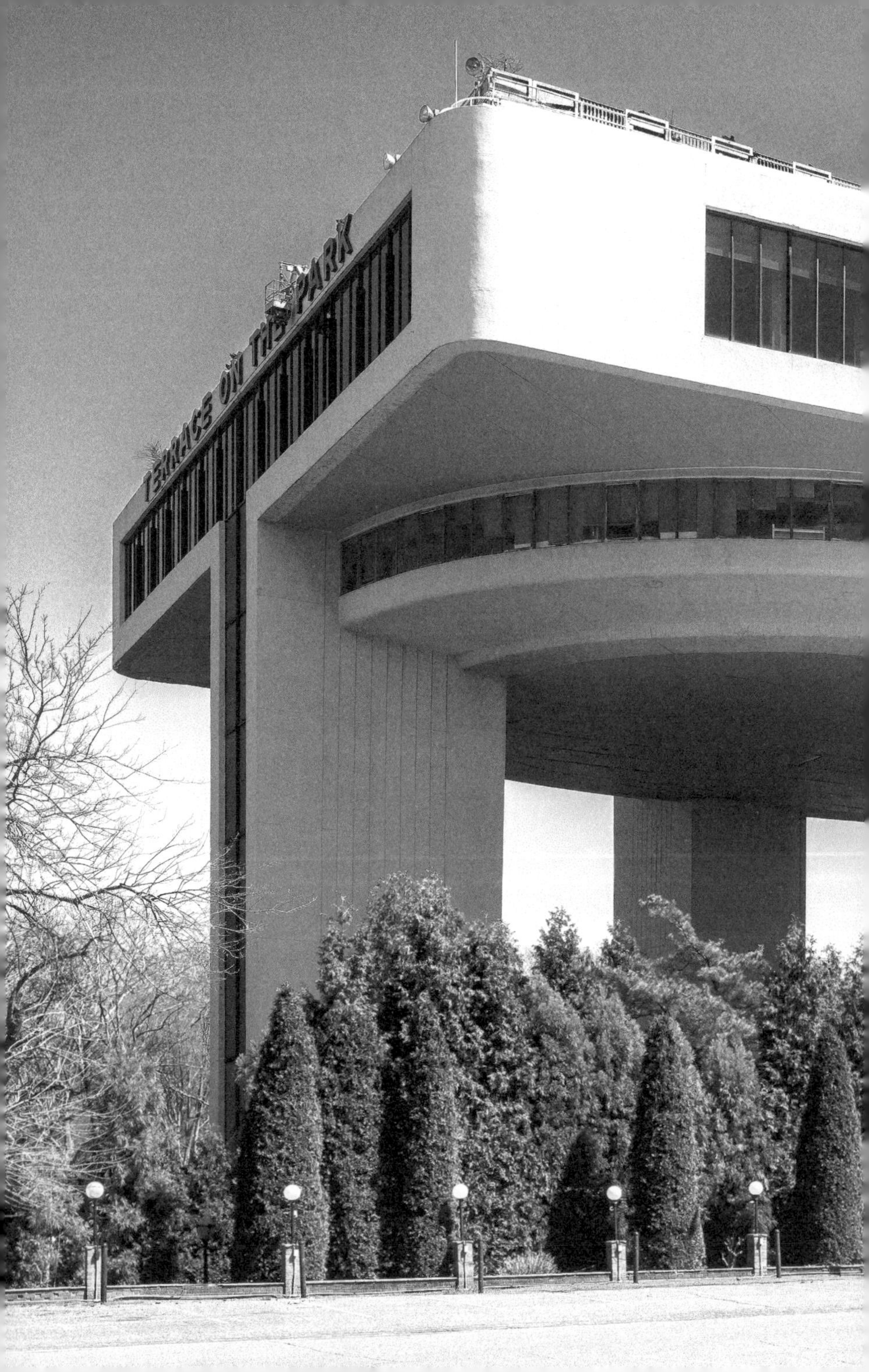
TERRACE ON THE PARK

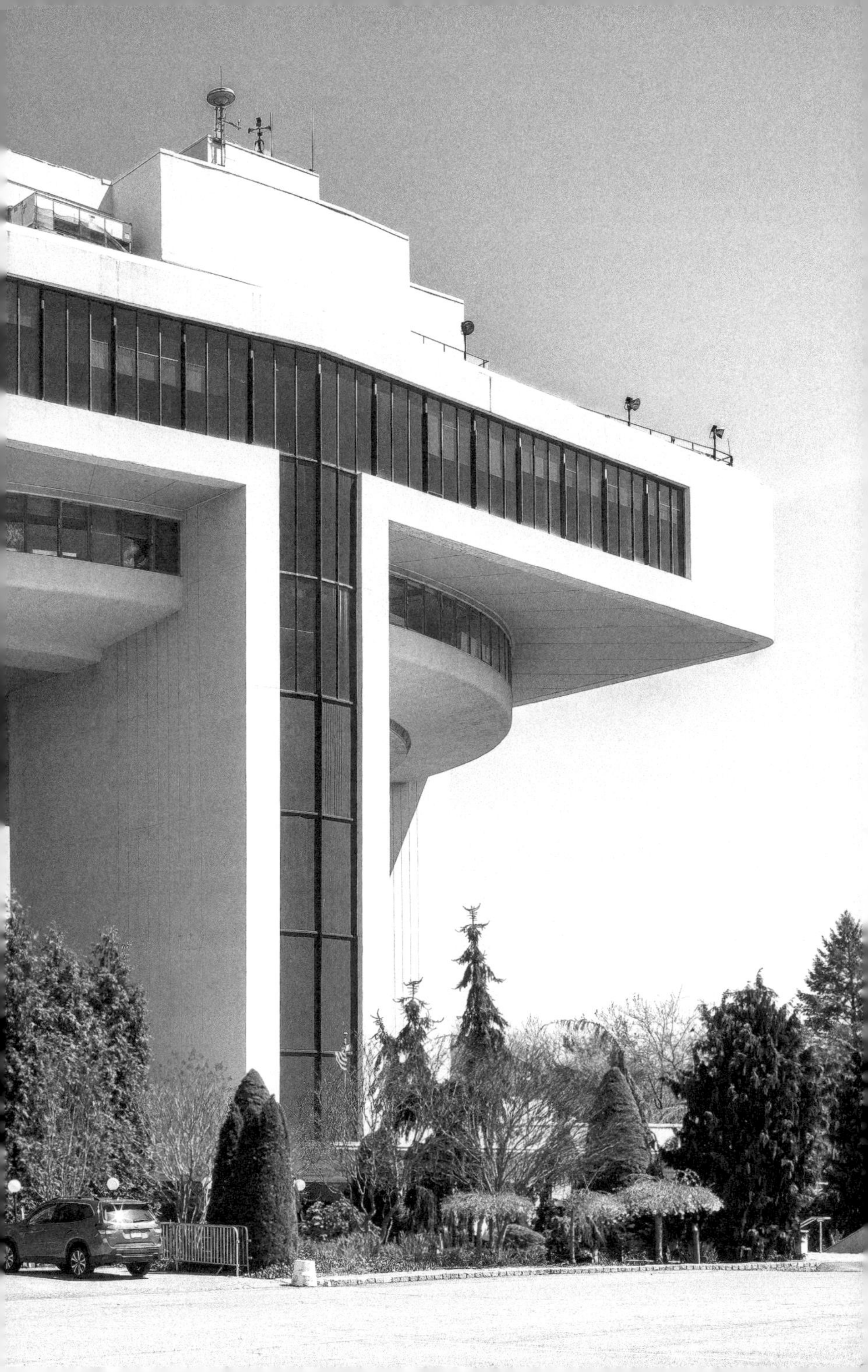

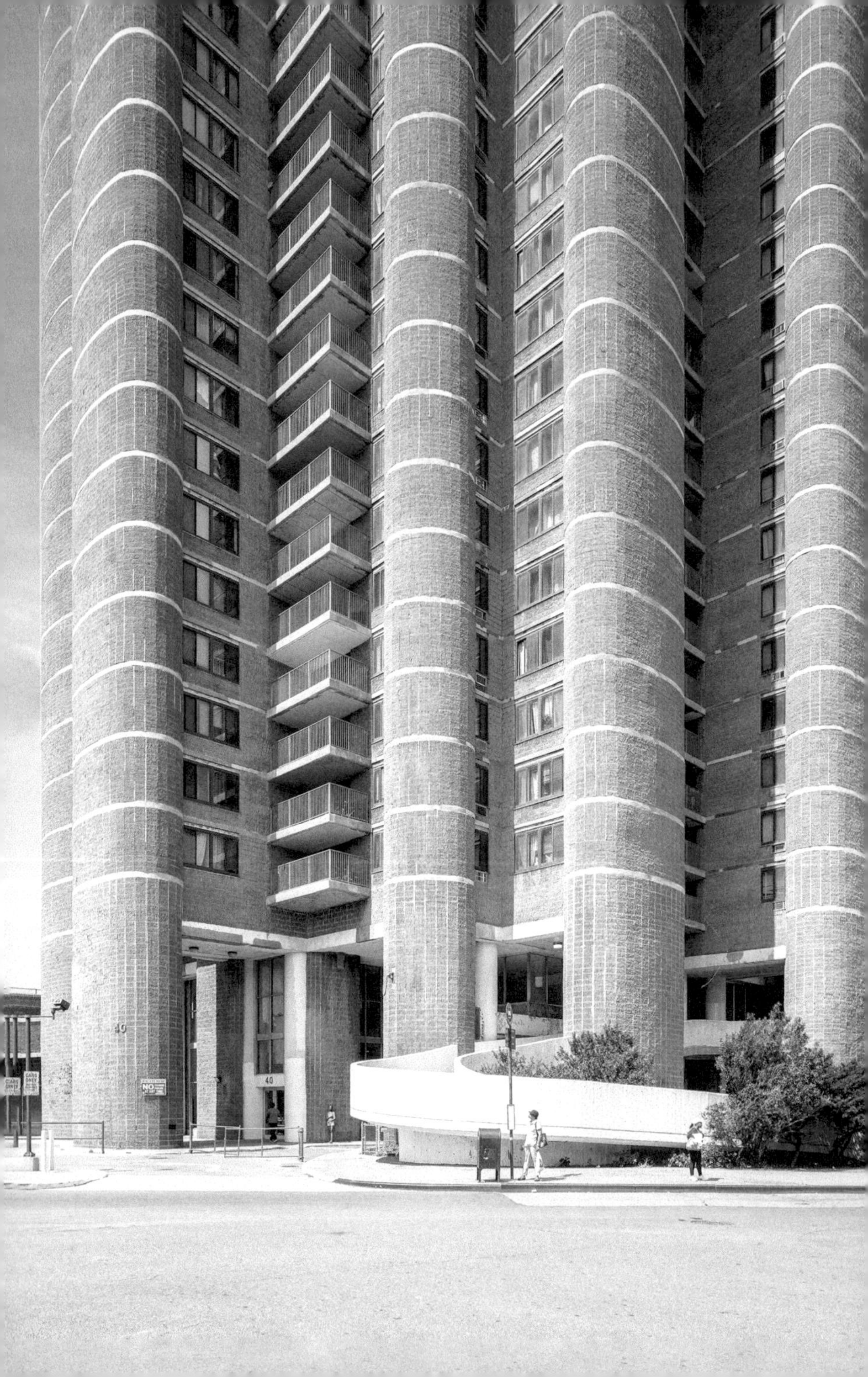
40

(50) Tracey Towers

Paul Rudolph, 1967–72
20 and 40 West Mosholu Parkway, The Bronx, 10468

Brick slabs define many residential structures built through New York's Mitchell-Lama Program for middle-income housing. In contrast, the Tracey Towers are all curves. Paul Rudolph worked in association with Jerald L. Karlan on the design that features his signature prefabricated concrete blocks, their heft given an expressive quality through a coarse corduroy texture. Stacked in lofty columns at varying heights, they cluster around the cores of the complex's twin towers. When completed, they were the Bronx's tallest buildings at 400 feet. They remain a landmark in a borough with few high-rise statements.

They were constructed using the air rights over an MTA train yard. The project followed Rudolph's time from 1958 to 1965 as the Department of Architecture chair at Yale, where he also employed his signature ribbed concrete technique on the Art and Architecture Building in 1963. Although he designed other works in New York City, like Middletown Plaza [35] and the 1973 Lewis S. Davidson Houses in the Bronx that likewise feature ribbed concrete blocks, the Tracey Towers are his most monumental and showcase his virtuosity in giving an elegance to the weighty material.

In spite of the sinuous exterior, the apartment layouts are largely ordinary, as indicated by the right-angled balconies and windows nestled within the fluted columns. One tower is 38 stories, the other is 41, the differing elevations allowing for a parking garage at one base. It is accessed by a spiraling entrance ramp, while inside, curved seating alcoves accent the lobbies.

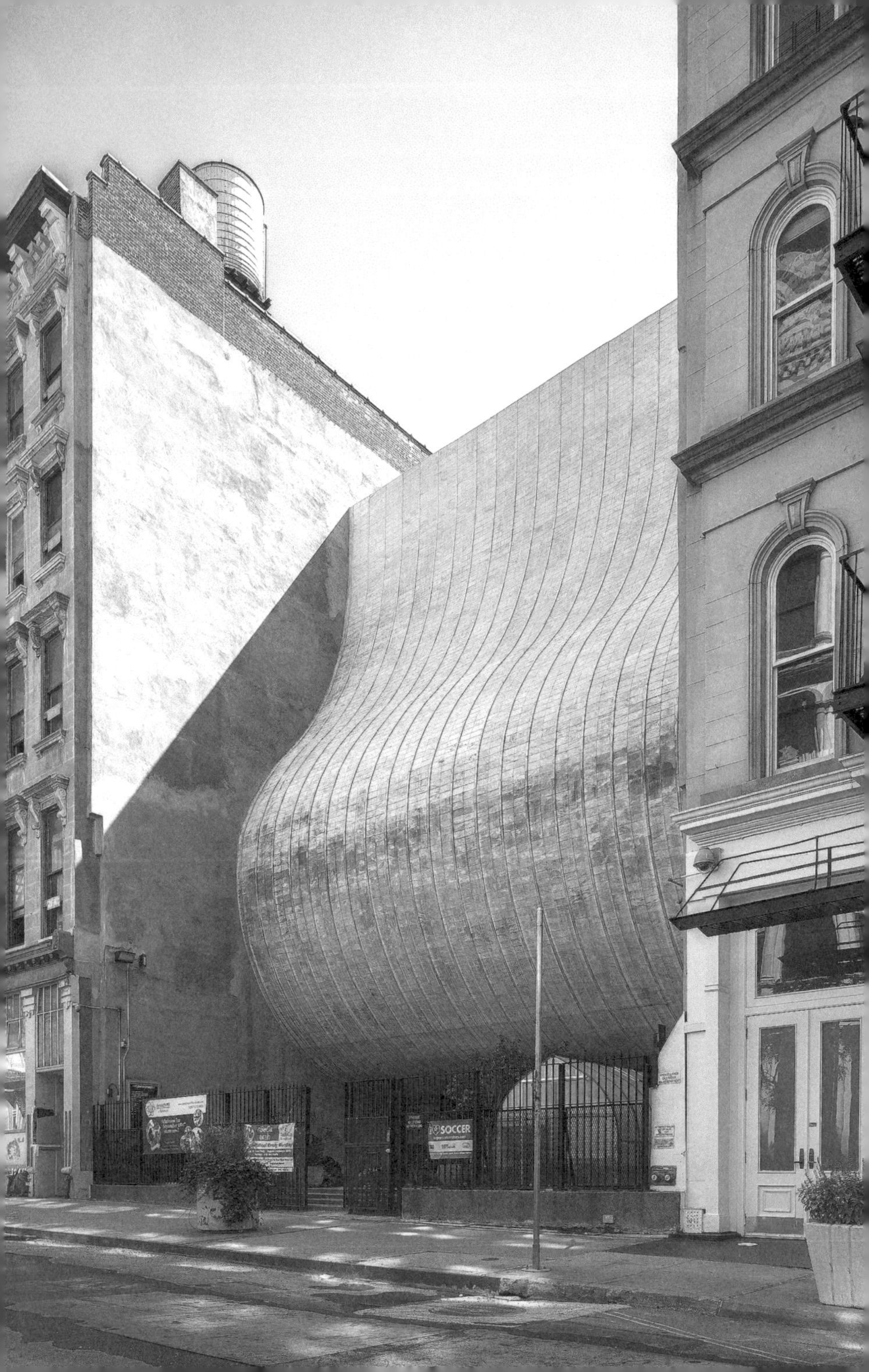
SOCCER

51 Tribeca Synagogue (Civic Center Synagogue)

William N. Breger Associates, 1965–67
49 White Street, Manhattan, 10013

A 19th-century block is interrupted by a floating windowless wave. Three concrete shells create a curve that billows forward and swoops back. William N. Breger used the site's restrictions—just 50 feet wide—as inspiration for an urban retreat. It has taken on some grime over the years, so its covering tile no longer has its shine. Still, it remains striking, particularly the sanctuary where that rolling form pulls inward to give an intimacy to the space. Clad in wood paneling and bathed by a long skylight, it is not only an eloquent use of materials but a practical one. No electrical amplification or lighting is required on Shabbat for the Orthodox Jewish congregation.

The Civic Center Synagogue was founded in 1938 in a loft to offer weekday services to workers in the area. It briefly had a home on Duane Street, completed in 1957, which was condemned through eminent domain; this land was provided as a replacement. The Bronx-born Breger was an assistant to Walter Gropius before establishing his own firm. His other major New York City projects were blocky nursing homes; for this, he brought a lyrical idea for a modern synagogue, realized with structural engineer Paul Gugliotta. Initially, its services were packed. Attendance fell off so that by the late 1980s, it was considered for demolition. Revived as the Synagogue for the Arts, it hosted poetry readings and art shows, before being renamed the Tribeca Synagogue in 2013 to reinforce that community connection.

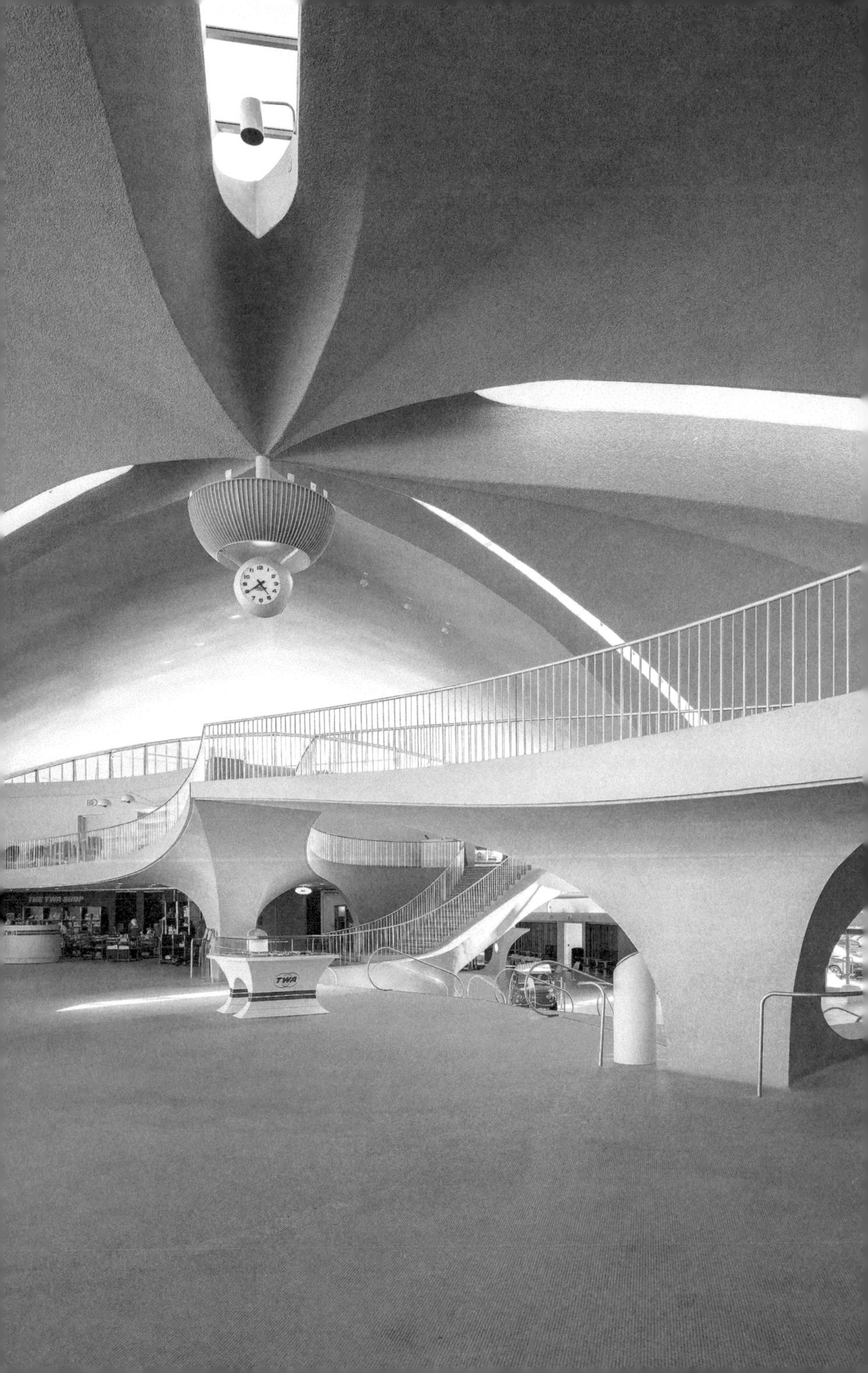
THE TWA SHOP
TWA

52 TWA Flight Center

Eero Saarinen & Associates, 1956-62
Terminal 5, John F. Kennedy International Airport, Queens, 11430

Everything sweeps upward in this former Trans World Airlines (TWA) terminal. When it opened at what was then Idlewild Airport, it encapsulated the optimistic spirit of the postwar Jet Age. Finnish-born architect Eero Saarinen used thin shells of reinforced concrete—in some places only seven inches thick—to create fluid forms. The huge wings of its roof seem about to lift off from the supporting Y-shaped piers. The vaulted interior is softly curved around soaring staircases. Large arches of windows let in sunlight. A concrete balcony offers a view of a 1963 clock hanging at the point where the four shells of concrete that make up the structure intersect.

It was one of Saarinen's last projects; he died in 1961 before its completion. Over the decades, it became obsolete as it could not accommodate new jumbo jets. The death knell for TWA sounded in 2001 with its third and last bankruptcy. The terminal then sat empty for almost two decades.

It was finally restored and reopened as the entryway to a hotel in 2019, brimming with nostalgia for a glamorous time of flight. Everywhere are the red and white colors of TWA's corporate identity. Guests access their rooms in two new buildings—their designs subdued to not compete with Saarinen's masterpiece—through the crimson-carpeted tunnels that once connected to airplanes. Passersby can also partake in restored features like the sunken lounge in the lobby, its built-in seating a respite in a more frenetic era of travel.

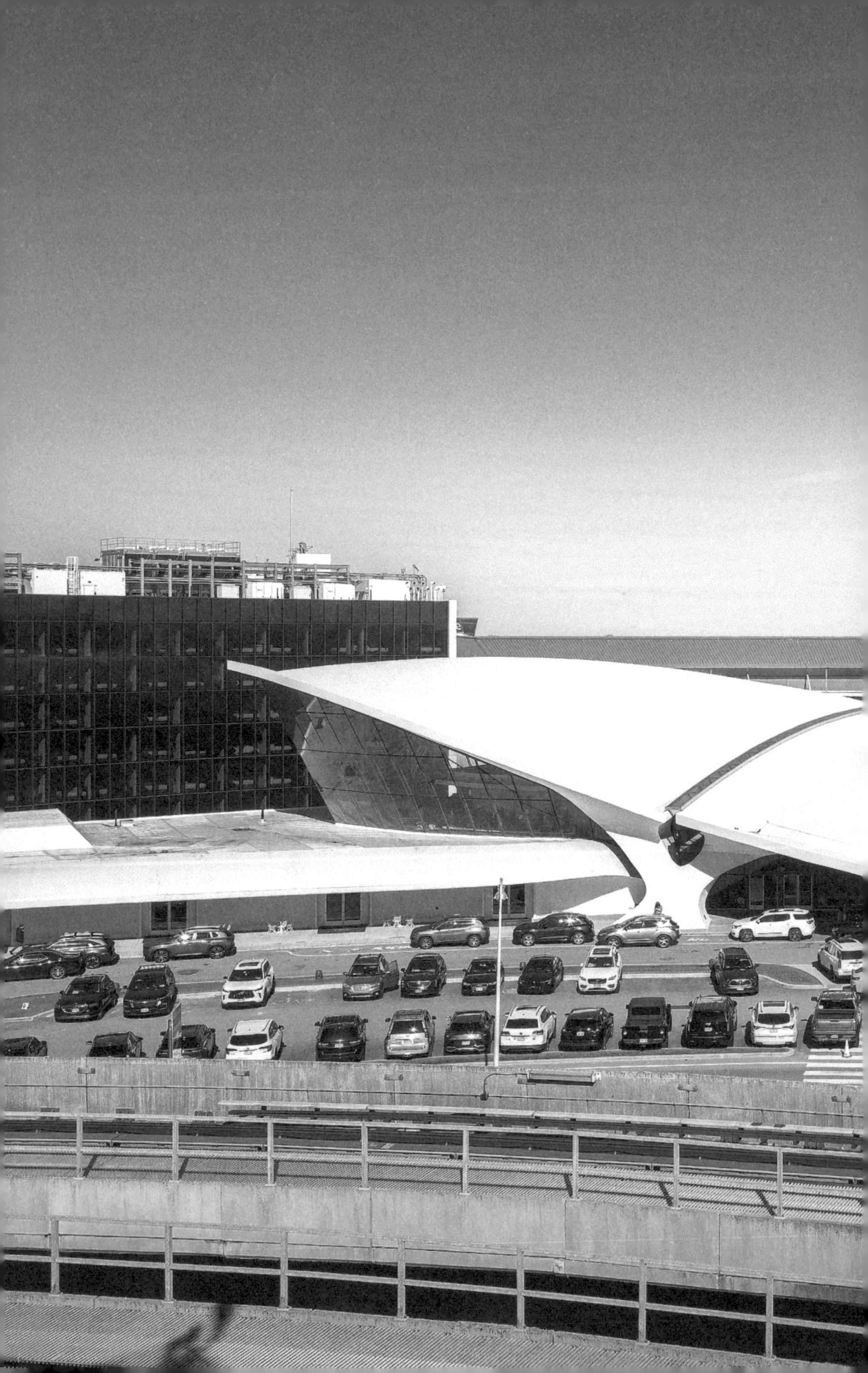

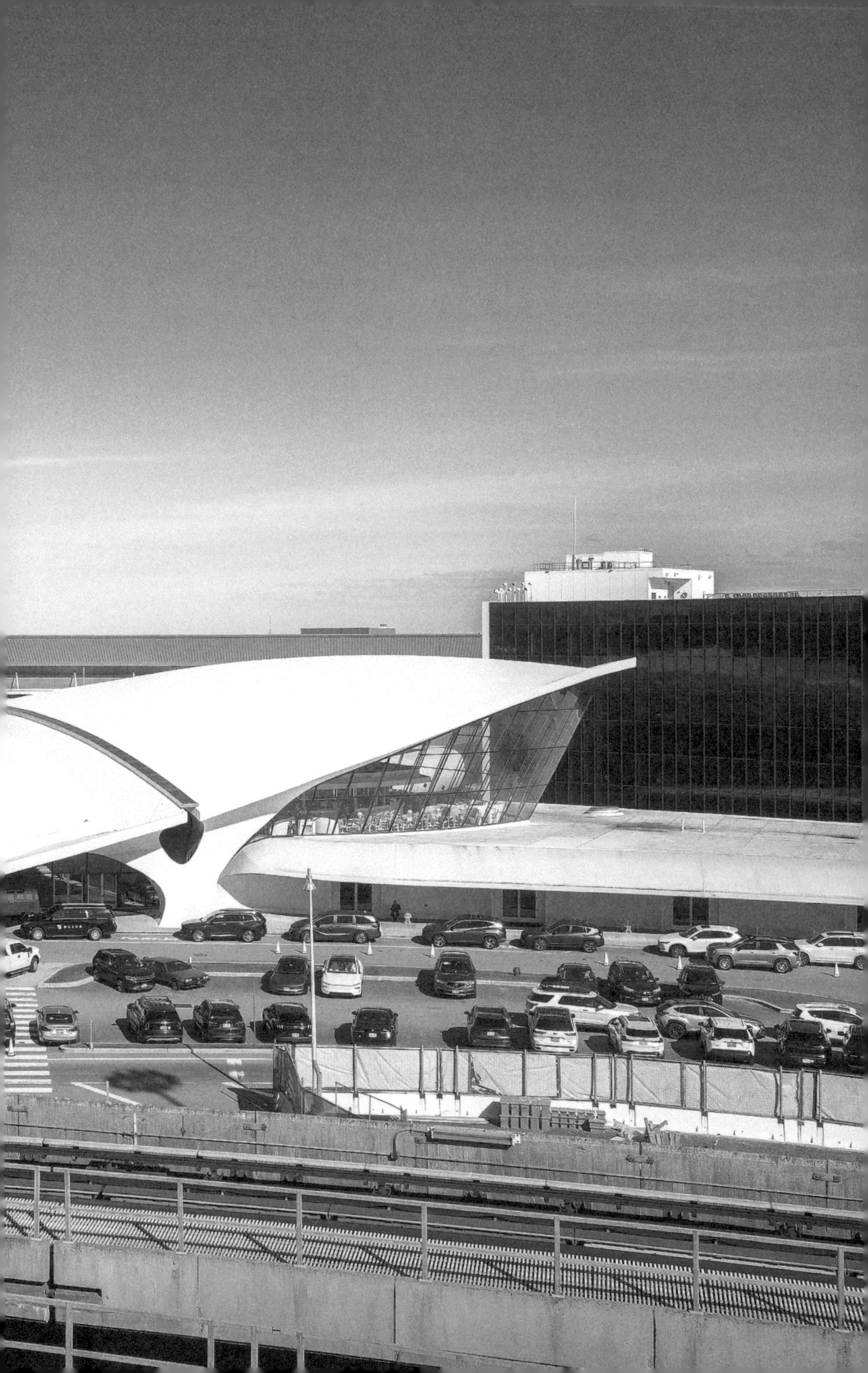

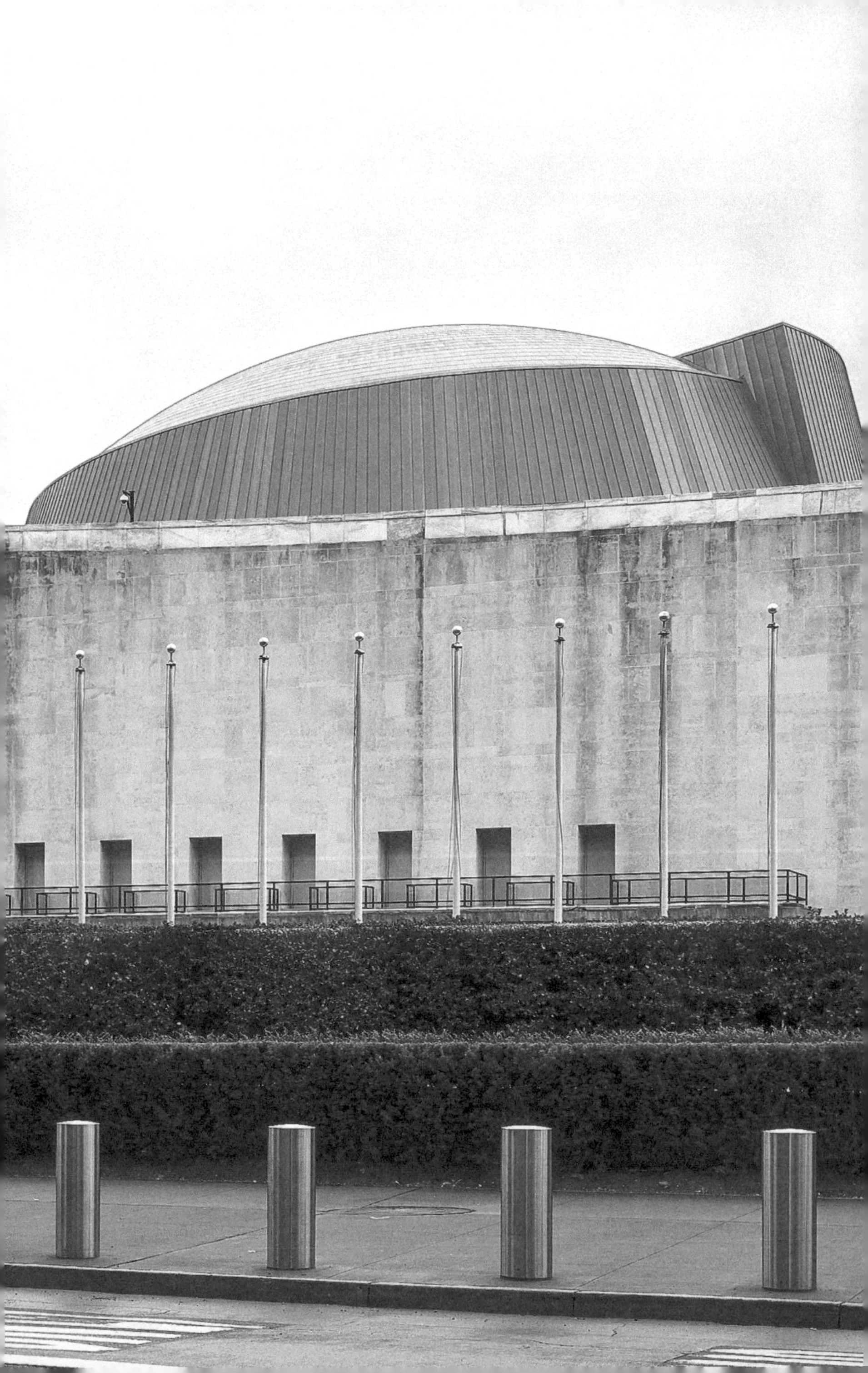

53 United Nations General Assembly Building

United Nations Headquarters Board of Design (Wallace K. Harrison, Max Abramovitz, Oscar Niemeyer, Le Corbusier), 1948–52
405 East 45th Street, Manhattan, 10017

The completion of the United Nations (UN) complex alongside the East River was more than a construction project; it was a symbol. The international organization was formed in the aftermath of World War II with the hope that working together across borders could prevent such violence from happening again. At the opening of the General Assembly in 1952, Trygve Lie—the UN's first secretary-general—said, "I am sure that men often worked harder and with more interest because the rivets they were driving, the stone they were setting, the concrete they were pouring, and the wires they were fastening had for them, in this instance, a special significance and meaning."

Slaughterhouses had been the main business on this Manhattan shoreline for over a century. A superstar team of global architects led by Wallace K. Harrison was organized to turn the land into the UN Headquarters. Each brought their flavor of Modernism in sometimes conflicting views.

Construction started in October 1949. While the glass slab of the Secretariat thrusts upward, the low-slung General Assembly bends downward, as if pushed by the weight of the central dome. Much of the final design was synthesized from the proposals of Oscar Niemeyer and Le Corbusier. Both were advocates for the expressive possibilities of reinforced concrete. Here, the sweeping steel-framed form was clad with limestone and marble, giving a stately sheen to the building that holds meeting halls and council chambers for the member states.

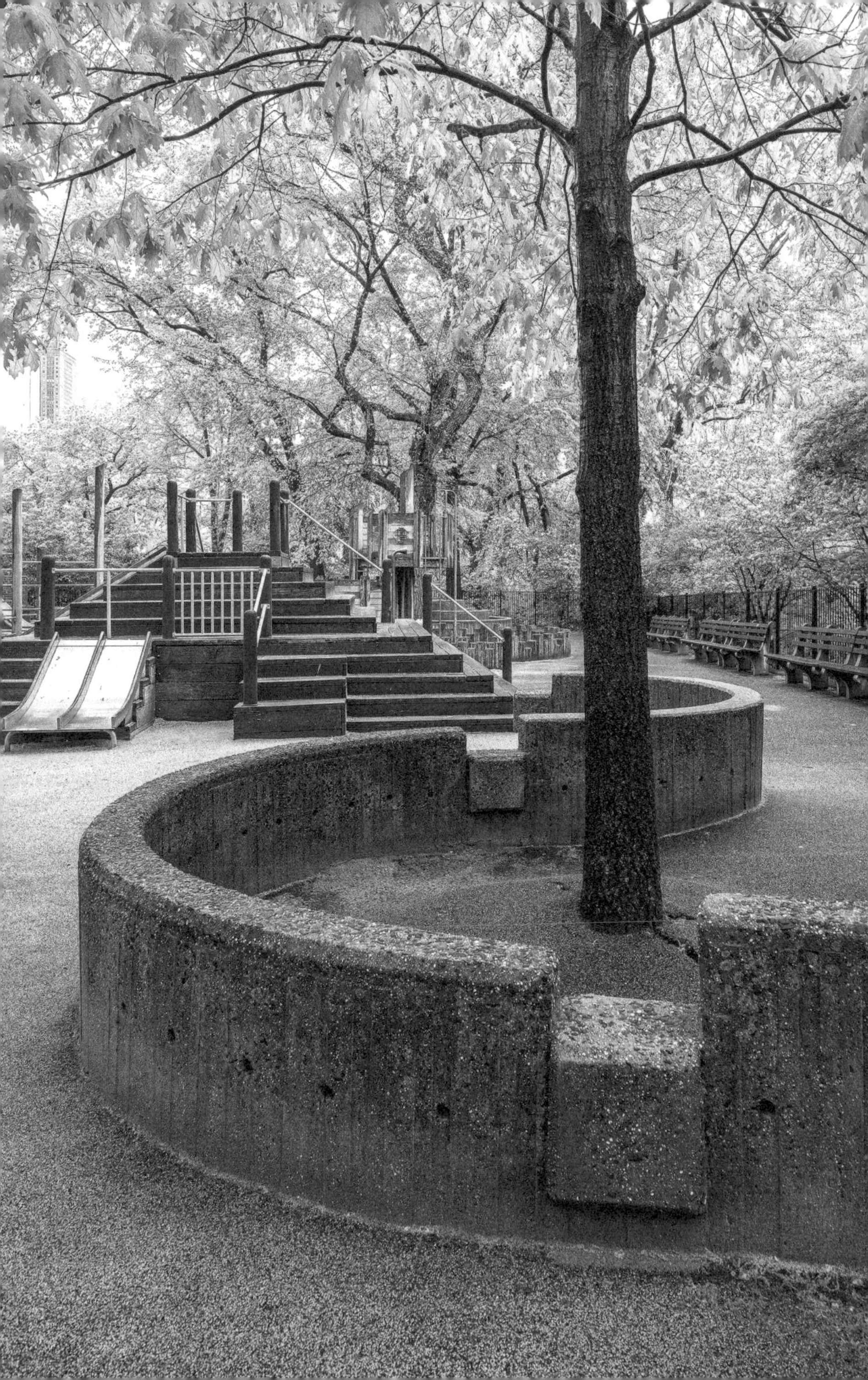

54 West 67th Street Adventure Playground

Dattner Architects, 1966–67
Central Park at West 67th Street, Manhattan, 10023

Richard Dattner observed that when children are left to their own devices, "they choose an environment rich in experience—experience over which they have some measure of individual control," and it's frequently the dirt around a tree or the water in a fountain that draws them rather than designed play equipment. He was one of the first to bring the adventure-style playground from Europe to the United States, creating what are better described as "playscapes" than "playgrounds" for how they encourage imaginative exploration. He was inspired by M. Paul Friedberg's 1965 play area with its maze of concrete structures (demolished in 2000) at Jacob Riis Plaza in the East Village. Dattner likewise used resilient concrete to build pyramids, tunnels, slides, wading pools, and other features for kids to scramble over and under.

He eventually designed five playgrounds on the edges of Central Park throughout the 1960s and '70s, with the Adventure Playground at West 67th, opened in May 1967, being the earliest. It was erected at a popular play spot saved in 1956 by local mothers who took a stand against the bulldozers sent by Robert Moses to dig it up for a parking lot. Dattner based every aspect on research into how children played, and this focus on child development helped kick off a whole movement of interactive playgrounds that supplanted equipment-filled lots. It underwent some updating in 2015 that maintained the vision of the original design, including its concrete and granite climbing mound, curved walls, and amphitheater steps.

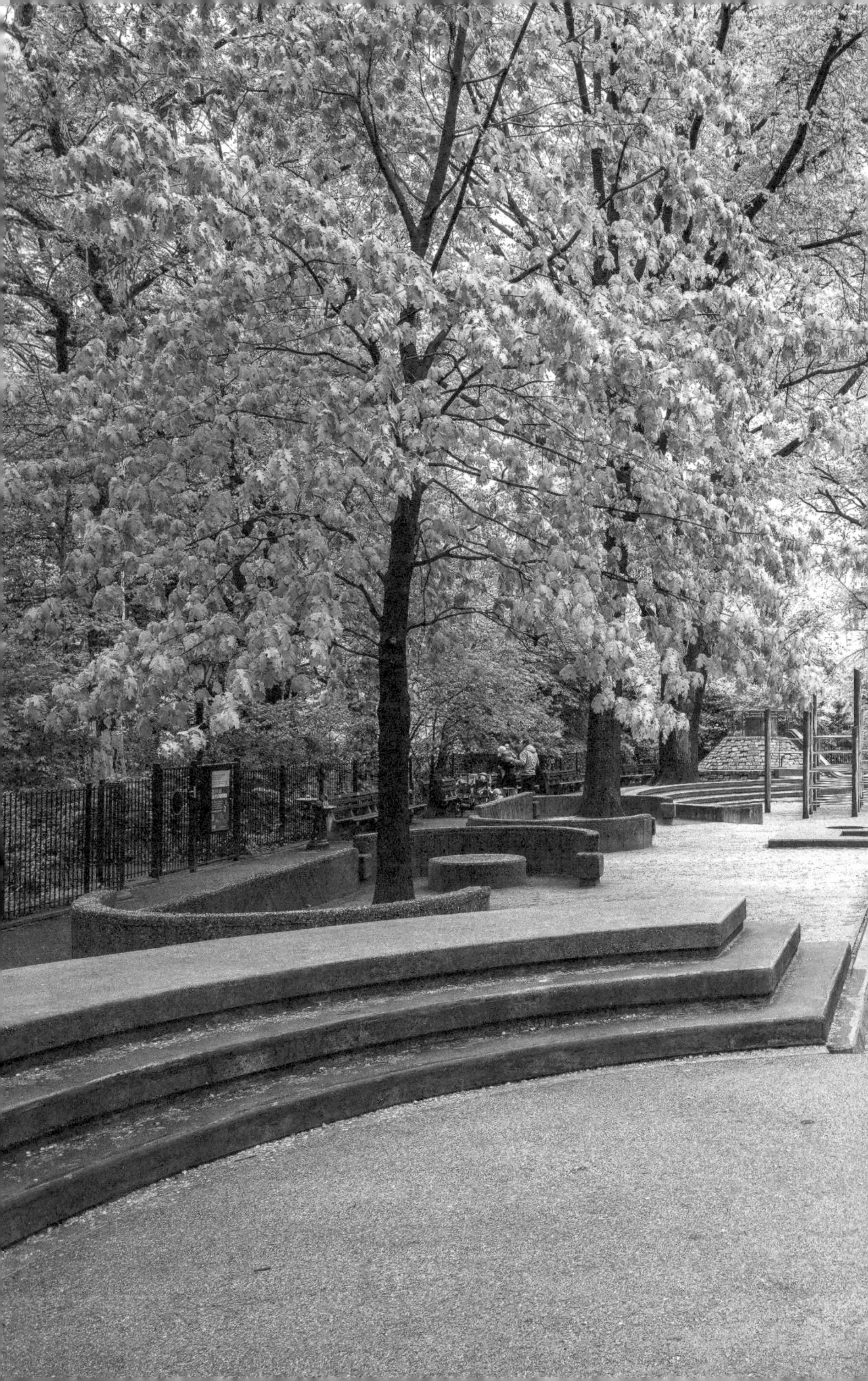

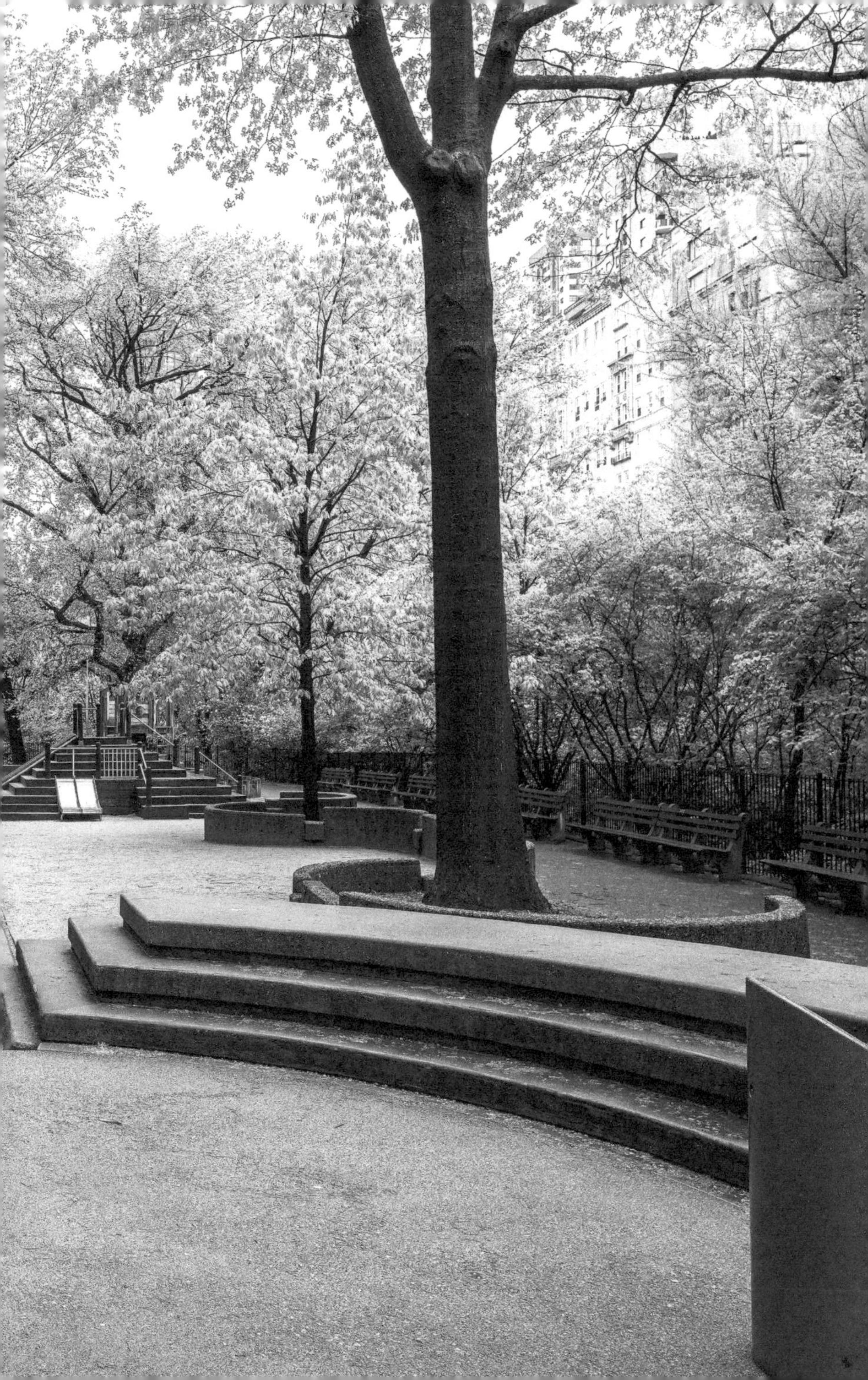

Index

Blue Crow Media
London, United Kingdom
bluecrowmedia.com

First published 2026

ISBN 978-1-912018-46-8

A CIP Catalogue record for this book
is available from the British Library.

Written by Allison C. Meier
Photographed by Jason R. Woods
Published by Derek Lamberton
Designed by Tuomi
Printed by Livonia Print

This book and other titles are available
to purchase from bluecrowmedia.com.